Death among the Fossils

DEATH

AMONG

THE

FOSSILS

ISADORE DURANT

University of New Mexico Press Albuquerque

Library of Congress Cataloging-in-Publication Data

Durant, Isadore, 1945–

    Death among the fossils / Isadore Durant. — 1st ed.

        p.   cm.

    ISBN 0-8263-1950-5. — ISBN 0-8263-1951-3 (pbk.)

    I. Title.

PS3554.U665D4   1999

813'.54—dc21   98-40790

                                                        CIP

To A.

Barbore 1985: The Find

The wind whipped up the gully in a hard gust, slashing him in the face with grit lifted from the alkaline exposures, driving sharp particles up under his wraparound sunglasses. He turned his back to the wind, blinked, wiped his eyes to clear them, and reached again for his canteen. Glancing at his watch, he forestalled the motion. *Only ten-thirty . . . this water's got to last till noon.* He pulled a blue American handkerchief from his shorts pocket and wiped his face, set his hat at a steep angle down over his brow, and turned again into the wind. Walking down the rocky floor of the gully, he swept his eyes over both sides of the slopes. His pace was slow, attuned to the rhythm of his eyes as they searched through the scatter of lava cobbles, fragments of eroded calcrete, broken crusts of the recent land surface, looking for the telltale blue-black sheen of fossil bone.

It had been nearly four hours since Balebe had started walking alone down from the head of this winding gash in the ancient Batchilok Formation. The wind had then been a light breeze, cool and pleasant on his skin. The sun had just been rising, deceptively distant and gentle, over the eastern mountains. Now its radiation actually stung his skin, and as on other such mornings he was beginning to pant lightly under the pressure of its heat. *First time in my life I've sunburned . . . and I used to make fun of* wazungu *with their sunscreen lotions . . . here I am borrowing Bob's. He's really*

1

had his fun out of that one, talking about making me an honorary white man!

A rock outcrop along a southerly twist of the gully offered a slim shadow, and he stopped there to check his bearings on the aerial photograph of the region. Crouching in the scanty shade, he removed the clipboard with the photo from his small backpack, found the curve of the gully in the picture, verified its orientation with his compass. *Should be two kilometers more down to the Bir Kalichi drainage, hope to God Bob isn't late again.*

The wind died in the little curve of the gully, and immediately he felt the sweat plastering his shirt to his back, under his watchband, trickling down the backs of his legs. He rose from his crouch and moved the band up his arm, noting an even greater contrast between the skin under the band and the deep reddish-brown of the rest of his arm.

"Damn! If Mum could see me now! She always said I was too much of an Irish redhead for this equatorial sun," he muttered. He moved out of the shade and sighed as the sun hit him. "How the hell Shafer expects anyone to actually find anything after ten a.m. is beyond me. I wonder how many hominids have been missed by men walking by in a stupor."

He began to scan again, tracing the light tan streak of a volcanic ash bed across gaps caused by erosion. The cemented layer of ash formed the highly visible upper boundary of the Batchilok Formation. Potassium-argon dates on samples collected by the Belgians last year indicated that hundreds of square kilometers had been blanketed by a violent eruption of poison gas and incandescent ash nearly three million years ago. The gas was long gone, but the ash remained, now as a narrow band of easily crumbled rock, cropping out over the badlands of southwest Barbore. The fossil-rich deposits lying under the ash were even older, perhaps as much as another half million years. Chances of finding new hominid fossils of such great age had brought Dr. Bob Shafer to prospect these badlands, and had led Balebe to work with him.

A cluster of bone high on the southern slope of the wash caught his eye. He moved closer. *Limb fragments, looks pretty good sized, bovid or primate?* Balancing precariously on a ledge, he reached up to the scatter of mineralized fragments, pushing the top few away, revealing an articular end a bit down slope. *Bovid, large gazelle size, shit . . . oh Lord, I really am starting to speak American! I'd best mind my tongue around the Guvnor when I get home. Oh,* please *let me find something this last day!*

A few meters ahead some stones slid down the wall of the gully, followed by finer sediments. He walked on, past a huge hippopotamus jaw lying exposed in the floor of the wash. All its teeth were perfectly preserved. The back ones were opalescent black, the tusks gray-streaked. The teeth were beginning to weather, breaking into splinters. *How scandalized I was at first that they weren't collecting things like this, even when Laporteau explained that they'd fill the Barbore Museum's storage facilities in one season. It's we collectors who are swimming against the tide of time, pulling fossils out of their rightful course of self-destruc—*

Then he saw it. There was no mistaking the arch of teeth exposed midway up the gentle slope on his right. "Hominid! Beautiful! It's not a robust *Australopithecus,* look at those incisors—it's *Homo!*"

He looked around, trying to calm himself. "My God, this is really happening! I found one!" His heart pounded as he edged nearer, scanning the surrounding slope, his gaze returning again and again to the palate with its curve of teeth.

"It's perfect!" he exclaimed. "The third molar's just erupting, died coming into full adulthood. God, I've never seen anything so beautiful! There's got to be more around here."

He raked the surrounding slope with his eyes, growing more systematic as his breathing began to slow. "Right, Thanatu, get a grip on yourself. Look up, check to see it's under the tuff. Thank heaven it's showing here. Yes, it looks okay, but it could have slid down the hill from above and then recemented itself on the slope. We'll only know if we excavate."

He glanced at his watch. "Christ, what's the time, eleven-thirteen. Must have found it about eight minutes after—let's look down slope, nothing showing, though it's all the same sediments, fine-

3

grained, maybe that accounts for the preservation. God, it's beautiful! Look lower, nothing but lava . . .

"Allah! It's the mandible, lying right under your feet, you fool! Oh, Lord, I'm famous! Balebe Thanatu is going to be famous! No more patronizing, 'And isn't your father the attorney general of . . .' "

He carefully backed away from the slope, taking it all in at once, the lower jaw lying between two lava cobbles at the bottom of the gully, the maxillary teeth arching out from their encasing sediments. He took his hat off and rubbed his hand over his springy reddish hair.

The first Asalian student of paleoanthropology finds a hominid! Of course Nane and his men had been finding fossils for years, but the rest of the world sees him as some extraordinarily talented human retriever dog that Pierce keeps in his kennel . . . none of that here, Jack. You've got a Fulbright scholar, an African, who's going to describe this little beauty himself!

Remembering his rendezvous with Shafer, he glanced again at his watch—only twenty minutes until the time they'd set this morning. He whipped out a small notebook from the back pocket of his shorts and made some quick notes. He then scrambled up to the top of the gully opposite the fossils to check his bearings. Pulling out the aerial photograph he squinted at the surrounding terrain, lifting a clear plastic overlay that traced the outcroppings of the Batchilok Formation and repeatedly consulting the photo's detail. Finally he reached up and took a safety pin from his hat brim and with it made a pinprick directly on the photo to mark the find's location.

Weighing the photo down with a lava cobble, he unbuttoned the Brunton compass case on his belt and took bearings on the two most prominent peaks on the horizon. These figures jotted in his notebook, he slid back down to the gully floor. He reached again into his rucksack, removed a thin metal stake with a loop at the end and a roll of Day-Glo orange surveyor's tape. He tore off two strips of the tape and tied them through the loop. He then slowly shoved the stake into the ground near the jawbone.

Balebe quickly packed his gear back into the rucksack and then reached into an outside pocket of the pack, extracting a small camera. He adjusted the settings and took one close-up of each fossil. After a moment's hesitation, he turned and searched the opposite gully wall. Finding a niche, he placed the camera in it and set the time exposure lever. He hopped across the gully, pointed at the fossil in the slope and grinned back at the beeping camera. After the beeps had reached a crescendo and the shutter clicked, he hastily packed the camera away. He checked his watch and sighed. Giving the fossils one lingering look, he turned and began to trot down the gully toward the Bir Kalichi River.

Betrayal

The junction of the little gully with the Bir Kalichi was deserted when he arrived. Shafer was late again. Balebe grimaced. "Oh, come *on!*"

He walked across the broad sand bed of the dry river toward the shade of the huge trees lining the other side of the river course. The only green in a landscape of buff, brown, and black, their branches were heavy with the nests of birds. He sat down in a patch of shade on the sandy riverbed, listening to the falling tones of doves, the repetitious *hoopoopoopoo* of a hoopoe bird a few meters downstream. He was restless, impatient for Shafer's arrival.

Finally he discerned the whine of an engine laboring in the distance, gradually growing deeper, augmented by metallic clanks and crashes as Shafer cowboyed the battered Land Cruiser up the sand river. A moment later the vehicle slewed around the downstream curve. Near-empty water bags draped from the rear viewmirror strut swung wildly as the car rocked over the undulating floor of the watercourse. Balebe rose from his place in the shade and walked across the blazing sand to meet it.

The Land Cruiser jerked to a halt opposite him. Shafer had dust on his brows and his face bore lines of grime from his hatband and sunglasses. His sandy hair was stiff with dried perspiration, his aquiline nose sunburned and peeling. Shafer leaned out of the cab. "Well, how'd it go?"

Balebe's heart began pounding again, but he struggled to remain casual. He reached for a half-empty water bag, unscrewed the top, and tilted it by a corner, bending to catch the stream in his mouth. Stepping back, he wiped his mouth and smiled. "Found one," he said, looking Shafer straight in the eye.

"A hominid? You're kidding! You're not kidding! Where, for Christ's sake?"

"About two and a half kilometers up the drainage. A beautiful maxilla and mandible. It's definitely *Homo*." He struggled to maintain a calm appearance.

Shafer jumped from the cab, grabbed Balebe's hand and pumped it. "Wonderful! Great! God, I knew they were here! Good job! Christ, you're a cool one, Thanatu!"

Balebe allowed himself a wide smile. "It was just below some long bones that looked suspicious but turned out to be bovid—it's beautifully preserved, pretty definitely below the tuff, M3's are just erupting, the maxilla is still *in situ*. There may be more in the hillside!"

"Now there's a little more *enthusiasm,* fella! You made my day. Let's go see it! How far up can we drive?"

"Oh, at least halfway."

They jumped into the Land Cruiser, and Shafer slewed the wheel sharply to the right to make the entrance to the little drainage. They bucked and rolled over the stream bed, slowing to a creep as they scraped over lava boulders. Finally Shafer said, "Okay, we go the rest of the way on foot." They set off at a jog up the wash.

Balebe kept checking his bearings as they went along, irrational fears that it had all been a hallucination passing through his mind. Within half a minute, both men were panting heavily from the searing heat. The sun blazed directly overhead. All shade had vanished.

"Around this bend, I think . . ." They rounded the bend and saw the little flagged stake about sixty meters up the wash. Shafer quickened his pace to a run. Balebe matched it. Then, about two meters from the stake, Shafer stopped and glanced questioningly at the young man.

"There, between the stake and that big lava cobble, there's the mandible. The maxilla . . ."

Shafer was already crouched over the mandible, staring. He then looked up and followed Balebe's pointing finger. His eyes fastened on the curved arcade of teeth glinting almost unbearably in the noonday glare. After a long moment, he expelled a heavy breath. He removed his hat and ran his hand through his sandy hair. Still on his haunches, he turned and grinned up at Balebe.

"I *knew* they were here, and how sweet it is to get one! What a beauty! Not like that scrappy shit poor old van de Hoven was finding at Lake Logo! Balebe, this is a real gem."

The student smiled back at Shafer mutely. His head swam, and he didn't know if it was the effects of the sun or the surge of pride and elation he felt. *My father will have to come off his high horse now . . . it's too good to be true!* He waited expectantly for a signal from Shafer, for more conversation, but the older man seemed to have withdrawn into himself completely. After a long interval, Shafer rose, but instead of turning to Balebe, he backed away from the finds a bit and sat down on a lava boulder facing them. He reached into his shirt pocket and pulled out a pack of cigarettes, shook one out, and lit it with a gold butane lighter. Staring steadily ahead, he smoked for several minutes, without a glance at the younger man.

Balebe felt a ghost of unease rise up inside him. *What's going on, shouldn't we be going back to camp?*

At last, seeming to come to a decision, Shafer took a strong drag on his cigarette, rose, tossed the cigarette down, and ground it out under his heel. Uncasing his camera, he turned to Balebe and said, "Go back to the car, get a roll of toilet paper and a couple of collecting bags." He turned away abruptly and began to frame the fossils in his camera lens.

Balebe stood stunned. "But shouldn't we just leave them and come back with an excavation crew?" he blurted. "There may be . . ."

"There'll be no excavation this time, Thanatu, just go get the bags!" Shafer barked.

"But you're not going to leave the hillside unexcavated!" Balebe cried. "Erosion could take whatever may be in that slope off by next season, and Jan's crew could easily . . ."

"Precisely, Jan's crew could, and they're not going to see this site!" Shafer snapped.

Balebe was momentarily speechless. *He means to deceive the Belgians!* "You can't mean you're not going to tell them!" he asked in disbelief.

"Exactly, my friend, and if you want a Ph.D. in this lifetime you'd better get with the program." The older man whipped off his sunglasses and fixed Balebe with an icy glare in his gray eyes. "I've waited too damn long for a find like this to give it up to a stupid shit like van de Hoven. You've seen how they constantly screw around in the field. If it weren't for the money, I'd never have agreed to join up with that pompous creep. I had my fill of his conceitedness and airhead paleontology at Lake Logo. But beggars can't be choosers, right Thanatu?"

Balebe's skin had gone clammy, and he felt ill. *I can't believe this . . .* "Look, Shafer, what do you propose to do? How could this possibly work?"

"'What do I propose to do?'" Shafer mimicked. "It's easy. We leave the field tomorrow. You and I take out the specimens now and hold on to them. The Belgians drive north to Andaba, as planned, we cut south across the Batchilok, *as planned,* via the Bir Kalichi, and we have ourselves a little discovery on the way across the border to Asalia. Surprise!

"Van de Hoven is heading straight back to Brussels, but we're already committed to a stop in Wangara, to compare our primates and pigs with the Ruba specimens in the Asalia National Museum. When we get to Wangara we announce that we found the fossils on the last day in the field, after the Belgians were already en route to Andaba, *and* in an area that jerk Jan thought was sterile! It'll be a news conference at the museum, just us two, okay?"

Balebe sighed and shook his head. "I must tell you that I feel very uneasy about this, Bob. Jan may not be a genius, but he and his institute did put up most of the money for the expedition, and without Michel we'd have been totally lost in this stratigraphy."

"Look, Thanatu, how many times do I have to say it? We found it. They didn't. Laporteau is a damn good stratigrapher, but he's not a paleontologist. This is the real world, man. This is a very, very big opportunity for both of us. With a find of *Homo* this early, the foundations will be falling all over each other trying to get in on next year's field season. So what if the Belgians are pissed? They can't disprove our story, *and* next year we won't need their money. Screw 'em!" Shafer turned back to the fossils and lit another cigarette.

Balebe's mind was reeling. *I'd always thought the stories about Shafer were sour grapes on the part of less lucky or successful people, but now, Christ! There's Melanie Baine's being thrown out of Barbore, and the rumor that Bob was behind the allegation that she was a CIA spy. That set her career back years, nearly finished her. And the grad students' talk, about Bill Hudson's aborted dissertation, and that woman, what was her name, the one who flunked her comprehensives after confronting Shafer? It's all true,* he has *ruined people. He could do it to me . . . This is as bad as my father's bloody politics! I need time to think this through, to find some way out . . .* He stared unblinkingly at Shafer, casting about for a response.

"All right, Thanatu, we're playing hardball now. You're either on the bus or off it. If you make trouble for me, I can get that Fulbright taken away. Too much partying and not enough nose to the grindstone, a typical African student story—they've heard it before—and you'd be on your way home in no time. You managed to get yourself into one of the three best fossil hominid programs in the world, bro, and if you cross me, I'll see to it that you won't qualify for janitorial service in any major university, much less a degree. You know I can do it. You don't really want to throw all that away, do you?"

Balebe shook with a surge of desperate rage at the man's arrogance, and he nearly leapt at him. He struggled to control himself. *I've got to bargain for some time to think!* He calmed his breathing enough to speak. "Right, Shafer, you're a devious, exploitative bastard, but you're holding all the cards. It's as you say."

"Good, I knew you'd see reason, Balebe! Besides, you're still gonna get credit for this, along with your professor, right? Now go get those bags and the TP, okay?"

Balebe returned from the car to find Shafer already scraping away at the earth around the maxilla with his knife.

"Get that mandible and wrap it, Thanatu. Wrap it up good, but don't make a football out of it, okay? I'm going to want you to keep the bones in your bag, since nobody'd figure a nice guy like you would have anything to hide."

Balebe complied, watching Shafer gingerly tunnel around the other piece, exposing more of the bone above the teeth. He kept working around the fossil with his knife, enlarging a little moat all around the piece. "Nice piece of zygomatic in the left side. Other side's snapped right at the base, though . . . wait a minute, here we go, it's loosening up . . . that's right, baby, slow and easy now . . . aha!" The piece suddenly slumped down a few centimeters, into the paleontologist's waiting palm.

Shafer turned toward Balebe, cradling the fossil in his hand. "This little beauty is gonna make a couple of people *very* unhappy," he grinned. "That old bitch Anthea Pierce is going to have to eat it on this one, and her wonderful nephew David is not going to like it either. There goes his whole model for hominid evolution! Oh, my, my! Just let's see them try to get the foundations to go for that West Ruba project now!"

A new wave of nausea hit the young man. It was all very well for Shafer to plan a frontal attack on the Pierces. He wasn't an Asalian, with everything to lose from antagonizing such prominent compatriots. Even with his powerful father, Balebe knew the Pierce family could present formidable obstacles to his career, and he had taken such great care to cultivate at least David as a friend and sponsor. With Anthea's attitude toward Africans, he wasn't sure he'd ever earn anything more than neutrality from her, but at least he had achieved that. Perhaps being half European redeemed him in her eyes. But it had actually been David Pierce who'd suggested

10

that he study with Shafer after completing his bachelor's degree at the University of Wangara.

He now recalled in vivid detail that conversation in Pierce's museum office. "I rather hate to say it, Thanatu, but I suppose the best thing you can do at this point in your career is to go to America and work with Shafer. As you know, Dr. Shafer and I have our differences regarding the pattern of human evolution, but he's undeniably bright. You'll get good training with him, make some good connections—and American money is what we'll ultimately need to really open up this country's fossil resources."

Pierce had paused and swiveled his chair to stare at a photograph of Mount Ruba on the wall behind his desk. Still facing away from the young man, he continued in a sardonic tone. "Moreover, in the short term, it will be a politic move for you, since Shafer will be working in Barbore rather than here for the next few years. That will keep him, and you, out of Anthea's orbit. I may be able to take my problems with Bob philosophically, but Anthea really has a pathological hatred of him. So you mustn't get too close to Asalia while in Shafer's company. Anthea isn't getting any younger, but she could still make a lot of mischief for a young person such as you over the next few years."

Pierce swung back around to stare Balebe in the eye, pointing at him with the stem of his pipe. "But mind that you don't let him put you at a disadvantage. He's a deeply ambitious man."

It had all seemed so feasible at the time. A few years with Shafer, then back to Asalia with a joint position in the university and the museum, connections with American and Belgian colleagues bringing in money for collaborative efforts, a rising career with David's blessing and at least grudging consent from Anthea Pierce. Now, it all is thrown into jeopardy with this fraud, combined with Shafer's urge to lord it over the Pierces. Christ!

"Snap out of it, Thanatu! We're already an hour late for lunch, and they'll come looking for us if we don't get moving!" Shafer had finished wrapping the maxilla and was stuffing both in a collecting bag. "Put this in your pack and keep it with you at all times. And for God's sake, act casual!"

They walked back to the vehicle in silence. Shafer took charge of the delicate task of backing it down the gully to the first small feeder channel that allowed them sufficient room to turn around. Shadows were beginning to show on the eastern side of the gully as the sun moved west. They made the junction quickly, and Shafer turned the vehicle upstream toward camp. But before they plunged down into the sand of the main channel, he stopped on the firmer delta of the feeder channel.

"We've got one more thing to do," he said, looking up at Thanatu as he set the emergency brake and killed the engine. He reached behind the back of the seat and drew out a *panga,* testing the edge of the bushknife while smiling at the youth.

A shiver of fear hit the young man. *Jesus, what's he going . . .*

Shafer heaved himself down from the Land Cruiser. "We've got to have a flat tire and fix it. That's why we're so late for lunch, hey, bwana?"

Deception

Balebe turned on his side as quietly as possible and stared into the dark. Less than a meter away Laporteau's breathing was fuzzing into a light snore. After a totally miserable evening in camp, the young man wanted to keep the Belgian from developing any more suspicions than he might already have. He sighed softly.

He had been unbearably tense as they entered the camp well after three in the afternoon, the artfully slashed tire bouncing in the bed of the Land Cruiser. As van de Hoven and Laporteau rose from their canvas seats under the awning and came to meet them, Balebe was sure that he would somehow give away their find, in his eyes, his movements, his speech. He struggled to picture his other entries into camp, greetings to the Belgians and the Barboro workmen, exhausted trudges to his tent to drop his gear, the washings-up behind his tent, some semblance of the camp routines, a past now irrevocably sundered. But his mind remained fixed on the two fragments wrapped in cloth collecting bags at the bottom of his rucksack.

Shafer had heightened the agony by insisting that he pull out and show the baboon mandible he'd found earlier in the day. *Christ! What if I pull out the wrong one?* Despite a rehearsal and marking the bag containing the find with an ink blot, he still was barely able to suppress his trembling as he reached into his pack and handed the specimen bag to Shafer.

"Good, Balebe, it's a very nice one, indeed," van de Hoven said, adding, "I know we are all disappointed that we have not found the hominids, but your *Theropithecus* will make a nice little paper in *Nature*—how small it is! Bob—you must let the boy publish this as senior author, *ja?*"

Shafer leaned back against the hood of the Rover and grinned at van de Hoven in unfeigned delight. "That's a great idea, Jan, he deserves it!" He turned and looked Balebe straight in the eye, continuing to smile broadly.

Balebe stared back, unable to believe the gall of the man. *Yes, we have a little private joke, you swine. You're even more cold-blooded than I'd thought!* He turned abruptly and went through the motions of unpacking the vehicle as Shafer glibly explained their flat tire and asked van de Hoven how their day had gone. Shafer's chitchat was so casual, so open, believable. *If this is how he lies, I'll never believe a thing he says ever again!*

Shafer turned again to Balebe and caught his eyes for a second. "Say, you'd better go on and get those Darvons from my first aid kit. Try lying down for a while, okay?" Turning back to the others, he said, "Balebe here has a really bad headache—too much sun, and a little too much excitement, maybe. I've convinced him to lie down for a while before dinner."

Christ, he's a smooth bastard! Balebe thought, but lowered his eyes and nodded. "Sorry to be a bother," he muttered as he slung his pack over one shoulder and took the two empty water bags from the door of the car. As he turned to walk toward the cook fire, he saw Laporteau gazing at him, a Gauloise cigarette dangling from his lip, a speculative expression on his face. *Oh, God, he knows some-*

thing's wrong! He lowered his eyes and strode on to the kitchen area.

Hanging the water bags over a branch by the fire, he greeted Hamid, the Barboro cook, and the other field assistants in rudimentary Barboro, thanking God that his shaky grasp of the language precluded a full account of the day's events. Pushing into the tent Shafer and van de Hoven shared, Balebe found the metal first aid box under Shafer's bed. He sat on the bed and opened it. *I wonder whether to just go through the motions or to actually take a couple of capsules. May as well act out the charade to the fullest. Perhaps they'll relax me a bit.* He rose and went to the water bag and cup hanging by the door. He stared at the backpack on the floor of the tent as he washed down the capsules. *Christ, I can't go through with this! Why am I so afraid of the exploitative bastard?*

The odor of Laporteau's cigarette wafted into the tent. He turned to find the stocky Belgian gazing at him with a slightly quizzical expression. His heart began to pound.

"*Bon,* Balebe, is there something besides the headache wrong?" he said softly.

Balebe took a deep, shaky breath. "As a matter of fact, Michel, I . . ."

"Hey, kid, I thought I told you to lie down for a while," Shafer stepped into the tent and tossed his pack on the floor. "You really don't look too good, does he, Michel? Go get some rest while I ask Michel here about the sedimentary environment of the little *Theropithecus.*"

Balebe's nerve failed him. He nodded and grabbed his pack, leaving without another look at Michel. He trudged on to the tent he shared with Laporteau, slid his rucksack under his bed, and began unlacing his dusty boots, stripping off his clothes.

Sitting on the bed in his undershorts, he was overcome by a sense of unreality. He wanted terribly to look at the specimens to make sure they were there. His habitual fastidiousness forced him to his feet again, to slide on his sandals and go outside to wash with the basin of water provided by Hamid.

He gazed out over the badlands to the east of the promontory on which their camp lay and shivered as he sponged himself. *Where will this end? . . . There is still time to unmask this swindle . . . Do I really prize my precious career so much? How the hell will I get through the night sharing the tent with Michel?*

Dinner was a nightmare. He used the excuse of the headache to cover his abstraction and lack of appetite. Shafer continued to shock and amaze Balebe with his ability to lie. Over the simple stew and the red wine van de Hoven had produced for their last night in camp, Shafer broached the subject of a change in departure plans.

Taking a sip of wine, Shafer said, "You know, Jan, I've really got an urge to have another look at some of those beds along the Bir Kalichi on our way out. I really think they've got more potential than you believe."

Van de Hoven shrugged. "As you wish, Bob. I don't agree concerning their potential, but it will do no harm. I am only concerned that you don't have problems with the car if you go overland instead of using the Demitchi-Wangara Road. Look at what happened today."

"Don't worry, Jan, the Toyota's in great shape, and Balebe knows how to change a tire real well by this time!"

Balebe managed a small smile at Shafer's joke, wondering at the man's gall. Laporteau, as usual, had said little at dinner, restricting himself to a few wry comments in the face of van de Hoven's volubility. To Balebe's surprise, Laporteau had not pressed him later in the evening. In fact, he'd sat up with Bob over their last bottle of brandy late into the night, coming to bed well after one o'clock. Balebe was able to pretend to be asleep.

Now, as this last night in camp was half over, he listened to Laporteau's gentle snore and the incessant sound of the wind blowing through the tent ropes, the branches of the trees. Every minute took him further away from the point of revealing the find, into closer comradeship with the man today's events had taught him to despise.

He again recalled David Pierce's words last year: "He's a deeply ambitious man." "Mind you don't let him put you at a disadvantage . . ." He sighed again, rolling onto his back with a faint squeaking of the canvas cot, and stared into the darkness.

Departure

Daybreak brought unaccustomed noise and activity to the camp. Shafer and Laporteau directed the Barbore workmen in striking the tents, rolling them up, and stowing them in their storage bags. Hamid was noisily boxing up all the cooking gear except his huge sooty teakettle, all the while arguing in Barboro with the youth helping him.

Van de Hoven was sitting at the one remaining table, double-checking that the American and Belgian teams each had documentation for every collected specimen, sorting through the originals and carbons of the field catalogues, muttering under his breath in Flemish as he recapitulated the field season. Balebe checked the wrappings on the fossils and packed them into cartons now emptied of their tinned food. *Fine irony, this! Shafer's putting me on to jobs that set the hook deeper.*

By half past eight, when they stopped for biscuits and milky tea brewed in Hamid's kettle, the campsite was utterly transformed. They stood sipping the sweet, smoky liquid amidst stacks of folded cots, tables, chairs, piled-up boxes, and the low mounds of the bagged tents. This was not the first field camp Balebe had ever seen taken down, but despite his anger and worry he was struck by the transformation of the place back into its former state. Only the well-trampled earth and a few branches lopped from the thorn trees were testimony to their four-week stay. Straining the dregs of his unstrained tea through his teeth, he handed the cup to Hamid and walked off to stand on the headland where he'd bathed every night for these weeks. *Well, you're certainly not the kid you were when you arrived,* he thought bitterly.

Laporteau cried, "*Allons-y!* Let's go!" and began directing the loading of the vehicles. Empty gasoline barrels were lashed in the back of the Belgians' Land Rover pickup, followed by tents and furniture, all covered by a flysheet tethered firmly with rope. Van de Hoven and Laporteau shoved their personal gear behind the seats of the other Rover. Shafer and Balebe stowed their luggage,

16

sleeping bags, the boxes of fossils, and the field documents in the back of the Toyota. Finishing their loading, Hamid and the five workmen watched expectantly as Laporteau divided up the remaining tinned food and dry goods into five heaps and gestured for them to each take one. They then piled their own meager baggage into the back of the second Belgian Rover.

Van de Hoven seated himself on the stone at Hamid's cooking place and opened his paybook, gesturing for the Barbore to come near.

"Oh Jesus, here we go," fumed Shafer, tapping a cigarette out of his pack and lighting it. "This'll probably take a coupla hours."

Laporteau reached over and pulled a cigarette from Shafer's Benson and Hedges before Bob could return it to his pocket. He lit it and shrugged. "Have patience, *mon ami,* there are only six today. Remember when he played this game with twenty-seven at Lake Logo!"

Turning to Balebe with a dry smile, Laporteau explained. "My colleague has an involved formula to calculate the pay, which depends on the actual hours worked. Because it is not a flat rate, everyone tries to get a good deal from him, and we get a lot of lost time in the process. But he must satisfy himself that no one is getting too much. *Flamand typique, eh?*"

Balebe managed to smile and then turned to walk down the track a little way, as much to get away from the presence of Shafer and the personable sedimentologist as to avoid the increasingly loud haggling by the dead fire. A few meters down the powdery track, two sand grouse landed, tensed at his approach, and took off again into the bush. The weight of the backpack slung over his shoulder was a constant reminder of his duplicity, and he longed for the moment when the Belgians would leave.

After some time, one of the horns blasted, and he heard engines starting up. He turned and quickly walked back. Laporteau and Hamid were in the cab of the Rover pickup, and Warrmarra, the youngest of the field workers, had wedged himself between two tent bags. Van de Hoven and the other workmen were in the other.

Shafer leaned against the Toyota and shouted to the Belgians,

"We'll cable you when we get to Wangara. Take it easy on the escarpment!"

Van de Hoven raised his hand and nodded. "Good, Bob, have a safe journey—maybe better luck next year with the hominids!" Laporteau gestured to his partner to head out first, and the vehicle rolled slowly down the track. Laporteau put his vehicle in gear and drew level with Shafer and Balebe. "Say hello to those lovely ladies of Wangara for me, Bob. I wish I had your opportunities. Ah well, next summer, at the paleoanthropological congress! *Bonne chance,* Balebe, you will make a fine anthropologist, and very soon!"

Balebe's eyes locked for just a moment with the Belgian's hazel ones. He nodded mutely and raised his hand in farewell.

Laporteau released the clutch and rolled off. Warrmarra grinned and waved to Balebe as the Rover rocked down the uneven track. The cars rattled over the rutted track, lost to sight long before their sounds faded. Shafer turned toward Balebe and said, "Better relax, Thanatu, this'll be a long, slow ride until we get to the border." Turning away and looking straight ahead he added, "Not a bad job of acting, kid, you had them snowed. Go take the bones and put them in my flight bag now."

For a moment Balebe stared at the distant mountains, immobile. Then he turned without a word and headed for the Land Cruiser. The thought of two days' journey alone with Shafer filled him with loathing. But at least he was heading home.

Wangara, 1985: Homecoming

Balebe woke to the sounds of crockery rattling rhythmically atop the soft thump of sandaled feet moving along the corridor. A soft knock on the door, "*Chai,* Baleb*ah,*" the voice of old Kaniugi, who always played with his name, since with that pronunciation it meant "mango" in Kaniugi's mother tongue. A rattling thump of the tray on the hall carpet, Kaniugi's retreating steps.

"*Ayah,* Kaniugi, *asante sana.*" He rose from his bed, shivering in the gray light of the early morning. "Tea at dawn," he muttered. "Bloody upper-class habit went out in England in the thirties . . . oh well, it takes the chill off." He felt even more victimized by the morning chill of the Asalian highlands after a season in the heat of Batchilok.

He opened the door and lifted the tray off the floor where Kaniugi had left it: teapot, strainer, the blue cup and saucer, creamer with warm milk, sugar, his old sterling spoon from Connaught. Kaniugi and Mariamu never forgot. He walked back to the bed, set the tray on the bedside table, and sat down, wrapping his bedclothes around his shoulders.

Outside the doves were reciting their syncopated coo, so much more interesting than the ones in the States. The fussy twittering of mousebirds rose like static against the doves' rhythm. Moving through the familiar ritual of morning tea, he let his mind wander back over his arrival the night before.

It had been past midnight when the Land Cruiser finally swung onto the dual-lane carriageway that signaled the northern outskirts of Wangara. Dim orange street lamps did little to light the side of the road. The people walking on the dusty verge were barely visible in their dark clothing. After the pure air of the countryside, the smells of the city were overpowering—diesel exhaust, wood smoke, food cooking at roadside stands, the vague hint of incense from the Indians' bungalows.

Balebe peered into the tea shops by the side of the road, where kerosene lamps barely outlined the shapes of men seated at the long tables. *Home, finally . . . I love these* chai *shops, the gentle, funny conversations, I hate the poverty, the corruption, what am I doing to change it, studying fossils? What's the old man up to with the arrests, the disappearances, and now Shafer's got me by the short hairs. Damn the man!*

Shafer had offered to drive him out to the house, and at this hour he could scarcely refuse, however much he wanted to be shut of him. At the second roundabout he said, "Take Andani Road east." Shafer grunted and swung hard right, across the path of a speeding red Ferrari piloted by a turbaned Sikh. The blare of the Ferrari's horn faded behind them.

Andani Road traversed the northern edge of the city's affluent suburbs for several kilometers before they turned right up the Mbagama Valley toward his parents' home. The night air turned cooler and moister, less smoke-laden, as they sped past the dim outlines of manicured hedges and high fences with warning signs— *Mbwa,* "Dog," *Mbwa Kali,* "Fierce dog," and finally, just down the road from his parents' house, the MacPhersons' laconic "DOGS." Balebe noted that since last year the enameled signs of professional guard agencies from downtown were on more walls and gates. "Ultimate Security Ltd." piqued him into a smile despite his rotten mood. *Must have the Bomb.*

He and Shafer had both sat silently for most of the day, wrapped in the fatigue of two days' bone-jarring travel over the worst tracks that western Barbore and eastern Asalia had to offer. Balebe had welcomed their tiredness as an excuse for avoiding conversation with Shafer. His bitterness was as physically palpable to him as the dust that covered his sweat-stained clothing and skin.

Almost there, how will I manage with Father? Shit! If he finds out, he's likely first to reproach me once again for having taken this "mad road to inconsequentiality" and then to do something that will take all this entirely out of my control! He wouldn't dare detain an American, but what would *he do . . . what if the rumors about the disappearances are true? Shit!* Rage welled up again, as much at his father as at Shafer this time. He shifted restlessly in his seat.

" 'Nother coupla minutes and we'll be there, hey? Your Dad sure has nice taste in real estate, Balebe."

The young man only grunted. *If you only knew, Shafer, if you only knew what he did to get this "real estate," you'd have probably thought twice before pulling this shitty little stunt with me. The Rhys-Davids had broken no laws, really, even if they were terrible racialists . . . having their property confiscated and being deported in the turmoil, that was Ezekiel's revenge.*

"The turn into the driveway just past that jacaranda, to the left. You'll have to stop at the gate while the askaris come to check us.

I'll get out and walk in, if it's all right with you," he said, striving for civility.

"No problem, kid, it's really late and we don't need to socialize tonight. Remember to be at the museum by ten tomorrow, so we can go over our press release, okay?"

"Right—here we are. I've got my bags, thanks. Can you find your way back to town?"

"Yeah, I never lose my way, you know that." Shafer's grin stood out in his grimy face. "See you tomorrow."

Balebe stepped down from the Land Cruiser to the massive gate and peered into the driveway past the swathe illuminated by the headlights. Two men in heavy greatcoats moved quickly down the drive toward them with the distinctive bobbing gait of the western pastoralists, their clubs held loosely in their hands. They broke into grins when they saw him, thrusting their hands through the grating for two firm, dry handshakes even before the gate was unlocked.

With a quick good-bye, Shafer threw the Cruiser into reverse and was gone as Balebe stood exchanging news with the askaris. The simple act of inquiring after families and work, for news of the house and his parents, lifted some of the weight of the last four days from him, but his need to be evasive in his replies to their inquiries about whether he'd found anything brought it back at once.

"*Ayah,*" he said, turning the conversation to an end. "I want to greet my mother and father," he said, in the simple Swahili these rural men used. "Just go," said the guards, "we will see each other tomorrow." He turned and walked up the long drive, feet crunching on the gravel.

As he reached the first step of the entrance, the heavy wood door opened, revealing Kaniugi's lined face. Except that he was a little more stooped, Kaniugi looked no different to Balebe than he had when the old man had ordered him around the kitchen at tea time fifteen years ago. He stepped up and over the threshold, taking Kaniugi's extended hand in his, gripping his own right elbow with his left hand to add strength to their greeting.

"*Salama,* Balebe, *habari za siku nyingi?*" Peace, what news of these many nights?

"*Nzuri,* Kaniugi, *habari zako?*" Good, what news of you?

This second language, used as much as English in his childhood, sounded so sweet that it drew him in again to the chain of pleasantries, the peace of old gestures and familiar roles. He kept the initiative in this exchange, steering the questions away from the field season. His eyes roamed past Kaniugi, over the fresh flowers in the brass vase on the Chippendale table, up the wide staircase, toward the paintings of native birds that lined the hallway.

He wiped his boots on the rough sisal mat inside the door, looked at the shining expanse of dark wood parquet down the hall, and stooped to untie and remove his boots before even setting foot in the house. They were heavily laden with the beige dust of the dry places, only lightly tinged with the red clay of these highlands.

"Your mother is waiting in the library. Your father is already sleeping. I will prepare a bath for you."

Balebe nodded and let Kaniugi relieve him of his gear. "Very good, thank you, Kaniugi." At least he would be spared his interview with his father until tomorrow. He walked quickly down to the library door in his stocking feet, tapped, and opened it. His mother was sitting in her favorite chair, next to a low fire in the grate. She rose immediately and rushed across the room to him, arms outstretched.

"Welcome home, my dear, how filthy you are! Haven't you had any time to wash on this expedition?"

"Not for the last three days, Mum. Do stop hugging me, you'll smear this muck all over yourself!"

"Never mind, you were a good deal more repulsive the first time I saw you and I hugged you nonetheless! How have you been?"

He'd dreaded this. She'd drawn back, still holding both his hands, and was searching his face with her cool green eyes. It had always been impossible to lie or dissemble with her.

"To be honest, Mum, I'm in a bit of a mess. Shafer has turned out to be a real scoundrel, worse than I could ever have imagined, and right now I can't figure a decent way out of the fix he's put me in.

But I'd rather you'd not tell the Guvnor until I've had a little more time to work this out on my own."

"Ah, Balebe Patrick, it isn't politically sensitive, is it?"

"Not in the usual sense, but within the paleoanthropological community it's going to be a real scandal if the truth gets out, and my whole career is in jeopardy if it does as well. Yet—the bastard thinks he can get away with what amounts to fraud, and I can't let him! Oh God, Mum, if I'd only listened more closely to David Pierce!"

His mother drew him over to the fireside and down to the old sofa. Without a word, she went to the liquor cabinet and poured a half tumbler of Jameson's. Handing it to him with her eyes fixed on his face, she sat beside him and waited a moment before speaking. Then she reached across and laid her cool hand on his arm.

"I don't suppose you'll be wanting to give me the details just yet. So keep your counsel. But remember, I am always here to listen if you want to have it all out."

He took a mouthful straight down, glad of the burning in his throat, then smiled at her. "Yes, I know, and you know that I'm grateful." He didn't add, *And I know you've never betrayed me to my father.*

As if following his thoughts, she straightened and said, "Your father has an early meeting with the vice president tomorrow and sends his regrets that he couldn't welcome you home tonight. He'll not be expecting you at breakfast, but he'll come home for tea and will want to see you then."

"How have things been?" The question was open enough to give her room to say what she might.

She brushed back her hair, streaked with more gray than it had been a year ago, and stared into the fire. "Oh, you may have been keeping up with the political infighting in the *Weekly Report* . . . It's been worse than the press lets on. Your father's been very preoccupied about the economic crisis, what with inflation giving the extremists something to pick at, and elections coming up in autumn. They've had to send troops out to quell riots in some of the markets up north, which hasn't made him any more popular. Some

23

of his enemies have been increasingly rude in Parliament. It's not been an easy time."

She turned back to him and smiled. "However, Malama has just got a first on her secondary exam, and Adiari's team's been taking prizes at every soccer tournament in the country. Semira has come to stay while she waits for her baby—you can imagine how proud Mariamu and Kaniugi are. We're all so happy to have her back and to be anticipating her firstborn. Nathan's really off to a very good start with his car repair business, and Kaniugi's becoming quite satisfied with his son-in-law, even if he isn't Pakyu."

Balebe smiled, remembering the uproar when Kaniugi's daughter, Semira, had announced she intended to marry "this boy Nathan," as Kaniugi had jeeringly called him. Balebe wondered if Kaniugi ever in his secret heart blamed bringing Semira up in his own parents' interracial household for this fit of tribal ecumenism on his daughter's part. Despite Kaniugi's hostility to the idea of Semira's marrying a Chacha, Nathan had persisted, having the great tact to offer Kaniugi the traditional Pakyu bridewealth, although his own ethnic group followed different customs, and he so thoroughly modern a young man in any case. The relationship seemed to be maturing well, with Nathan again conceding to his wife's people's tradition in sending her home from their rooms behind the garage for her lying-in.

He smiled. "If Nathan's half as savvy at his business as he is with his in-laws, he'll do well. I'm glad Semira's found someone who cares as much as he does."

He gazed at his mother affectionately over the rim of the tumbler. *All these years in a place so different from green and rocky Connaught, Mary O'Reilly, and how well you've done.* As always, he found it hard to imagine what had drawn his parents to one another in that Manchester classroom. Sometimes, on those rare occasions when his father had taken more than his usual single whiskey and some of the hardness had slipped from his face, he could see another, more attractive man. He felt that his parents' verbal dueling, which ranged from brilliant banter in times like that to full-blown confrontation in the worst moments, must have been the vital link, the avenue of affinity that first opened between them when both were struggling on tiny student stipends as strangers in the land of their colonizer.

As the years passed here in Asalia, and Ezekiel Thanatu had become an increasingly powerful and feared man, the distance between his parents seemed to widen. He wondered if his mother had ever thought of leaving, returning home to the land she had left at eighteen and revisited only once since coming to Asalia. *But you'd never leave us, would you, Mother, no matter how hard a man your husband became. We have always held you hostage.*

He drained his glass and set it on the end table. "Kaniugi was drawing me a bath. I mustn't let it get cold."

She smiled again, and took his hand. "It's wonderful to have you home, whatever the mess and fuss."

He leaned to kiss her cheek and rose. "It's wonderful to be here. Thanks for staying up, Mum, I needed a little respite. Please see that I'm up early. I've got to meet Shafer at the museum at ten."

He'd mounted the stairs, turned into his room. His eyes wandered over the familiar furniture, his mother's paintings of the Rift Valley, the crowded bookshelf. *Home, really home.* Entering his own room, he saw that Kaniugi had stacked his dusty bags on an unfolded back issue of the *Gazette*. He smiled. *Ever on the offensive against dirt! May as well set out the dirty clothes for washing. Hell, they're* all *dirty by Kaniugi's standards!*

He unzipped his backpack and reached into it, began to draw his camera out from its packing in his spare sweatshirt, and froze.

The memory of the photographs he'd taken of the fossils struck him, so hard he lost his breath for a moment. He straightened, staring at the doorway.

"Allah! What a fool I've been! The photos have the date on them! He doesn't know I had the camera with me! I have proof that Shafer's lying about the discovery date!"

He tore the camera out of the bag. "Jesus! Why didn't I think of this in Barbore? I could have put an end to this madness three days ago. Thanatu, you're an imbecile!" His hands were trembling as he uncased the camera and set it to rewind. He pulled the back open and took out the roll of film. "Oh, God, don't let me bungle this one!" he whispered.

He stared at the shiny metal cartridge cradled in his hand, breathing hard. *Where to get it developed—damn! It would be easy if it were the States, with all those automated photo labs where no one gives a damn, but here, even if they've got the machines, they scrutinize every last frame.* He stood up suddenly, gripping the cartridge. "Dhanni's father's store! I'll have to enlist her aid, but I don't want to implicate her. Thank God it's print film, not slides! Damn! I won't have time to develop it before the press conference, but I can tell Shafer I've got them, nonetheless. It's the only leverage I've got, at this point."

He went over to his desk and scrabbled in the drawer, drawing out a clean film canister. Popping the film into it, he slid it under his pillow, feeling better than he had in three days. He smiled and announced, "Time for the first hot bath in six weeks!"

The memory of the bath's welcoming warmth, and of the amazing sedimentation of dirt into the water, brought him into the present moment. The sunlight now shone brightly through his window and the doves had stopped calling in the garden. The film and the night's rest in his own home had strengthened him, and his interval away from Shafer had allowed his resolve to grow.

He picked up his watch from the nightstand. *Eight-twenty, time to get dressed and cadge a ride from Mum. With any luck, Shafer will see reason and announce the find properly . . . perhaps we can cook up a face-saving story. If he doesn't cooperate, I'll just have to unmask the fraud before it goes any further. Oh, the Guvnor wouldn't relish hearing about this in the morning paper! God knows, he should be glad, since confronting Shafer will probably put his firstborn son out of paleoanthropology forever . . . perhaps a degree in economics would please him. I bloody well hope my sticking to my principles does something to cheer him up.*

Tossing off the bedclothes, he walked across to his dresser, grabbed his sponge bag, and started out the door to wash up for the confrontation. He stopped, turned back to the bed, snatched up the film can, and walked down the hall.

Another Betrayal

It was twenty to ten when Mary dropped him off at the Asalia National Museum. The parking lot was crowded with vividly painted charter buses unloading out-of-town schoolchildren. He noticed Anthea Pierce's old Renault parked over by the archaeology labs, and his heart sank. "Oh great," he muttered to himself. "All we need to top this off is a confrontation between Anthea and Shafer! They say Anthea swore to shoot him if he ever set foot in the Ruba area again. Bob really didn't have to be so offensive about her in that magazine interview, but it's in character."

His heart began pounding as he hurried past the main entrance of the exhibit halls to the new office building. *God, how could I have been such a fool as not to confront him in the field, to expose him in front of Michel and Jan? This will be ten times worse, letting them know now. At least we can handle it man-to-man before the press conference—then it just goes as far as it needs to. What will the Belgians think of me?*

As he started up the steps to speak to the woman in the reception booth, he heard Shafer's voice echoing out from the conference room ahead to his left.

"So that's about the size of it, ladies and gentlemen. It's a really revolutionary find that forces us to revise our entire view of the emergence of the genus *Homo*. In a moment, you photographers can come up to take a few pictures. But first, I want to be sure to thank our Belgian colleagues for all the logistical support they provided us during the field season before our find. Without their aid, we would not have been able to be in the field long enough to make the find, even though they had unfortunately left before it was discovered. I also want to thank my student, Balebe Thanatu, son of Asalia's attorney general, for his help in the field. He was an invaluable aid to my fieldwork." The instant Shafer stopped talking, a din broke out as reporters competed in shouting questions.

Balebe stood frozen outside the room, a wave of shock washing over him. *The swine! I can't believe the depths he'll sink to . . . he set me up to miss this press conference! The lie's now headline news! I'll smash him! I'll kill him!*

The courtyard of the building in front of him disappeared in a red mist. He grasped the strap of his camera bag to steady his hands. He dared not move. *No. I will not, will not give him the satisfaction of my publicly disgracing myself.* He took a deep breath. *I've got to get the photos developed right now! I'll set this bastard straight today.*

He turned on his heel away from the clamor in the conference room and strode away from the building, back across the parking lot to the taxi rank outside the exhibit hall where the schoolchildren were still queuing. He leaned into the first cab's window. "Downtown, Patel Cameras, let's go quickly."

A short time later, the cab had penetrated a narrow street near the Neville Hotel. Paying off the driver, Balebe strode into Patel's. The clerk behind the counter greeted him gladly, "Ah, Mr. Balebe, welcome, welcome! You are lucky, Miss Dhanni is in! I will call her!" He disappeared behind a beaded curtain into the interior of the store.

Almost instantly, a lovely young woman of South Asian ancestry rushed through the curtain, long black hair flowing behind her as she rushed around the end of the counter. She gave him a dazzling smile as she extended both hands. "Balebe, my dear fellow, how wonderful to see you! How have you been? Are you home from America for a while? Have you been finding any fossils? Oh, do come on back and have some tea—Sammy, please bring us some tea and biscuits!"

She gestured him back through the doorway and then down a corridor into her office. Grainy black-and-white enlargements of action shots of car rallies and sports events covered one wall. He recognized several Asalian long-distance runners in the prints. But his eye was caught by a series of high-contrast portraits of western pastoralists on the wall opposite.

Dhanni smiled at him as he examined them, settling back into a leather desk chair and crossing her stylishly trousered legs. "Do you like them? I've been experimenting again. Daddy thinks I

28

should stick to the tried and true, but it's got rather boring for me, and my photo expeditions allow me to get away from the family for a while. How I love the west, the people, the openness, the land!"

They paused while Sammy brought in a tray of tea. Balebe turned back to the photos for a moment and smiled. "They're super, Dhanni—you've really captured something there, despite the avant garde processing style. Much truer to the spirit of the Shurr than any of those foreign photogs have managed. How *is* the family?"

Dhanni's face clouded a bit. "Oh, you know, same as ever, everyone's fine, though Dad's got to be careful of his heart. It's worse for me now that I've finished university. Mum and the aunts are really frantic that I haven't found a 'nice boy' and got settled into a bungalow in Meadowlands. I've had any number of excruciating arranged outings with suitable young men, and long cross-examinations afterwards." She sighed and said in an undertone, "I still am sneaking around to see Ben—he's definitely not the kind of nice boy they have in mind."

Their eyes met briefly in sympathy. All through their last two years at university, they'd been part of a little crowd of young Asalians who'd clubbed together out of personal affinity rather than ethnic or religious ties. Stories had gone around about them, but "the seven" were really just good friends, until Dhanni and Ben had fallen deeply in love. The others had covered for them, allowing them time to be alone while ostensibly out with the group. Although Dhanni's family had lived in Asalia for three generations, descendants of railway laborers imported from the Indian Raj, neither they nor Ben's Pakyu family would have approved of a date between the two, much less talk of the marriage both young people wanted.

"God, Dhanni, how much longer are you two going to be tiptoeing around like this?" he asked in equally quiet tones.

"Only until he finishes his law degree. We'll be able to support ourselves then, even if our families cut us off." The pain in her eyes was so apparent, despite the lightness of her tone.

Asalia, what bitter fruit you give your children to eat, he thought.

29

"Look, Dhanni, I've come to ask you a huge favor. It may take your time, and please say no if it's inconvenient, but if you can . . ."

"Anything, Balebe, just ask."

"Right, it has to be utterly hush-hush, at least for now, so I need you to do this all yourself. I've a roll of color print film I need to have developed, and prints made of a couple of the frames. You're the only person I can trust with the work—can you do it?"

"Why, of course. My, this *must* be important, I've never seen you so cloak-and-dagger!"

"Yes, Dhanni, this is very serious."

"Goodness, my dear boy, you've certainly moved into an exciting world since leaving us!"

"More exciting and disillusioning than I had ever thought, Dhanni, and I have only dim hopes of resolving this mess cleanly. Let's get on with it now, can we?"

"Well, actually, Balebe, you're in luck beyond your wildest dreams! We've just installed one of those fabulous automatic photo machines up at our new store in Meadowlands. It's been a real money-maker, since we set it up out in the shop and people can watch their film run through!"

She glanced at her watch. "It's not opening time at Meadowlands yet. You haven't a car, have you? Well, then, I'll lift you up there and run the film through myself straightaway. The beauty of it is that even I don't really have to see the prints, and you can keep your cloak-and-dagger stuff to yourself!"

He broke into a delighted grin. "It's not too much bother to run me up there? I had no idea that there was one of those machines in the country!"

"Well, we had to pay the usual hundred-percent duty on it, plus all manner of "*chai*" to the Customs people—you know how they can be when angling for a bribe—but what's one to do with one's money, anyhow? And as far as this entire episode goes, your secret's safe with me. I won't even tell Ben!" Her eyes sparkled. "Although, if it's ever okay to tell, let me be the first to know! Now, let's get the car!"

Confrontation

An hour later, Balebe unfolded himself from Dhanni's Mazda, promising to call her soon. He strode back toward the museum office building, his rage now contained in an icy calm. After a brief conversation with the receptionist at the entrance booth, he went upstairs to the Palaeontology Department. Nodding to the curatorial staff's greetings, Balebe walked down the long corridor to where they told him Shafer was working.

Shafer was seated in the section containing the Ruba pig fossils, at a table covered with unwrapped specimens from the Batchilok. He was wearing a clean tan safari suit Balebe knew had never seen the field, and his sandy hair seemed to have been trimmed and styled since yesterday. His flight bag, still containing the fossils, lay on the floor next to his chair.

He looked up and his face assumed a subtle, mocking smile as he saw Balebe approaching. "Well, well, oversleep or something, kid? The conference was over an hour ago. It's out on the wires now, and how sweet it is! Want to help me with these pigs?"

Balebe leaned on the table, bringing his face close to Shafer's. He spoke in a low voice, so as not to attract the attention of the department's staff working at their desks fifty feet away. "You do the damned pigs yourself, you unprincipled bastard! I am here to tell you what I want, and you are going to give it to me, without an argument."

He pressed on, before the words forming in Shafer's mouth could be expressed. "Take a look at these, you sod," he said, tossing down the three color prints.

"This is the maxilla, the mandible, and me, dated August twentieth, right on the film. This is proof that you've lied to the press, lied to van de Hoven, and used me. My father runs the courts and police in this country, and people he doesn't like have disappeared. I could quite easily let him know what you've done. However, I won't, at least not if you cooperate with me."

Shafer had leapt to his feet and now leaned on the table, too,

31

looking down at the photographs, utterly still. He finally raised his eyes to stare at Balebe. "What do you want, Thanatu?" His face was gray.

"It's simple, and you get off easy, Bob. What I want is out—out of your graduate program by January at the very latest, and into another Ph.D. program of equal status, with no fuss, no questions. I want to work with Melanie Baine."

"Oh great, Thanatu, make it easy for me. That bitch hates my guts!"

"And with very good reason, if the rumors I've heard are right—and now I'm willing to believe everything I've heard. You really *did* become her lover, playing up the romance of joint research in her new fossil localities in the Batchilok. Then you started the story that she was a spy, didn't you? Once you got her thrown out of the country, you moved right into the Batchilok beds."

"Hey, Balebe, give me a break, we were consenting adults! And the woman didn't have any idea what to do with that area, and I did!"

"Christ, Shafer, you're the most amoral bastard I've ever met! I really think you don't know you're doing anything wrong—you'll be damned lucky to die a natural death!

"Okay, okay, you've got me on this one. I'll bet the negatives are in a nice, safe place, hey? I could probably take you down on this one, since you were willing to cozy up to me until now, but it's not worth the trouble. I'll send a telex to Melanie this afternoon and see what we can work out."

The two men stared at each other in open dislike from either side of the table. As Shafer opened his mouth to add something, the door of the department was flung open, and David Pierce's unmistakable voice asked the section head where Shafer was. A moment later, Pierce stood before them, in an icy rage. Balebe's heart sank. He had never seen Pierce this angry. The man's dark brown eyes seemed ink black as he glared from one to the other.

"Shafer, what *is* it that you've been doing? I've just got off the phone with Jan van de Hoven. He called from the Andaba Hilton, where he just got word of your announcement. *Why* doesn't he know anything about the find? He's beside himself, man, threatening to pull all Belgian support from your next expedition, to complain to the Barbore Ministry of Antiquities about your project, and get your permit pulled. He's also threatening *me* with loss of support for our joint projects in Ruba, because I let you put on this press conference in the museum!"

Pierce pressed on. "It's bad enough your imposing on my hospitality in order to rub my face in the triumph of your theory, but you've gone much too far in alienating Jan. The man is raving mad, Shafer! I insist you make a full explanation of why you chose to use our facilities in a way that jeopardizes my institution's future with the Belgians."

Balebe felt himself slipping into a panic. He glanced down the corridor of the collections to see the entire Palaeontology Department staff attending to the exchange. His own future depended on the next few moments, and on the words of the man he had just excoriated.

Shafer looked down for a moment, casually swept the photographs together and turned them over on the table. He then heaved a sigh and met Pierce's eyes. "Phew, David, I guess I really blew it. Even if Anthea used to hoard fossils in the old days, this press conference was a mistake. Balebe here was just giving me hell for not phoning the Belgians and telling them ahead of time about our find on the way out of the field. I just got carried away. I mean, this is pretty heady stuff, and we only made the find three days ago."

He shrugged and gestured to Pierce. "I admit I made a big mistake not giving the Belgians more credit in my announcement. But, dammit, they didn't find it! And Jan kept telling me that there was nothing to find down the Bir Kalichi!"

Shafer raised his hand as if fending off an objection. "I know, I know, that shouldn't count!" He stopped, sighed, then continued. "David, I made a mistake. I abused your good offices in letting me use the museum to make the announcement. Chalk it up to enthusiasm. I am genuinely sorry. Hey, Balebe was already reading me the riot act."

Pierce, his face still grim, turned to Balebe. "So, you, too, thought it was a bad idea to take this course."

Once again stunned by Shafer's facility at weaving half truths and outright lies into a plausible whole, Balebe nodded and said in a low voice, "Yes, I think it was a dreadful mistake."

"Well, maybe there's hope for you yet, Thanatu. Please remember henceforth that while you may be attending an American university and associating with Americans, you are a citizen of this country, and that you owe your country, if not your own family, a higher level of integrity than might be the norm among those with whom you consort."

Pierce turned back to Shafer. "Bob, get on the phone in my office right now and see if you can patch this up with Jan. This state of affairs simply must be remedied immediately." Without another word he turned and strode out of the collections.

Balebe met Shafer's eyes and said to him in an undertone, "You're scum, Shafer, and I don't want to dirty myself any more by dealing with you. I'll give you this filthy little fraud on the Belgians—what matters most in the end is that the fossils have been found and will be published."

Shafer began to reply, but Balebe cut him off. "I never want to have anything to do with you personally again. Get me transferred to San Felipe State. I'll hold onto the negatives, but don't worry, there'll be none of your sordid blackmail schemes, only this: if I ever see you making mischief for people as you've done here, I'll expose you for the exploitative bastard you are." He, too, turned and walked out of the collections into the bright afternoon sun.

Wangara, 1986: Meetings

At eight o'clock in the morning, the city of Wangara was gray and cool. Outside the Neville Hotel, a knot of tourists shivered in their summer outfits as they queued for the zebra-striped minibuses waiting to take them out to the game parks. Brown-feathered kites wheeled over the concrete canyons of the city's heart, keen-eyed scavengers oblivious to the din of rush hour traffic.

On the terrace cafe of the Neville, Bob Shafer poured a second cup of coffee from the silver pot on his table and tapped out a Benson and Hedges from his pack. His sandy hair was well-styled and showed considerably more gray at the temples than it had on his previous visit the year before. He wore a well-tailored American suit and Italian shoes. A leather briefcase lay on the chair next to him. He lit his cigarette and leaned back, smiling faintly at the tourists in front of him. His eyes wandered from them across the broad boulevard to his left, lingering on the crowd of pedestrians bunched up at the traffic light.

The crowd surged toward him across Taifa Avenue with the green light. Shafer watched it resolve into individuals who reflected the currents that ran together in this capital of trade and tourism in sub-Saharan Africa. A turbaned Sikh in a khaki safari suit strode ahead of three stylishly dressed black women with elaborate braided hairdos who strolled across engrossed in animated conversation. As they reached the near curb, the women took care to step around a legless beggar swinging himself along on thickly callused knuckles. An Arab in a thousand-dollar suit and an embroidered skullcap jostled two young European men in jeans, scuffed jogging shoes, and backpacks who stood gawking at the Neville's breakfast terrace. These and others mingled briefly with the shivering tourists and souvenir hawkers outside the hotel, then moved down the street.

Shafer checked his watch, put a red twenty-diyani note on his check, and rose to join the crowd heading south on Kabime Street. A half block down the street, he stopped to drop a ten-diyani bill into the upended hat of the legless beggar, who'd now taken up his accustomed post along the sidewalk near the tourist hotels. The man grinned and stuck his hand out to Shafer, who bent and shook it, exchanging a few words in Swahili before moving on.

Shafer moved with the skill of considerable experience through the crowded pavement, striding across Umoja Avenue at a near run just in front of two onrushing buses. Having gained the far curb, he changed his direction, walking east along the avenue toward the Pankolo Conference Centre.

This morning the Pankolo Conference Centre was attracting an assortment of people who differed in appearance from either the tourists or the indigenous mix of downtown Wangara. Predominantly white and male, but with some white women and a few Asian and African men mixed in, most were a shade too casually dressed for business, yet overdressed for tourism. Like Shafer, many carried briefcases, except for those with day packs over their shoulders. A modest marquee set into the side of the Centre bore the legend "Welcome 3rd Paleoanthropological Congress."

Greetings sounded in the cavernous entrance to the main hall, dominated by the statue of Bethwick Pankolo, first president of Asalia. Small groups of people stood in animated talk, waved to new arrivals, shook hands, greeted others, and formed into new clusters.

Shafer strode into the entrance and glanced around. Quite a few conversations stopped, and many eyes followed him as he moved toward one such group, composed of Michel Laporteau, clad in a dark gray suit and white, open-necked shirt, a wiry man in khaki shorts, white shirt, and worn tweed jacket, and a lean blond woman in a finely cut beige dress topped by a fawn suede jacket. Shafer smiled and shook hands with each of the men, then put a casual arm around the woman and pecked her cheek. Only those closest to the group could see how Melanie Baine's face froze as Shafer touched her.

"Michel, how the hell are you? You've lost some weight since last summer in the Batchilok! You're lookin' good!" Shafer said, directing his first remarks to the Belgian sedimentologist.

"Pas mal, mon ami, the ladies appreciate the slender form more these days, eh, Melanie?" Laporteau raised an eyebrow at the woman suggestively. He tapped out a Gauloise from his pack and lit it, still smiling.

"Christ, Michel, you never do let up, do you," said the man in the tweed jacket. "You're looking a real lady-killer yourself these days,

Bob. I know American academics make piles of money compared to us expats, but do you really have enough to afford those shoes?"

"Well, Colin, the book's been doing well, and the lecture circuit's going okay too, after the Barbore find. Besides, in the States we've gotta dress for success, unlike you Brits, who can show up anywhere in shorts and knee socks, right Melanie?"

Melanie Baine looked Shafer full in the eyes for the first time and said, "Some of us seem to need more success than others, Bob. If you'll excuse me, I have to go find Balebe before the session begins." She turned and swiftly walked away.

"*Touché,* Bob, I believe she made a direct hit," Laporteau chuckled.

"Good-looking woman, Melanie, but cold, too cold. I prefer something a bit warmer, don't you, Michel?" Shafer bantered back.

Colin Jones interposed, "Well, while you two discuss the relative merits of hot and cold running women, I'll see whether the Centre's barman can be chatted up for a bitter before the tedious speeches begin. I require some fortification against these pomposities by the Big Men in the Government Opening Another Meeting at the Splendid Pankolo Conference Centre. I liked this place better when it was a racecourse. Care to join me?"

"Nine's a bit early for me, Colin, try me later," Shafer replied, and Laporteau shook his head.

Laporteau smiled at Jones's departing back. "I will never understand the priorities of the British. But he is correct that these opening speeches will be a bore. However, it is the price we pay for the free rides to exotic places, no? I don't suppose you know whether David Pierce will try to reply today to your *Nature* paper on the Batchilok find?"

"Well, David dropped me a note saying that he was only going to speak as head of paleontology of the museum of the host country today, and that he'd deal with my materials tomorrow when we are both scheduled to present papers."

"Ah, the fireworks will start tomorrow afternoon, then? As I remember, you are second, after Pierce, in the session?" Laporteau asked.

"Yeah, thank God we have this afternoon and tomorrow morning off for the museum tours. I need to relax a little before speaking before the assembled masses. Jesus, Michel, *everyone* who's anyone in paleoanthropology is here."

Shafer took his pack of cigarettes from his jacket pocket, tapped another out, and lit it. "I *know* my Batchilok find itself blows David's model for the origins of genus *Homo* out of the water, but the guy's such a smooth operator that I still get nervous about debating him. I mean, that English public school manner and all the *savoir faire*—it pisses me off that he's been able to put so much over just on his manners alone!"

Laporteau arched a brow and said, a little diffidently, "Ah, but until you had made that find, either his view or yours was equally tenable, *n'est-ce pas*? I agree that David is very able verbally, but there has been more substance to his work than you would imply, my friend."

Shafer rocked back on his heels, exhaling another lungful of smoke. "Yeah, Michel, I guess you're right. But he and Anthea have been getting money from the foundations for years, just on their reputations and upper-class manners, while the rest of us have to scrabble around for the damned airfare!" He ground his cigarette out under his heel and changed the subject. "Anyway, how's it gone out in West Ruba this summer? I hear that some of the localities are very rich."

Laporteau grunted and nodded, "Some yes, some no. I have been spending most of my time mapping the exposures in detail and documenting the sedimentary environments, so you would have to ask David—or better yet, Juma, about the fossils. However, one does observe as one walks, and occasionally one does see something very interesting . . ."

"Richer than the Asoka localities we worked back in eighty?" Shafer queried.

"Well, at least so, and definitely older than those and the other East Ruba exposures Anthea has researched. The old woman is now a bit, ah, put out, that she never searched the other side of the river, only to have David find these more ancient deposits when she is too old to work on them!"

"Hmmm, figures she'd be pissed, even if it is her nephew that found them!" Shafer chuckled. He looked up at the clearing morning sky. "Still, those were great days out there, Michel, you and me, Melanie, and old Anthea prospecting and excavating. As a first field experience, it was superb! God, what I'd give for a day of that right now, just to unwind a little!"

"Hmm!" Laporteau nodded. "You paleoanthropological types are so emotional with your materials. The subject appears to attract those who will have their theories be a matter of life and death! I myself prefer a discipline in which one can work with a certain *sang-froid*, reserving the passions for other arenas. Anthea has been making my life completely decomposed for the last two weeks, preparing for the field excursion to Ruba for the congress participants—so much emotion over these old remains!"

He took another drag on his Gauloise. "Incidentally, I have a suggestion for a very intriguing way to unwind, Bob, if you—ah! We are now supposed to move inside and compose ourselves for the formalities. I believe that the young Thanatu's father is speaking. The more I think of it, the more perhaps Jones had the right idea."

Laporteau and Shafer joined the crowd filing into Uhuru Hall.

Missing

The following afternoon at the Pankolo Conference Centre, few people lingered outside the hall before the afternoon session. Most had wanted to secure seats for what promised to be one of the most electric exchanges of the century, the face-to-face debate between Pierce and Shafer over the implications of the Batchilok find for their different theories of human evolution, with a scheduled hour of open questions and comments from the floor. The various other actors, prominent and less so, were eager to pose questions to each and to express their own viewpoints.

The interior of Uhuru Hall was wood paneled, a huge mural showing the progress of the nation of Asalia adding color along the front wall. Lighting in the audience section was muted, but the stage, with two podiums and stands for illustrative materials, was brilliantly lit.

Many in the audience were standing, waving and calling to friends several aisles over. As two o'clock approached, however, most sat down, and the talk inside the hall lowered to an intense buzz. At two precisely, Jan van de Hoven walked stiffly from the wings and approached the right-hand podium.

"Ladies and gentlemen, I am happy to welcome you here to the second day of the Third International Paleoanthropological Congress." He paused for a moment, as if collecting his thoughts. "I am supposed to be introducing to you the two men from whom I know you all want to hear, Dr. David Pierce and Professor Robert Shafer. I will beg your, ah, indulgence for a few minutes, since one of our participants has not yet arrived." He left the podium and disappeared into the wings.

The noise of the audience rose to a new level of intensity. In the second row to the far right, Colin Jones leaned back and called to Michel Laporteau in the row behind him, "Oi! Is it Pierce or Shafer who's late? Want to lay a fiver on Pierce?" Laporteau smiled and shook his head, returning to his conversation with an American geologist.

About ten minutes later, van de Hoven reappeared, looking more ill-at-ease than before. "Ladies and gentlemen, I beg your pardon, but one of our participants still has not arrived, and we have not been able to contact him at his hotel . . ."

The crowd surged into conversation. It was Shafer who had not yet showed up! "Please, ladies and gentlemen, I beg you, please!" van de Hoven raised his voice over the noise. "I must make a further announcement!"

The crowd quieted to hear what van de Hoven had to tell them. "In view of Professor Shafer's absence, Dr. Pierce has chosen to defer his presentation until such time as Professor Shafer is available to hear it in its, ah, completeness. So, we are calling a fifteen minute recess at this time, and then, if Professor Shafer does not appear, we will commence with the rest of the afternoon program. All participating peoples should be advised to be prepared to give their talks at that time."

As van de Hoven left the podium, the conference room broke into an uproar. People jumped over the backs of seats to reach friends, and most people surged toward the exits, talking animatedly.

In the entrance, Colin Jones sought out Melanie Baine. "Well, Melanie, it seems Bob has finally gone too far with his grandstanding. Or perhaps he's come a cropper somehow. Quite unlike him to miss his moment of glory, don't you think?"

"Yes, it is rather out of character for Bob to miss a chance to humiliate someone like David. What does he have to gain by delaying this, when he has the upper hand, given the implications of his Batchilok finds?" Melanie shook her head. "I don't understand it at all." She turned to face into the light breeze, her blond hair lifting in the wind.

Michel Laporteau had drifted up, Gauloise dangling from his lip, and listened to their exchange. Colin smiled wickedly at Melanie. "You didn't finally put some arsenic in Bob's Wheetabix, did you, my dear?" Laporteau smiled wryly and took another drag on his cigarette.

"As much as I would once have liked to, Colin, I long ago decided it wouldn't be worth the trouble," Melanie replied, smiling. "Besides, so many others have equally good cause to do it . . . But this is very strange."

Colin chuckled. "Yes, there's always the Pierces, and old Jan himself, and what about that young Thanatu fellow you've taken on as a student? I heard a rumor—oi! There's the signal from Jan for the rest of the afternoon session! Rather anticlimactic, eh?"

"Yes," Laporteau joined in, "one wonders how David Pierce will, ah, handle this problem."

With the rest of the conference participants, Laporteau, Jones, and Baine filed back toward the auditorium. Just then, a high-pitched shriek rang out from above, and many gasped and stopped in their tracks, including Melanie.

Jones glanced up and then at Melanie with twinkling eyes. "A little jumpy, what? Pay it no mind, it's just a couple of the bloody kites fighting over some rubbish they've nipped. Whatever's got hold of Bob's rather bigger than that, I'm sure!"

Twilight

The halogen street lights were beginning to glow a weak pink in the dusk when the conference participants drifted out of the Pankolo Centre in small groups. Michel Laporteau stood for a moment at the curb facing the Centre, inhaling his Gauloise and jingling change in his pocket. He turned to watch the sun's rays shining from behind the clouds hanging at the western edge of the highlands. The lamplight gathered intensity, casting orange pools of light along the lightly trafficked avenue as the brief equatorial twilight darkened. He stood, silently, as most of the participants moved away toward their hotels.

"Oi, Michel, how about a Dubonnet at the Neville?" Jones's voice broke his solitude. The wiry Welshman strode toward him, still in shorts and knee socks, worn tweed coat flapping in the rising breeze.

"*Bon,* yes, why not, my friend. Have you heard anything more about the search for Shafer?"

"Nothing more than what we heard an hour ago. The CID is now involved and it's a full-fledged manhunt. Bloody embarrassing for the country, and for that boy Thanatu's father, eh?"

"Is it possible, perhaps, that some terrorist group . . . ?" Michel inquired, smoothing his dark hair.

"Well, my source at police HQ says not likely, since CID believes that a terrorist group would have made some public announcement by now. There are no signs of violence at the hotel. In fact, it doesn't seem that Shafer's bed was slept in. Knowing Bob, perhaps that should not be alarming news. Damned strange, though, Bob always had his priorities set, with fossils first and *femmes* a clear second."

He leaned a little closer to Laporteau. "Latest word is that several of our esteemed colleagues have been called in to 'assist the police with their enquiries,' as they say."

Laporteau stared hard at him. "Are they suspecting a particular person, then?"

"Hardly, it seems they're just going on a fishing expedition, trying to find out who last saw Bob alive, when, where, and so on. The window of opportunity seems to have been between the end of yesterday's morning session—or rather after the lunch that Bob had with Dieter Kresch and company—and early this morning. I suspect our esteemed colleagues are being grilled about their alibis for the span in question. Oh well, let the coppers do their jobs, and let the barmen at the Neville do theirs!"

The two men, so similar in height but so different in build and attire, turned their backs to the now dim western sky and walked along Pankolo Avenue. At the next corner, they trotted across the road and made for eastern Juwayi Street, where a door let straight into the Neville's Long Bar.

Once inside, they moved up to the crowded counter. Jones waved to one of the white-coated barmen for attention. "Elephant Head *moto!*" he barked, tossing a twenty-diyani note on the counter and gesturing at Michel.

Laporteau asked for a Dubonnet on ice and sighed. "Warm beer, you English never cease to fascinate me."

After an interval of silent reflection on the satisfactions of his drink, the Belgian cocked his head sideways at Jones. "How did the museum laboratory tour go yesterday, Colin? You have been so preoccupied preparing displays for the visiting scholars. Was it a success?"

Jones ran his hand over the thinning hair atop his head and nodded. "Yes, it actually went off very well, after a regular balls-up of a morning, running about, getting the archaeological side of things set up. David handled the fossil hominids and the like."

He wiped a bit of foam from his leathery upper lip. "It was especial hell to get something decent together on the Ruba sites, holed up in the bloody awful old wing of the museum that Anthea fancies. The light's bad, the dust is thick enough to excavate, and what's worse, the old woman's been in looking over my shoulder every day she's in town."

Michel sighed and tugged at the cuffs of his shirt, evening them up exactly at the ends of his dark suit jacket. "Yes, Anthea has been very preoccupied with all details in the field as well. I am exhausted from the rigors."

Jones snorted and took another drink. "Right you are, and I don't mind telling you that it's been a regular nightmare to work with her since that article by Shafer came out two years ago, and now with the Batchilok find and the conference on, it's reached a fever pitch. She's determined that the Ruba evidence should refute his position, and his statement that she's sloppy in her analyses."

He waved an arm and went on. "So, not only has she been rooting around endlessly in the Ruba hominid material, but she's also been breathing down my neck, virtually ordering me to find proof of her position in the stone tools! It's hard enough to get the damned things sorted and measured and produce some neat-looking pie diagrams, eight weeks after a field season—but to make them testify to the species of their makers! Huh!" He took a long swig of his beer.

Laporteau grimaced and nodded. "My condolences, Colin, Anthea is a difficult woman at the best of times, but since this problem with Shafer began, I have heard that she is not *rationale.*"

"Well, whatever it is, she's become obsessed, and I'm the one taking the daily outpourings of spleen," Jones replied. "Michel, when she gets on the subject of Shafer, the woman's positively homicidal." Jones stopped his glass midway to his mouth and swiveled around to look Laporteau full in the eyes. "Jesus wept, you don't suppose . . ."

"Hmpf, well anything is possible, *mon vieux,* but please recall what Melanie said earlier today. There are so many with motivations against Bob. After all, both of these women, although for entirely different reasons, and then, what of David?"

Jones nodded, and gestured to the barman for another round. "Yes, I see what you mean. If Bob has been done in, David is the obvious choice, since he was about to be done in, metaphorically but royally, himself. I mean, there's no way that his ideas about the origins of the genus *Homo* can stand up under the challenge of Shafer's Barbore find. It's not so much that he's had to eat crow since the *Nature* article's come out as the fact that Shafer was obviously setting out to take such glee in ridiculing him. That could send even someone as cool as David over the edge, I should think."

Michel shook his head, sipping his Dubonnet. "I will never understand you paleoanthropological types. Always so involved with your egos in your work. I myself am delighted to be a student of the quiet sediments, where one can work with more detachment. It makes a more tranquil occupation."

Jones grunted and took a sip of his new drink. "As for Melanie—I'd never for a minute believe the girl would dirty her hands with anything like a murder! Fastidious, she is. But you were in the field with her and Bob during La Grande Passion and all that—what do you think? Would she have it in her to bump Bob off?"

Laporteau looked quietly into his drink for a moment, then raised his head with a little grimace and stared at the mirror behind the barman. "Ah, it's a difficult matter, Colin. You know, at that time, when we were together in Anthea's field camp, we were all very young. The Melanie I knew then—well, she has completely disappeared. You were in England then, so you never saw this girl when she was young. Lovely, as she still is, but very open, *une jeune fille,* really." He sighed, "She was so in love with Bob, and Bob seemed to be reciprocating."

He cocked his head and gave Colin a sidelong glance. "Of course, with Anthea's camp rules, they had little time to demonstrate to each other. But Melanie was *très belle,* glowing, in that way that women do when they give their hearts . . ." He sighed. "After her field season in Barbore, when she was deported, I have never seen that young girl again, although I have known her all these years."

Jones looked down at his drink but remained silent, and after an interval, Laporteau resumed with a sigh. "Who is to know the human heart, Colin? She was so utterly crushed when I saw her in transit in Bruxelles, after she was expelled from Barbore, like a smashed bird. I tell you, I was in fear that she might take her life."

He looked up and cleared his throat. "But, then, she rallied—she once again began to come to meetings and to publish. But she was *une femme changée,* always on guard, always completely *chic, bien défendée*—you understand?"

Jones shifted uncomfortably on his bar stool. "Er, yes, I see what you mean. Damned poor form if Bob did get her put out of Barbore, wretched thing to do." He glanced at the door and straightened on his stool. "Ah, there's Melanie, now, looking a bit grim. Oi! Melanie, over here!"

Melanie Baine pushed through to the bar. Her usually immaculate blond hairdo was a bit tousled, and she was clearly upset. "God, it's good to see familiar faces! I've just been grilled by the police and really need a drink—double vodka on the rocks—with a twist!" she called to the bartender.

She gratefully sank down on the stool offered by Laporteau. "*Merci bien,* Michel, give me one of those stinking Gauloise, please, I need a cigarette. Thanks." She grimaced with distaste on her first puff, but kept smoking. "Jesus, I can't believe I used to like to smoke . . ."

As the barman served her drink, Jones looked at her expectantly. "Well, don't leave us guessing, Melanie! What did they ask? Does it seem they're treating it like a kidnapping or what? Do you have an alibi? No, Michel, don't shush me, it'll do the girl good to talk about it!"

Melanie took another drag on the cigarette, gagged, and stubbed it out in Michel's ashtray. "Sorry, I just can't finish this. Well, Colin, they seem to be debating between kidnapping and homicide right now."

She shook her blond mane and smoothed her skirt with a wry smile. "It seems Balebe's father knows enough about our professional infighting to know who Bob's, ah, least friendly parties are, and we were all lined up in the waiting room, to be given the interrogation routine—me, David, Jan, and a couple of others . . ." She took another gulp of her drink and patted at her hair. "Oh, they're terribly polite and deferential, ladies first and all that. But it still gave me the creeps to be sitting on a squeaky oak chair with these three bulky guys clumped around me."

She glanced at Jones and smiled. "And yes, I have an alibi, that is, if they don't think Anthea and I are in league with each other. I had dinner with her out at her house last night. She was being ushered in, incidentally, just as I left. You can imagine the uproar."

Jones rolled his eyes. "Say no more." Laporteau muttered under his breath in French, and Melanie managed a chuckle.

Beginning on his third beer, Jones said, "Well, then, homicide is an option, you know. Anthea's actually threatened his life, as we were saying before you came in, and there are moments when I wouldn't put it past her, but David seems an equally likely prospect."

Melanie nodded. "Yes, this was going to be a really hard defeat for David's ideas about the descent of *Homo* from *Australopithecus* in the late Pliocene. But he's *too* perfect a suspect. Who'd want to commit a crime that you're clearly going to be the prime suspect for? Besides, he's got an iron-clad alibi for most of the span during which Bob must have disappeared."

The Belgian sighed. "Yes, he was officiating the museum tour all afternoon and then attending the tedious dinner at the Belgian Embassy last night, at which we endlessly endured Jan's field stories, until we were all too stupefied to respond. At least they served *cuisine française.*"

He turned toward Jones. "But among suspects, should we not even include van de Hoven? He certainly had reason to be angry with Bob since last year. He was simply impossible in Andaba, after Bob's announcement of the find from here. I tell you, he was like a madman, accusing Bob of hiding the fossil, even after Shafer telephoned and tried some pacification. Even for days afterward, he was completely enraged. It was a blessing to retreat to Bruxelles after he went on to his institute."

Jones nodded. "Mmmm, it was all around the museum that Pierce and Shafer had a huge blowup after the press conference when Bob announced the find. About van de Hoven not knowing ahead of time and then phoning David and giving him what for. But

Jan *can't* have had anything to do with Bob's disappearance. I mean, if the man had, he'd have been apprehended at the scene, and Bob would be amongst us now! I've never met such an incompetent! But don't get me started on Jan!"

He ran his hand over the top of his balding head, eyes fixed on the ancient fox-hunting scene suspended behind the bar. "There isn't a Belgian Mafia, is there? I mean, the only way Jan could have pulled it off would have been to hire someone to do it."

Melanie choked on her drink and began to cough. "Colin, you say the damnedest things! But that was what I needed to get me out of this mood. I mean, I'm stuck between being secretly glad Bob's disappeared on the eve of his triumph and fear that acting too happy will land me in jail! I've got to go now, yes, you *will* take this money for my drink! I'm supposed to go back and meet Anthea outside police headquarters, and I don't dare be late. Bye!" With another pat at her hair, she dove back into the crowd and disappeared.

Jones stared after her. "Lovely girl, that, don't for a minute believe she'd do Bob in, though God knows, she'd have reason."

Laporteau shifted on his stool and looked down at his drink. "There are still others, you know. I tell you, something strange happened last season in the Batchilok with that young Thanatu. He acted not himself our last day in camp, and then so soon after Bob's announcement of the find, he is transferred to Melanie's university. I suspect something of Bob's mischief there, although I am not certain . . . and the boy has a formidable father."

"Er, yes," Jones said, quickly scanning around them and gauging the distance between himself and the nearest barman. "I wouldn't put it past Bob to have fiddled the boy out of the discovery! He did it to the Belgians, why not to him?"

He lowered his voice a bit and leaned toward the Belgian. "The elder T. is definitely someone to be reckoned with. I wouldn't care to put myself on his bad side, as a permanent resident and employee of the republic."

Jones straightened and gestured to the barman for another beer. "At any rate, you're looking remarkably composed for someone who's been making all these last-minute arrangements for the congress excursion to Ruba. I must say that I was relieved to hear it was you, and not someone like that harebrained Jan, who was organizing the Ruba excursion."

Laporteau groaned, a twinkle in his hazel eyes. "Ah, yes, who can forget the disaster of the Casablanca conference, where they left it to van de Hoven to supply the refreshments for the excursion to the Rabat locales. It was most regrettable, to be drinking warm Fanta sodas and chewing awful crackers from Singapore, in a nation where such fine foods are easily to be found."

"Huh! At least you *got* crackers! I was out there translating old Demoine's tool typology for the British contingent, and we all ended up with absolutely nothing. Anthea was livid, as you can imagine! I myself was thinking about leaving the stupid sod out there at the quarry!"

Laporteau smiled. "Sometimes I think that at least half the, er, ardors?—no, the hardships—of fieldwork are simply created by the fieldworkers themselves. Simple stupidity, in most cases, and a lack of attention to the infrastructure."

"So true, Michel, so true."

They sat in silence a few moments, sipping their drinks. Then Laporteau smiled wryly at the fox-hunting scene. "You may be assured that the infrastructure for this excursion has been properly composed in Anthea's camp. When she has not been here in town, molesting you, she has been in Ruba, terrorizing the camp staff.

"I myself have had to make three trips in David's plane, with the miscellaneous food, liquor, and other amenities for the Ruba excursion. David is exacting about the details of the lunch in his area, but Anthea—she is not reasonable. Even yesterday, as the congress began, I was obliged to fly more fruit and vegetables and suddenly an extra minifridge to her camp! However, all the details for the dinner and overnight stay there are complete. We have only to wait two days until the congress adjourns."

He swirled the remaining ice cubes around in his glass. "It will still be awkward, providing lunch to thirty persons in such primitive conditions as West Ruba. However, there will be decent wine, and good boxed lunches from the Neville which David will fly out with the excursion participants. The main problem has been finding a suitable dining place. Something close to the airstrip as well as to the exposures where he found that *Australopithecus* mandible, yet also somewhat sheltered and pleasant, as much as that region allows."

He took another sip of his drink. "Juma and I spent two miserable days exploring possible situations which David had pointed out on aerial photos, only to find most completely unacceptable. However, we finally located an adequate site."

"So, you were just out that way yesterday?" Jones asked, fishing in his pocket for change.

"Yes, to Anthea's camp one last time. David will fly his camp staff and Juma's men out there tomorrow to set up the extra tents for the guests. They will also drive two more Rovers across the river to the West Ruba airstrip, where we already have one vehicle waiting." He heaved a sigh. "I am glad it is over."

Laporteau drained his drink and turned to Jones. "Now, it is almost eight o'clock and my digestion requires some satisfaction. Where do you wish to dine? I absolutely refuse to subject myself to tough goat meat, undercooked *pommes frites,* and warm beer at your old favorite, the New Victoria. Once was enough for my liver, but I would be delighted to share a meal with you at some more civilized place."

"Well, *chacun a son goût,* as you'd say," Jones replied, plonking a handful of change down on the bar. "Can we compromise with the Kashmir? I quite fancy their tandoori chicken."

"A splendid choice! And perhaps I can interest you in accompanying me later to the Pearl Club? There are some new young ladies there who are quite attractive."

"A bit pricey for me, old man. Remember I'm paid in local currency! But if you'll pay the cover charge, I'll have a beer or two and listen to the band. I hear the new blokes from Zaire are very good. I must be off early, though—another night like last night and I'll never be able to present my talk at the morning session on the Early Stone Age. I swear that McBradney woman scheduled me at eight-thirty to deprive me of my evening comforts!"

"*Bien,* you can avail yourself of the refreshments and the music, and I will make myself available to the ladies, for dancing and for as much else as they wish to consume."

"Christ, Michel, you're such a walking caricature, the oversexed Froggie! It's an experience, to have all my stereotypes so well justified."

"*Belge, mon ami, que je suis Belge!*" Laporteau smiled back, gesturing at Colin's outfit. "And you, with your shorts, knobby knees, and warm beer, nothing of the stereotype there, eh? I fear that, with our respective habits, we could be creatures in a cheap novel, eh?"

"Well, let's not get too carried away, old man. What say we write ourselves in for a little chop, eh?"

Wangara, 1987: Arrival

The man in front of Cynthia took back his passport and moved on. She stepped up to the window under the sign reading "Pankolo International Airport Immigration." A bored-looking young man in a sharp green-and-khaki uniform looked at her unsmilingly as she offered her passport and immigration forms. Despite herself, she felt a ghost of unease under his appraising glance. He studied her papers for a moment and then raised his eyes again, looking her straight in the eye this time, with a cool insolence mixed with a hint of sexual charge.

"You are a student of what?"

"Paleoanthropology," she blurted, without thinking.

"What?" he asked sharply.

"Uh, ancient humans, fossils, human evolution . . ." she stammered.

"Ahhhh, *hominids!* Yes, I attended a lecture Dr. Pierce gave at the national museum on our heritage. Do you believe humanity evolved here in Africa, as he says?" His eyes were still serious and mildly threatening.

Cynthia smiled. "As a matter of fact, I do. All the evidence points to it."

"Hmm," he nodded and returned to her immigration document. "Show me your return ticket. We don't want young foreigners coming here saying they're students and then dealing in dope and living off our economy!"

She handed over her ticket quietly, stifling her urge to protest. *Why am I getting the creeps so badly? Thousands of American tourists visit this place every year, it's safe, right? Just because Bob Shafer disappeared here last year doesn't mean every anthropologist does . . .* The memory flitted across her mind of Shafer's face during their brief introduction at the physical anthropology meetings in Tucson. His immaculate hairdo, his glance sizing her up as a potential conquest, the charming smile that perceptibly cooled as he took in the San Felipe State on her name tag. She blinked to banish the image and tried to look calm as the immigration official thumbed through her ticket.

Looking up from the last ticket of her return flight, he asked, "Where is this place San Felipe?"

"It's in the southwestern part of the United States—very hot and dry—like your Rift Valley. I am a student at the university there."

He nodded and turned her immigration form over, running his eyes down the lines. Cynthia saw him stiffen slightly on his stool as he reached the bottom of the page, with the name and address of her local host. When he looked up at her again, his face was subtly altered, impassive, devoid of any charge whatsoever. "You are staying with Ezekiel Thanatu." It was less a question than a neutral statement of fact.

"Yes, I am a classmate of his son's at San Felipe State University, in America."

The immigration official looked down again, reached for his stamp, and carefully fixed the seal of the Republic of Asalia in the lower left box of the form, dated and initialed it. Leafing her passport open to the page with her Asalian visa, he took another stamp and affixed a red triangle, writing her date of entry within it. He folded the immigration form precisely in half, placed it in the center fold of her passport, and handed it back to her, in an ritualized motion. Looking at her from some very remote place, he said, "You are very welcome to Asalia. As we say here, *karibu*. Enjoy your stay very much."

She thanked him and moved into the Customs hall to search out her luggage. *Balebe's dad must really have some clout here, to have such an effect on the guy.* Retrieving her bags from the luggage carrousel, she took her place in line.

She shuffled her bags along the floor to the customs counter, where the uniformed official was obliging a young African to un-pack both his weathered vinyl suitcases and a large carton tied up with twine. After considerable wrangling, the young man hur-riedly packed his bags back up and hefted them off the counter toward the double doors. As he pushed through, Cynthia saw a huge crowd, mainly of African people, peering eagerly through the gap as it opened and closed.

"They are coming to greet their relatives who return from over-seas," the customs official said with a smile, taking her passport and currency declaration. "Some of these young people go away for six or eight years, without possibility of coming home. Finances, you understand. So, their families are so glad to welcome them by coming to the capital when they finally return. We have to slow them down a bit here, to make sure they are not trying to bring in toaster ovens or VCRs without paying the proper duties. Sorry to inconvenience you."

Cynthia looked him in the face and smiled.

"No extra liquor or cigarettes, eh? Don't bother to open your bags. Welcome to Asalia. You can change your dollar traveler's cheques for diyanis over there at the bank kiosk. And mind you don't let those taxi drivers trick you. There are good buses to carry you into downtown Wangara for only thirty diyanis."

"Thank you, I have a friend meeting me here." She picked up her bags and pushed through the door, scanning the crowd for Balebe's face.

"Taxi, madam, taxi here."

"Taxi, madam, very good price."

"Cyn, over here!" She saw Balebe's waving hand over the heads of a group of country people, the men in worn suits and women in cheap cotton dresses. *Peasants, you can tell them the world over . . . somehow they remind me of the Kekchi in Guatemala.* She pushed through toward Balebe, who was smiling broadly. He stood out in this crowd, as much by virtue of his American denims and blue work shirt as his greater height and fairer skin.

"Boy, am I glad to see you!" she exclaimed, hugging him briefly. "Thanks for coming out to get me so early in the morning."

He grinned and picked up her larger bag. "It must be rather intimidating, landing in such a foreign place for the first time. I remember my apprehension going through customs at JFK when I first came to the States, even though I'd been to England several times before. Come on, the car's out this way."

They walked out into the clarity of the African morning. The air was unexpectedly cold, and Cynthia pulled on the sweatshirt she'd used overnight on the plane from London.

Balebe smiled at her. "You see, I told you it was chilly here. We're three-quarters of a mile above sea level, and the nights can be quite cool." He led her across into a parking lot and unlocked the trunk of a large black Citroen. "A bit ostentatious, I know," he said. "Things are different here." He seemed a bit ill-at-ease. She remembered the immigration official's reaction to his father's name.

"Well, I'm an anthropologist by training," she said, feeling at a loss herself for what to say. He gestured her around to the driver's side of the car, then laughed at her confusion.

"Remember that we drive on the left side of the road, so our driver's side is opposite yours! Hop in, I want to show you a bit before we go out to my family's home. The Wangara National Reserve is just across the way, we'll drive through it and see some game. How does that strike you?"

"Great! I've had breakfast on the plane, so I'm ready to see something of the country!"

They swiftly left the anonymous modernity of the airport, emerging into an open plain dotted with flat-topped thorn trees. Cynthia laughed and gestured. "Just like on the television specials!"

"You'll find much that you've seen before in films and television, but I think you'll get the most from it if you try to leave behind what you have been told about it," Balebe said, with an edge in his voice.

"Wow, that's a rather tall order, or wasn't that you by my side in that awful seminar Dave Jarvis gave on cultural constructions of reality?"

He grimaced and said, "Well, Cyn, as much as I deplore the endless But-What-Is-the-Meaning-of-Meaning that these cultural anthropology types get into, there is a grain of truth in all that. What I meant to say is that this is no more Wild Africa than San Felipe is the Wild West. Yes, there are wild animals, and some of our people wear few clothes and practice different customs. But that colonialist vision of the Unspoiled Paradise, pursued by nearly every tourist who comes here, never existed for us, and it's a bit insulting to act as if it did or does. In fact, I shouldn't go on about the wildlife with my father, if I were you. It's a bit of a sore point with him that white people come here to look at the animals and not to meet the people."

"Ah, I see what you mean. So that's why you're taking me to a game park first thing off the airplane, right?"

Balebe laughed. "Well, you must remember that I'm a rather cosmopolitan type, always seeking to oblige the foreign guest. Anyway, I love wild animals myself!" He turned the car off the main highway into a gateway emblazoned with the name of the national reserve.

After a brief consultation in Swahili with the gate guards, he turned the car to the left. "There was a lion kill out near the pools, we'll see if the pride's still on the kill."

As they rounded a curve, he braked to a halt. A group of three giraffes, two adults and a very young one, broke into a graceful rocking canter across the road in front of them.

"Wow, I've never seen them run before! Magnificent! And look how short the little one's neck is! It must be like the early ancestral forms. The control over elongating the neck vertebrae sets in during maturation! Amazing!"

Balebe turned to look at her, a smile on his face. "Ah, Cynthia, I've missed that active mind of yours this last month. Welcome to my home."

She smiled back at him, happy and faintly embarrassed at the same time. They were such good friends. A really unexpected match of perspective and humor that had delighted both of them, after Balebe had transferred in to be Melanie's graduate student, too, in the middle of the previous academic year. It was a small group, and they all of necessity spent many hours in one another's company, in required classes, working on projects in Melanie's lab, poring over journals and monographs in the library.

All the second-year students had initially wondered if this guy Thanatu would fit in, having been a student of Melanie's least favorite paleoanthropologist, and a foreigner as well. But Balebe had charmed them all with his modesty and subtle humor, showing none of the abrasiveness typical of Shafer and some of his other students. Over his first six months in the San Felipe program, Balebe proved singularly unwilling to talk about Shafer, in either positive or negative terms. When they did have to discuss Shafer's model of human evolution in seminar, he assumed a kind of British formality that contrasted sharply with his usual easygoing style. Cynthia had repeatedly wondered what had happened that caused him to transfer to San Felipe but felt it prudent not to try to draw him out.

When Shafer had disappeared over the last summer break, rumors of foul play and who might have done it had buzzed through the grad student gossip network. When Balebe returned from his visit home—and from actually being at the fateful paleoanthropological congress—several students had tried to badger him into expressing an opinion. He had remained as closemouthed as ever about Shafer, prompting some of the more malicious grads to suggest that perhaps he'd had something to do with what everyone by then was assuming was Shafer's death. The rest had staunchly defended Balebe's character behind his back, and, as the year progressed, fewer and fewer references were made connecting the young Asalian to Shafer.

I would remember all that now, here, where Shafer disappeared . . . Cynthia roused herself from her thoughts. "I've missed you too, BT . . . and thanks again for doing whatever you did to get me attached to Pierce's field group this year."

He put the car into gear and started down the road. "It was nothing. David wrote me saying that they could really use a second person to help with the technical side of field documentation, and with your archaeological background, you were the best choice. And a lot more fun than Tom Weller!"

Cynthia smiled at the thought of their incredibly well versed, incredibly dull classmate who seemed to know the specimen number of every fossil, every potassium-argon date, and every site locale. "God, a summer in the field with Tom could drive anyone to insanity—or homicide!"

"Well, he's working on fossil *Cercopithecus* monkeys in Bleck's lab this summer, poor guy." Balebe smiled.

"Yeah, but *he* doesn't think it's boring, BT!"

They drove slowly up a hill, through the brushy vegetation at either side of the road, in a companionable silence. After a few moments they reached the crest of the hill, and she gasped. Below lay a mosaic of grasslands, scattered acacia trees with that distinctive form she'd seen forever in still and moving pictures, dense foliage along two small streams converging from opposite sides of the long highland they had just crested. Balebe stopped the engine and set the brake.

"A bit overwhelming at the outset?" he asked.

She nodded, her eyes roaming over the undulating topography. "Look!" she cried, pointing at a herd of giraffes moving with their slow motion walk across the parkland below toward the small eastern watercourse. Suddenly a chorus of something like deep, gruff human shouts rose up from trees along that stream.

"Baboons, remember the old DeVore film in Anthro 101?" Balebe pointed to dark forms bouncing in the upper branches of two larger trees along the watercourse. "Something has alarmed them. It could be the lions or some scavengers on the way to the kill."

Again, they sat in silence for a moment, contemplating the scene.

Then he started the car and began a slow descent of the hill. As they drove into the brush, he asked, "How are things with you and Cliff?"

She sighed and looked at her hands. "Well, we've finally given up on it. The closer he got to getting his degree, the more obvious it became that I wasn't going to be the loyal lawyer's wife he had in mind. I finally told him that I wasn't going to stop my plans for fieldwork, and moreover, I wanted a career that would keep me going overseas intermittently. It was hard. He just couldn't seem to believe that I'd be committed to 'these romantic adventures' as more than a passing amusement on the way to being a 'responsible adult'—I mean, he actually used those words!"

Balebe gave her a sidelong smile combining amusement and pain. "God, he sounds like he should join up with my father! Maybe it's something they get in their legal education. I am sorry, Cyn. It's always hard to end an attachment, even if it's inappropriate. It's not your fault—I think he's a bloody fool to let you go."

"Thanks," she said, again faintly embarrassed by his unaccustomed personal frankness. Over the academic year, she and Balebe had usually been together in the group of paleoanthropology grad students. Even when they were alone, he'd kept to the role of platonic friend. Given their strong affinities of mind and outlook, she had occasionally wondered if this stemmed from his deference to her relationship with Cliff, or whether it was a matter of some other considerations, cultural or racial, she didn't know. By American standards, Balebe was black. He had talked to her a few times of the ambiguous roles he felt himself playing in an American context, as opposed to the equally ambiguous, but more familiar, ones at home, where he was something other than an average African. She had wondered if this were influencing his behavior toward her, or whether he was, as a matter of good breeding, committed to being a steadfast friend. Or whether, like Cliff, he liked her well enough but had another type of woman in mind for a lasting emotional attachment. There were so many cultural differences that, despite their mental affinities, she often found him hard to read.

"They should be around this next bend." They emerged from the turn to face a small, artificially dammed pond. About twenty meters to their right, a mass of tawny bodies faced inward toward one another, muscles tense and heads bobbing down into the center. A single black leg of a large antelope projected above the massed bodies, waving like a branch in a heavy wind with the surges of the feeding lions.

"Wildebeest, looks like," Balebe said.

As they slowly drove closer, two adult lionesses raised their heads to stare briefly at the car. Cynthia's eyes made contact with those of one lioness, who held her in a deep, golden gaze for a long moment.

She felt a palpable shock, held in that intelligent, evaluating look. "Whoa, I've just been given the personal once-over by a major predator!" She shook herself as the lioness turned back to her kill. "God, I'm glad I'm in a car!"

Balebe smiled and nodded. "Yes, they are rather larger and more frightening out of zoos, aren't they? Gives you a sense of what evolving in Africa really meant."

A fierce low growl welled up, followed by a higher yowl, and a cub the size of a collie flew through the air, landing about two meters away. He rose up, shook himself, and moved back to the huddle with a limp.

"Natural selection at work," she whispered.

"I know that's how it goes, but I don't have to like it. Poor little fellow!" he responded.

They watched for another quarter hour, until the sated adults rose and began walking heavily away from the carcass, licking the blood from their muzzles. The two lionesses settled down on the road and began washing themselves, while five cubs continued to tussle over the nearly stripped carcass. After another ten minutes, one of the females rose, uttered a hoarse moan, and turned to walk past the car. The other lioness also rose and gave a similar moan. The cubs began to leave the carcass with some reluctance, following the females down the road. Each was pastel pink, the tips of its tawny fur matted with blood. The last to leave was the limping cub, which hopped along favoring one hind leg and stopped for a moment to gaze up at the inhabitants of the car.

"Oh, God, don't look so damned appealing!" Balebe said in an undertone, shaking his head. He turned to look at Cynthia with a rueful smile, only to say in a soft voice, "Oh, Cyn, don't cry. It's the way life really is."

"I know, but it still hurts, he's so sweet and curious!"

"Well, he may yet make it, and we can't very well adopt him. I mean, imagine the uproar if the son of the attorney general were apprehended smuggling a literally bloody lion cub from our most famous national park!"

She laughed while wiping her tears away. "Ah, that's what I needed, a dose of the absurdity of the human condition. I fear I'm in for lots of shocks along the way to paleoanthropological knowledge."

He started the car. "Perhaps so, Cyn. I haven't yet taken you to the slums of Choka Sana, or the orphanage where my Mum volunteers. Save your tears for the people."

She glanced at him, again caught by his mix of humor and deadly seriousness about his country. "I do want to see that, too, Balebe. I may cry, but I don't want to be the oblivious tourist I know you loathe."

He held her gaze for a moment as the car accelerated through first gear. "You are a strong person, Cynthia, *karibu nchi yangu*." He glanced at his watch. "Lord, it's nearly lunch time. Mum will kill me if we're late. She's laid on a spread for you!" He quickly shifted up through to third gear, heading for the park's northern gate.

Welcome

As they emerged from the north gate of the park, the vegetation swiftly changed from brush to open fields, and she saw scattered houses set back from the road. Most had corrugated metal roofs that glinted in the midday sun. After about five minutes, the road they were on reached another larger one running east-west. Balebe turned the Citroen west, toward the spires of downtown Wangara that were visible on the horizon.

"We'll skirt the downtown on the Jamhuri Ring Road, because we're in a hurry today. I'll take you down to the city center tomorrow, to introduce you to a couple of my old school chums, as well as to the museum."

Cynthia nodded and sat back in her seat, for the first time feeling the weight of fatigue of her two-day journey from San Felipe. She yawned and stretched luxuriously in the car's plush seat.

"Starting to get a little tired?" Balebe asked.

"Guess so, nothing a cup of coffee couldn't fix."

"I'll make sure you get some at lunch. But you should let yourself rest for a few hours this afternoon. You know, the time zones are nearly exactly back to front from San Felipe, so by your body's reckoning it's now, oh, two in the morning."

"Uh-huh, it's beginning to feel that way," she replied, yawning again. "God, I'm going to be a wreck at lunch."

"Never mind that, we're surprisingly tolerant of foreigners here." Balebe smiled. After a moment, he chuckled. "I remember one incredible time I got invited to David Pierce's flat when I was still an Aspiring Boy Anthropologist. He'd had the gall to invite Anthea herself, of whom I was and am still terrified, who came with an old school chum of hers from England. The two of them had clearly been having "sundowners" since noon and were bickering constantly in the sitting room. The woman, whose name I forget, had just got off the plane from UK that morning and turned out not to be able to hold her whiskey so well as Anthea."

He glanced sideways at her, a wicked smile on his face. "When we were called into the dining room, we all sat down, and this unfortunate woman took one bleary look around the table and went face down into a dainty little bowl of peas sitting beside her plate. Well, Anthea gave her one withering glance and said, 'I trust there's no liquid in that bowl, David,' and went back to sampling her roast. We ate the whole bloody meal with this poor woman passed out in her bowl of peas. You can imagine the awkwardness for a sixteen-year-old!"

"Balebe! Did this really happen? I can't believe it!"

He laughed. "*Kweli, dada!* I'm telling the truth! It rather broke the ice between David and me, since he kept waggling his eyebrows at me all through dinner, as if to reassure me it was more funny than mortifying. And I suppose since I neither ran screaming from the room nor used the wrong eating implements, I passed some baseline test for Anthea as well, since she's been brusquely cordial with me from then on. Actually, she rather fancies my Mum, so that helps."

He smacked the steering wheel with his hand. "Oh yes, now I remember, the woman's name was Blanche. At the end of the meal, Anthea pulled her up from the table, muttering, 'Come on, Blanche, time to wipe the peas off your face and present a good front to the natives.' Oh, she's fierce, Anthea is."

Cynthia chuckled. "I knew she was eccentric, but this puts a whole new cast on things—we aren't going to dinner with her, are we?"

"Well, not here in Wangara, but we will spend the night at her camp in Ruba on our way out to the new localities. Not to worry—she's quite soft on young women scientists, and she'll tolerate me. You did buy the bottle of malt whisky at Heathrow Duty Free, as I suggested?"

"Right here in my plastic bag, along with something for your family as well."

"Very good, you're catching on! Your bottle and mine should grease the wheels of social intercourse in Anthea's camp considerably."

Cynthia noted that the scenery out the window had changed, the scattered tin-roofed huts giving way to larger commercial buildings and a few compact clusters of semidetached houses. The road curved into a larger boulevard with two lanes running in each direction and a median strip planted with tropical flowers and succulents. Little groups of men and women, dressed much like the peasants at the airport, except that the women had brightly colored cloths wrapped over their dresses as extra skirts, were hand weeding and hacking up the earth around the plants with machete-like bushknives.

"Those are *pangas,* right?" she asked.

"Yes, this is our labor-intensive approach to highway maintenance. As you can see, we have many more people than machines."

The traffic had thickened since they joined the main highway. Cynthia found herself flinching as Balebe wove the car through a near anarchic flow of smoke-belching buses, Land Rovers, trucks, and sedans ranging from Morris Minors through Mercedes. They careened around a traffic circle. Halfway around, she shut her eyes as a huge army transport truck full of grinning soldiers and adorned with a large red "L" traversed four traffic lanes to exit left, to the blaring of many automobile horns.

"That's 'L' for 'learner,' isn't it?" she asked.

"You got it. We believe in sink or swim here in Asalia! It takes a little getting used to, I know," Balebe said, while leaning on the horn as a Land Rover cut in front of them with inches to spare. "The main rule of the road is the Biggest Wins, although if one has a simply awful small heap, one can gain the advantage over Mercedes owners who don't want to scratch their precious autos."

"This really is worse than Mexico. I didn't think that was possible." Cynthia averted her eyes from another near miss.

"Not to worry, we're almost to Ring Road, which will keep us out of the worst downtown traffic." At the next roundabout, he bore to the left. Almost immediately the road began to curve away from the towers of the city center and rise into more densely forested hills. Apartment buildings and large homes stood back from the road. Some bore the names of government ministries and educational institutions. Vehicular traffic did thin somewhat, although the number of pedestrians seemed to increase in comparison with that along the boulevard they'd left.

Cynthia gazed with interest at the diverse population walking along the red dirt sidewalks. While most men and women wore Western dress, she occasionally caught sight of a tall pastoralist

63

warrior in traditional dress, or an old woman with the shaved head and clusters of bead earrings typical of Chacha married women.

The road rose further into lush green highlands and ran past even larger houses set back from the road behind imposing gates. "This is where most of the government ministers live, as well as some bigwigs with international organizations based in Wangara," Balebe told her. "We live further out to the northwest. It's still a bit untamed out there, and if we're lucky we might get to see some green monkeys in our garden."

"Wow, this really is Africa, isn't it?"

"Mind you don't leave your bedroom windows open when you're out of the room. The little devils will come right in and make a mess, in every sense of the word. Here's our road."

They turned left. " Mbagama Road, which began immediately to climb along the steep side of a small valley. Lush little garden plots of bananas, squash, and maize were planted in the bottomlands and climbed part of the way up the hillsides.

Balebe glanced over at Cynthia, saw her staring down into the farmland. "This entire area was some of the richest Chacha land, well-watered and defensible. When the English came, the settlers grabbed it up, by fair means and foul, first for coffee and tea plantations, and then in the forties for big suburban homes. Loss of this land was one of the big grievances of the independence movement. But, then, I saw you've been reading a copy of Mbathire's book on the plane and probably know all this already."

Cynthia shook her head. "Don't stop talking. This brings it all to life. I would never place the areas simply from reading about them . . . this is part of the Mugomali Ridge, then?"

"Yes; we're almost home now. It's to our left up ahead." He slowed the Citroen and turned through two heavy wrought-iron gates into a gray gravel driveway that contrasted with the red earth it overlay and with the green lawn on either side. They drove up the drive about a hundred meters, to the imposing house built of the same rough-hewn stone blocks Cynthia had seen in many bungalows and mansions they had passed on their way.

Balebe pulled the car around the right side of the house and stopped. "Here we are," he said, as they got out of the car. "I hope you don't find it too off-putting," he added, again with that hint of awkwardness.

"Well, it does present a contrast to Mrs. Simms's rooming house in San Felipe, but I think I can manage the shock," she replied, mimicking Mrs. Simms's strong Southwestern twang.

He smiled and went back to the trunk to retrieve her bags. "You'll have to enter through the front door, it's a bit of family tradition that visitors must always be received properly."

As they walked up the front steps, the big door opened, and Cynthia saw an older man with a seamed face beaming at her. *This must be Kaniugi.*

"Kaniugi, this is Cynthia Cavallo, my friend from America," Balebe said in English. "Cynthia, may I present Bwana Kaniugi Nyau."

No accident of manners on Balebe's part that I was first presented to him! she thought, grasping Kaniugi's hand.

"Welcome, welcome, Miss Cynthia," he said. "We are happy you are visiting with us."

"*Asante sana, ninafuraha kuonana nawe,*" she replied, marshaling her best Swahili.

Kaniugi raised his brows and interrogated Balebe in the same language. "You've been teaching her Kiswahili?"

"No, she studied it in America with a Tanzanian. She probably speaks it better than you do!"

"Hey! Don't say that!" Cynthia exclaimed in English. "I know very little, really. I hope to learn more while I am here."

"You will learn," Kaniugi replied, picking up her bags. He turned to Balebe and continued in Swahili, "Your mother is waiting for you in the garden. Hurry and wash your hands!" He began climbing the staircase to the second floor.

Balebe smiled, gesturing for her to follow Kaniugi. "I'll never be too old to be ordered about like a four-year-old!" he muttered. "You can do a quick wash-up in the WC—remember the bathroom here is literally that, a room with a tub, period. It's the WC you'll want for anything else."

Cynthia felt her head spinning as she started up the stairs. *A little jet lag vertigo? Or is it just the fact that I've come from an airplane to a lion kill to an English manor house, complete with parquet floors and watercolors of wildflowers.*

Kaniugi led them down the hall to a room facing the front of the house. "Mama Mary's study. You stay here." Turning to Balebe, he told him to show her the WC and not to waste time, the meal had been ready for a half hour, and the bread was drying out. Balebe made placatory noises and asked that a cup of coffee be prepared for Cynthia right away.

She took a rapid look around the room as Balebe absented himself to wash up. A single bed against one wall was dwarfed by two huge teak desks side by side along the front windows. The wall opposite the bed was dominated by a long bookcase on which a variety of art paper and watercolor paints supplemented books on East African peoples, plants, and animals. Another row contained volumes of poetry, with about a dozen medical texts thrown in. An easel was shoved into the corner between the bookcase and a teak wardrobe.

"My mother paints," Balebe said from the doorway. "Some of the finest renderings of Asalian landscapes that I've seen, but then I'm biased. More of that later, when you've time to tour the house. Come wash up and meet the family."

They took a back staircase that led them down into the kitchen, where Kaniugi and an older woman were conferring over the stove in a language Cynthia assumed to be Kipakyu. The woman came forward smiling and placed a tray with a steaming cup of coffee, sugar, and creamer in Balebe's hands. She shook Cynthia's hand warmly, then waved them on through the doors to the dining room, saying in Swahili, "Welcome, welcome, I am Mariamu, we will talk later. Go out to eat lunch now!"

Balebe nodded toward a set of French doors on their right. "We're eating on the verandah, just through these doors."

As they stepped out onto the flagstones of the verandah, a woman of medium height rose from her chair. "Welcome, my dear, I've heard so many good things about you from Balebe. I'm so glad that we can begin to repay the many things you've done to make him more at home in America."

Cynthia grasped her hand, which was a little cool even in the midday sun, and smiled. "Thank you for inviting me to stay here, it's very kind of you," she replied. "I hope we haven't delayed lunch too much."

"Not at all—has Kaniugi been harping on the time, Balebe?" She smiled at Cynthia. "Kaniugi insists the house run on a tight schedule. I've always found it rather amusing that an African is constantly badgering me to be punctual—but then we Irish tend to operate on our own time, too. Put the tray on the table, dear, and go call your brother and sister. They're playing badminton."

She smiled and gestured Cynthia to one of the bentwood chairs next to the table. "Don't wait to have your coffee, you must be terribly tired."

Balebe trotted down the stairs and disappeared around the right corner of the house, raising his voice to call his brother and sister from their game.

Looking out from the verandah, Cynthia was seized by a sense of unreality. A manicured lawn nearly a hundred meters wide dropped gradually toward what looked like the upper reaches of the steep valley they'd climbed in the car. Three tree-sized poinsettia shrubs were set seemingly at random on the lawn, just coming into bloom. An enormous jacaranda stood next to the verandah, its blossoms like a lavender fog over the red earth exposed beneath it.

She shook herself slightly and turned apologetically to Balebe's mother. "I'm sorry to sit here like a bump on a log—it's just that I suddenly find it hard to believe I'm actually here."

"Never mind, Cynthia, I know exactly how you feel. When I came out here, people of our means sailed with the Union Castle Line, the Viscounts and other airplanes were simply too dear for the common person. I was already carrying Balebe, and needless to say, I was sick from the time we left England until we docked at Mombasa. By the time we got off the train in Wangara, I was in a complete daze, and the whole place seemed some kind of dream."

She smiled. "You can imagine what it was like meeting Ezekiel's family in such a state! That was back in the sixties, the year of Independence, actually, and there was so much turmoil and uncertainty. I tell you there was many a time I wanted to get right back on a plane and go back to England! But we were too poor to have afforded a return ticket, and besides, there was Balebe."

Ah yes, he had to be born here, where else? . . . God, what a path you've chosen . . . "It must have been a very exciting time," Cynthia said lamely.

"Yes, and one of great opportunity," Mary replied. Kaniugi appeared in the doorway with a tray, and she gestured to him to bring it out to the table. "There were so many posts suddenly vacated as the English left, and Ezekiel was able to move straightaway into a job with the Ministry of Justice. His older brother kept pressuring him to go into politics, but Ezekiel was adamant that his talents would best serve the legal branch of the government. It caused considerable consternation in the family, because a younger brother is supposed to follow his senior brother's advice, especially when the father is dead.

"The family had the idea that Ezekiel could bring more influence and wealth into the family as a politician than as a civil servant. I daresay they were right." She glanced at Cynthia and nodded. "You mustn't judge them by Anglo-American standards, though. It's simply the way an African should behave toward his family. Especially a family who'd made many sacrifices to send him abroad for a law degree. As an Irishwoman, I saw no harm in that kind of approach. But I fear that Ezekiel had assimilated a lot more of British rectitude than I ever did!"

The two women's eyes met in common amusement.

Mary smiled. "That, in addition to bringing home a European wife, put him in for quite a bit of criticism. But he's always been very good at ignoring that."

Cynthia wanted to ask her so much. *How was it to be a pregnant bride among a family with such different expectations? How did Africans and whites deal with what must have been one of the*

68

earliest interracial marriages among middle-class people? Who were her friends? How have you come to adjust to this world so smoothly, it seems? But I hardly know you, and these are terribly personal questions. What a fascinating person you are!

Balebe appeared around the corner with a lean boy of about fifteen with the same skin tones as his but jet-black hair and a younger girl whose mass of reddish blond hair was held away from her face by a headband. They both were grinning and a bit damp from their exertions. Dropping their badminton gear at the bottom of the steps, they stepped up and went through their introductions, with a mischievous twinkle behind their politenesses.

As she shook the girl's hand, Cynthia was struck by the near-amber color of Malama's eyes.

Malama burst out, "Balebe says you've been to South America. Did you see llamas and alpacas?"

"Malama!" her mother exclaimed.

"Don't worry, I'd love to talk about it. Yes, I did see llamas and alpacas when I went to the highlands. We actually were digging in a desert right by the sea coast, and it was too low for llamas there, but I did travel up into the Andes. They have some special white alpacas at the ancient city of Macchu Pichu. The Indians put ornaments on their ears."

"Oh, that's like the M'posas decorating their cows!" Malama said.

"Do let Cynthia have a bite to eat, Malama! She'll be here for a week and there will be adequate time for further interrogations," Balebe laughed, passing Cynthia a plate of cold cuts. "My sister is a nut for geography and cuts out pictures of exotic places for her special scrapbook of places to go."

"What a wonderful hobby. I'd never imagined that someone who lived in such an amazing country as Asalia would want to go elsewhere!"

Malama swallowed a mouthful of sandwich quickly and replied, "I love to travel! We've been just about everywhere here, except to the top of Mount Ruba, and once I'm sixteen, Daddy says I may do that, too. Then there's no place else to go!"

Balebe laughed. "Ah, Malama, you're worse than the archetypal American tourist, with his list of the Wonders of the World, and the only aim of travel being to tick it off the list and move on!"

"I do not think that way, thank you, and what's wrong with keeping a list?"

Mary Thanatu interjected, "Speaking of travel, have you any plans to take Cynthia anywhere special, or will you be closeted with those dusty fossils in the museum all week?"

"Well, we really must, um, bone up on our chronologically key species before heading out with Juma Nane, but I thought after the field season we'd take a day to visit the Diwa Forest Reserve."

"Oh, splendid! It's really a magical place, and you must see it this time of year. The butterflies are superb now, and of course the elephants and caves are quite remarkable. More cheese, dear? It's one of our best products here in Asalia."

Cynthia nodded and took the plate, still chewing on her sandwich. Malama and Adiari got into a wrangle about the relative merits of boys' versus girls' soccer teams, and the grown-ups addressed themselves to their food.

Cynthia felt the disorientation swirl around her again. *It's all so overwhelming. Will I make some kind of faux pas here or at the museum? How will I assimilate the dental morphology and postcranial anatomy of twenty new species in a week, and go off to some park with elephants? God, am I really up to this cross-cultural, advanced research? It seemed like a good idea at the time.*

"A bit overwhelmed, Cyn?" Balebe asked.

She started and caught his eye. "Am I that obvious?"

"Well, I was just thinking of my own first week at San Felipe last year, when all I wanted to do was crawl into a dark hole and sleep, but you, Cliff, and Tom Weller decided to show me the sights. It was really very kind of you, I know, but the Grand Canyon and a dizzying array of prehistoric pueblos in four days was rather much for this Third World guy!"

She laughed, "Yes, made even worse by Tom deciding to provide you with an intense course in prehistoric Southwestern culture, complete with tree-ring dates and pottery styles!"

"Quite so. By day three I was not sure whether I was on the Mogollon Rim, in it, or whether that was just another ceramic type!"

They both laughed, and Cynthia caught Mary watching Balebe with a subtle, speculative expression. *What is it? Is there some concern here for your son? Well, I'm as confused as you are, ma'am.*

Balebe turned to his mother, and her expression instantly shifted into a fond smile. "Look, for the museum work we'll have to take a car. How do you think the Guvnor would take it if we used your Citroen, and you shared the Mercedes for a few days?"

"I think we could manage all but the first two days. This week I'm due to be at Saint Crispin's Monday and Tuesday consecutively, so those days would be awkward."

Mary looked over at Cynthia. "Oh, I do apologize for going over family details when you're clearly asleep on your feet. Do have a nap before dinnertime. Malama, take Cynthia up to her room, while Balebe and I make some arrangements!"

Stifling another yawn, Cynthia thanked her, rose, and walked back into the house with Malama, who asked what state she was from, and what city, and how many other states in America she'd visited as they climbed the back stairs.

Thanking Malama for her help, Cynthia closed the door, slouched on the bed, and checked her watch, sighing, "Three p.m., drinks at seven, dinner at eight, dinner at seven a.m., my time. Wonderful. Take these clothes off, they're really grody . . . maybe I can teach Malama Valleyspeak. Unpack the only dress for tonight. Hang it up? Forget it, it'll unwrinkle enough over the back of this chair."

She returned to the bed, folded the bedspread back, and climbed in. With a grateful sigh, she nestled under the cool sheets and closed her eyes.

Ezekiel

Cynthia walked downstairs to the verandah, a paintbrush in hand. As she emerged from the double French doors, a soft tapping drumbeat began. Balebe and his mother were sitting on the verandah, with David and Anthea Pierce. At the base of the steps a pride of lions was feasting on something. She shouted at the cats and they pulled back, revealing a skeleton with the face of Bob Shafer. She stood terrified as the soft drumbeat grew louder and a chant built up behind it. It was calling her name. She turned to flee and the drumbeat resolved into a knocking on her bedroom door.

"Cynthia, Cynthia, *please* wake up. Here's some tea," Malama's soft voice repeated.

Cynthia sat up abruptly, blinking her eyes to clear the horrible image. "Yes, thanks, be right there." *Phew, what a doozy . . . the old subconscious is really working overtime.* She opened her suitcase and pulled out her robe, flung it on, and opened the door.

Malama was standing there with a tea tray in her hand and a slightly martyred look on her face. "I thought you'd never wake up! Mum didn't want me to invade your privacy, but I was about to come in and shake you!"

"Thank heavens you didn't! I was having a horrible dream about lions eating someone in your backyard, and I probably would have had a heart attack if you'd grabbed me." Cynthia smiled, taking the tray. *I'm still a little shaky, may as well talk about it.*

"Gosh! You needn't worry about that here, this section of Wangara is very civilized, you know. Although when I was five, there was a leopard going about eating people's dogs. Mum wouldn't let us or Semira—that's Kaniugi's daughter, she's grown up and has a baby now—play outside without someone watching us. But that was years ago!"

Cynthia smiled at the girl, set the tray on the nightstand, and sat down again on the bed. "Well, this was not so much a dream about anything real as a fantasy. I dreamed the lions were eating Bob Shafer!"

"Ooh! That's the famous anthropologist who disappeared last summer, isn't it? The one Balebe worked with before he joined your university," Malama exclaimed, throwing herself into one of the desk chairs. "Maybe you solved the mystery in your dream. People do sometimes!"

"Hmmm," Cynthia smiled, taking a sip of fragrant tea. "It was not much of a whodunit dream, I think. I don't know why I dreamed of Shafer anyway. I really only met him once, at the annual Physical Anthropology Association meetings in Tucson two years ago. Maybe it's all the connections here, with your brother having been his student, my going to meet David Pierce tomorrow . . ."

"And my father being in charge of investigating his case! Didn't you know that? Well, I shouldn't bring up your dream with him, if I were you! It's a real sore point with him that they've not been able to turn up a single clue about his disappearance in a whole year. He and Balebe got into a battle royal last week over it!" Malama reached over, grabbed a sugar cube from the tray, and popped it into her mouth.

Glancing at Cynthia's travel clock, she said, "Wow, we've only got a half hour to get ready for dinner. I hope you're not one of those girls who spends hours getting ready!" She immediately clapped her hand over her mouth, a look of mortification on her face.

Cynthia laughed. "No, I'm not! When you've had to get ready for fancy dinners with the district superintendent of a Latin American country, while living in a tent, after a hard day of digging, you learn to streamline." She rose and began searching in her suitcase for her dress shoes.

Malama got up and made for the door. She stopped and stood for a minute, watching Cynthia lay out her clothes. Finally she blurted, "Are you Balebe's girlfriend?"

Cynthia looked at her and smiled again. "No, we're just good friends," nearly blushing as she uttered the cliché.

Malama nodded, only slightly abashed by her own forwardness, and whirled off down the hall. Cynthia picked up her cosmetic bag and walked down the hall to the lavatory.

But it's the truth, cliché or not. Weird to dream about Shafer, gives me the creeps! But whoever killed him—if he's dead—would've had to have been in Asalia, and the Thanatu family is even more involved than I'd realized. It's a little creepy, being here, meeting all the people who had something to do with him or his disappearance.

Twenty minutes later, she descended the front stairs and turned down the corridor toward the sound of voices and glassware. Walking into the living room, she saw Balebe and his mother sitting together on a small Chippendale-style sofa by a fireplace and a man in a dark suit standing gazing out the back windows toward the trees in the valley behind the house. Balebe saw her in the doorway and rose, but it was Mary who came forward to greet her with a smile.

"Ah, Cynthia, how did you rest?" She took Cynthia's hand and drew her over to the window. "Dear, I would like you to meet Cynthia Cavallo, Balebe's friend from America."

Ezekiel Thanatu turned, took her hand, and bowed slightly. "It's a pleasure, Miss Cavallo, or is it Ms. these days?" His deeply lined brown face was impassive, but a glint of amusement lit his eyes, which were an extraordinarily light brown shade. *Malama gets her lovely eyes from her father,* she thought. The pinstripe suit was without a wrinkle, the waistcoat set with a golden watch chain, and the striped tie impeccably knotted.

Cynthia was struck by the man's handsome features and his aura of power, something Balebe's descriptions had never included. A bit off balance, she replied, "I hope it will soon be Doctor, sir."

Ezekiel Thanatu threw his head back and laughed, still holding her hand in his. "Ah, yes, I see what my son esteems in you, soon-to-be Doctor Cavallo. Welcome to Asalia!" Releasing her hand, he glanced at his watch. "We still have a few minutes before dinner, will you have a drink?"

Cynthia glanced at Mary's and said, "A gin and tonic will be fine, thanks."

Ezekiel turned to the liquor cabinet and busied himself. "So many of our visitors fancy gin-and-tonic. But tell me truthfully, what do you usually drink at home?" There was a subtle, needling undertone.

"Truthfully, beer and the occasional margarita," she said, taking the cold glass, "but I figured, when in Rome . . ." glancing at Mary's drink.

"Come now, Dad, don't launch into your 'Out of Africa' diatribe before dinner," Balebe interjected from his seat. "Cynthia's a bit more sophisticated than that."

"I shan't, in deference to your feelings, my boy," Ezekiel said, bowing over his own neat whiskey. "However, if you had to sit, as I do, through interminable lunches with supposedly sophisticated men from the World Bank, UNEP, and other organizations, listening to them wax poetic about Wild Africa, you'd probably change your tune about sophisticated foreigners."

Cynthia was fascinated by the man and his manner. *Remarkable! He does speak pure BBC English.* She recalled the longest conversation Balebe had ever had with her about his father. In the dimness of Pablito's on the Friday of finals week, they'd shared an entire pitcher of margaritas while waiting for Cliff to come in from his law exams. Somehow, their rambling conversation turned to his father.

"He's a self-made man in every sense of the word. There's probably no one else precisely like him in Asalia. He managed to claw his way up the educational ladder during colonial times, being one of the few Asalian 'natives' the British saw fit to send to UK for an advanced degree. He was ruthless in schooling us in our speech. It was BBC English or nothing, no African intonations, no slang, and certainly no Americanisms. I remember his lecturing us about how he listened and listened to the missionaries' wireless while working in their home, mimicking the news broadcasts word for word until he'd lost all trace of an African accent. 'If I could do it whilst scrubbing the Wilson's floors, you three can do it while enjoying the most expensive education in the republic!' " Balebe mimicked, pulling a stern face.

"But isn't all this imitating the British somehow selling out to the oppressor?" she said, regretting her words as soon as they'd come out of her mouth.

"It's a lot more complex than you Americans spouting liberation rhetoric seem to think," Balebe said, with an unaccustomed show of emotion. "From his earliest boyhood my father was dedicated to reclaiming the lands alienated from the Wachacha. He took a path that few men would have the strength of character to choose. He refined himself into a tool for combating the English, using their own weapons. He was convinced that it was possible to fight the English with their own legal system. Accordingly, he honed himself into the perfect weapon, a black barrister."

Balebe had taken another sip of his drink and licked a fleck of salt from his lip. "It meant breaking with his family in ways that must have been painful. He has never spoken about his feelings in going against his father's, and then his eldest brother's, wishes regarding his education and career. But it caused a bitter rift. Despite the fact that he and I don't see eye to eye on many topics, I can't imagine a greater sign of commitment for an African than sacrificing ties to his family."

Cynthia was silent for a long moment. "I'm sorry, I had no idea. You're right—it's easy to think in clichés, but when you look at the people involved, it's more complicated."

"Yes, and probably the bitterest thing for him to swallow was coming home to a newly independent nation which had been won back not by law but by armed struggle and the tides of international economics. So much left behind, on a path so few had taken, and for what, really? He might as well have stayed on being a schoolteacher in our family's homeland, as his father had wished."

Cynthia had simply shook her head and looked at her glass.

Balebe went on, "Luckily for him, and ultimately for us kids, his mother kept the family ties alive. Wachacha women are very strong-minded. Oh, they'll defer to their husbands on the surface of things, but they'll often find a way to get around the old man's rules and have it the way they want anyhow. My grandmother did just that."

He nodded as Cynthia offered him another helping from the

pitcher. "Before my father went to England, when he was attending what was then Royal Wangara College, she'd walk twenty kilometers into town and back, ostensibly to do some special marketing, once every few months. My father would meet her in the market and exchange news.

"After he went to England, she hired a schoolboy to write him letters—she was illiterate. She paid for the letters out of her egg money. Their connection was very strong. She was the person who welcomed my mother, who pressured my uncle into blessing my parents' marriage. In fact, I got all this from my Mum, who learnt it from my father's sisters." He sat in silent reflection for a moment.

"My grandmother died when I was six years old, and it was the only time I ever saw another side of my father. Traditional Wachacha funerals, especially for people as esteemed as my grandmother, are very emotional affairs. The sons as well as the daughters are given free rein to lament their mother's passing. My uncle, being the oldest brother, was expected to be the strongest mourner, but my father quite outdid him. It was the only time I have seen my father in traditional Chacha dress and in such a state. I remember it well, since it was quite frightening to see my dad heaping ashes upon his head and weeping uncontrollably."

He had looked up from his drink and smiled wryly. "It's not a performance I've seen repeated since."

Looking at Ezekiel now, Cynthia could well believe that. The man was almost inhumanly contained and correct. *Well, you loved your mother deeply, and that's a point in your favor, sir. Was she your last link to the culture and values of your birth? Whoa! Enough of this psychoanalyzing, Cyn, what are they saying?*

"I hear you have some background in archaeology, as well as in physical anthropology," Ezekiel was saying, as he handed her the drink. "Your health," he added as she raised her glass.

"Yes," she began, after acknowledging his toast, "My undergraduate work was largely in archaeology . . ." She paused as Kaniugi appeared in the double doorway leading into the dining room.

"Ah, dinner's ready," Ezekiel said. "Shall we proceed to table?"

Dinner

Malama and Adiari appeared from the kitchen and joined them as they seated themselves. Cynthia was placed at Ezekiel's left, and Balebe across from her. Adiari sat beside her and Malama opposite her brother, with Mary at the foot of the table. Kaniugi brought in a roast surrounded by potatoes, which Ezekiel carved and served. Vegetables and relishes made their way around the table.

After they had settled into their meals, Ezekiel turned to Cynthia. "Now, I think we were on the topic of your past career in archaeology before we came in to dinner." Malama looked at her expectantly, and Balebe's face bore an inscrutable look.

"Yes, I concentrated in South and Central American prehistory before coming to San Felipe for graduate work," she replied.

"What made you change your field?" Ezekiel asked, cutting into another slice of roast.

"Well, I'd always been interested in human evolution and had wanted to study it, but that really wasn't possible at my undergraduate college. After a year of contract archaeology work, I applied to San Felipe State, intending to pursue my work in South American archaeology. But things happened to change my interests."

"Such as," Ezekiel prompted.

God, you just won't let this go, will you, must be all the legal training. "Well, by the end of my first year, I'd taken a basic graduate course from Melanie Baine that had reawakened my interest in paleoanthropology, especially in reconstructing biomechanics—that's how animals move around. And that year a famous paleontologist who'd worked on fossil sites here in Asalia and in the Near East was visiting. I took her interdisciplinary seminar on taphonomy—that's how bones become fossils—and I saw that I could really pursue a concentration in human evolution at San Felipe."

She took another bite of potatoes, hoping that the interrogation was over. Balebe caught her eye for a second and looked down at his plate again. *I really don't want to go into how Sam McIntyre virtually hounded me out of archaeology, when I wouldn't sleep with him on the Santa Rosalia dig, how Melanie, Dave Jarvis, and old Don Smith were the only faculty who knew what was happening and were sympathetic.*

"Did you ever go to Tikal and Palenque?" Malama asked, giving the last word a French pronunciation.

"That's Pa-len-kay, in the Spanish pronunciation. Yes, I have, but more as a tourist than an archaeologist. I worked on a dig in Belize in the summer between my junior and senior years as an undergraduate, and at the end of the season, several of us went on a tour of the major Mayan sites. It put our little end of the Mayan world into some perspective!"

"It's really quite impressive," Balebe interjected. "Last Easter vacation several of us from San Felipe went down to Mexico and saw some of these sites, among other things. To think that they did so much without any kind of sophisticated technology."

"The terraces and earthworks of the Chacha highlands were constructed simply with hoes and much labor," Ezekiel replied. "It's easy for urban-bred people to think it all has to be done with tractors or cranes. The *jembe*—do you know the word, Miss Cavallo?— in the hands of a determined people can be a most powerful tool."

"That's Kiswahili for hoe, isn't it?" Cynthia replied. "Yes, we often forget that people can employ very sophisticated principles without high technology. It's just that the ideas don't preserve too well in the archaeological record."

"I'm sure you have an example in mind, Ms. Cavallo?" Ezekiel asked.

"Yes," she said, "I'm thinking of the Inca stone masonry, which still can be seen in Cuzco, in Peru. They managed to break enormous stones with great precision, using the cycles of freezing and thawing in the cold highlands. They put water into cracks they'd open in the stone, let the water freeze, expand, and enlarge the crack, and so on, until the stone split apart. It just took time."

Ezekiel nodded. "Ah yes, I fear that in our modern world we forget the value of patience and persistence in small efforts. Perhaps we Africans can see that more clearly, since we have so recently come from another way of life in which patience was a key virtue. We Wachacha have a saying: 'The termite is small, but she builds a mountain.' Have you seen our termite mounds?"

"Oh, Dad, let me ask Cynthia about South America!" Malama interjected.

"Very well," Ezekiel said dryly. "I fear, Miss Cavallo, that our younger generation is losing the virtue of patience at an alarming rate."

"What would you like to know, Malama?" Cynthia asked.

"Do people really ride on llamas, and are they red Indians?"

As Cynthia dealt with Malama's questions, she noted the others around the table. Adiari seemed almost as interested as Malama in the topics she raised, but was less forward. Mary said little and kept everyone's plates supplied, yet clearly attended to everything said. Balebe seemed to be in a world of his own, somewhat withdrawn and given to brief glances at her that seemed to hold a trace of anxiety.

Kaniugi appeared again from the kitchen, a tray in his hand, and set it down on the sideboard. He began to clear the table as Adiari and Mary discussed the boy's coming soccer matches.

Cynthia said "Thank you" to Kaniugi as he took her plate. He just grunted softly and moved on, without making direct contact. *Did I do something wrong, thanking a servant? This is so weird, a black man waiting on a black family. Everyone ignoring him as he works for them, but Balebe telling me he's really a member of the family. "Things are different here," indeed! This master-servant scene is so alien, I've always hated it in Latin America, and here we are again, African-style!*

Her eyes had been following Kaniugi, and when she glanced across the table to Balebe, he was looking directly at her with that strange, mixed look again.

There was an interval of silence after Kaniugi had cleared the plates and set a fruit tart and a pitcher of custard sauce in front of Mary, who began to portion it out.

Ezekiel resumed his conversation. "So, Ms. Cavallo, may I call you Cynthia? If you don't mind a little more 'shop talk,' as it were.

You see, my son seldom tells me of his studies, although I'll admit that he's not entirely to blame for our lack of communication."

Ezekiel took the dessert handed down to him from Balebe and continued. "I'm afraid I've been rather resistant to the idea of my son's pursuing a field so, shall we say, irrelevant to the needs of a developing nation. However, he has, despite my best efforts to persuade him against it, persisted in this endeavor."

He paused for a moment to sample the tart. "He's inherited a good deal of stubbornness from the O'Reilly side, I fear." He cocked an eyebrow at Mary with an ironical twist of his lips.

Mary tossed her head. "Ezekiel, if you insist on monopolizing the dinner conversation, do have done with your genetical studies and ask Cynthia a sensible question! Perhaps you shall learn something worthwhile about paleoanthropology."

Malama stifled a snicker, and Adiari poured more custard sauce on his tart with great attention. Balebe looked martyred but kept his silence.

"What would you like to know?" Cynthia asked, seeking to steer the conversation back to some abstract topic.

"I would like your opinion of the utility of such a field as paleoanthropology to a developing country such as ours. What good does it do us to have people studying fossil bones millions of years old? Isn't this a pastime better suited to affluent European nations?"

Cripes! Put me on the spot, why don't you! she thought. The table had grown silent, and the look on Balebe's face was ominous. She smoothed her napkin on her lap, playing for a little time. "Well, I can only give you my opinion, sir, but I think it's perfectly reasonable for indigenous people in a country such as yours to study the fossils your nation possesses. Some developing countries in Latin America see their prehistoric sites as a national patrimony—of course, they're dealing with materials that do often relate to historically documented groups, such as the Aztecs and the Incas . . ."

Ezekiel had her fixed directly in his gaze, and she hurried on. "I do think it's worthwhile for an Asalian to get training and practice in the field. It will forever remain a white man's pastime until others make it their own. As far as usefulness goes, my own view is that a few people working in paleoanthropology in an inspired way will make a bigger contribution to the country than they might if they were doing some other, more 'useful' work in a less inspired way.

"Besides," she said, trying to lighten the mood, "someone trained as a paleoanthropologist can be useful. Many such people in the States serve the police as forensic experts, determining age and sex on bodies much more recent than the Pleistocene."

Ezekiel Thanatu inclined his head toward Balebe. "Is that so, Balebe? You've never intimated that you might prove so useful to the CID in their work."

Looking across the table, Cynthia was stricken by the look on Balebe's face. Rather than taking her up on the joke, he was clearly struggling to master deep emotions. He finally met his father's eyes. "Yes," he said, "physical anthropologists are being very helpful in Argentina, identifying the remains of the 'disappeared.'"

In that instant, Cynthia realized that she had inadvertently led the conversation into some awful family territory. At the end of the table, Mary's face was ashen. The two other children were looking down at the table, motionless, and Ezekiel stared stonily at his eldest son, who glared back. *Oh, God, what have I done . . .*

Surprisingly, Adiari broke the silence. "Speaking of disappearing, would you like to see where we kids disappear to, down by the river, Cynthia? I believe the green monkeys will be there, this time of day."

"Yes, thank you, Adiari, I'd like to see the monkeys very much." She rose from the table with the younger children. Thanking Mary for the dinner, she followed Malama onto the verandah. As she was leaving, Ezekiel stood up and without another word walked into the living room. Balebe remained seated with his mother at the table. Cynthia and the two teenagers walked down the steps and away from the house. They walked in silence for a minute. Cynthia felt unbearably awkward, at a loss for words.

Again, it was Adiari who took the initiative. "I'm really sorry you stepped right in the middle of a family feud." His young face bore an expression she'd seen before, on children who'd had to grow up too fast.

"You couldn't have known that my dad and Balebe had a huge fight last week about political matters. You see, over the last two years, my dad has had a number of people put into detention. He and others in the government say they're dangerous radicals who want to overthrow the government. Balebe disagrees about that, but what's worse is that over the same time, some other politicians and students have just disappeared. Taken away by people in plainclothes and never heard from again."

Malama broke in. "People say that Daddy has something to do with the disappearances, but he says he hasn't, that it's other people—or that's what he finally said when Balebe started shouting at him last week. It was the same fight that started out with Shafer."

Cynthia was chilled. *Oh God, not here too, not another dirty war starting up, under this well-manicured surface . . . and these poor children. Who can they believe, the father, the brother? Was Shafer disappeared? Why? God, did I put my foot in it!* "I don't know what to say. I'm so sorry I've made things worse," she said lamely.

Malama smiled and grasped her hand as they approached the ravine that led down to the river. "Oh, don't worry, we like you lots, and besides, we're all used to big fights at our house, they've been going on between Mum and Dad forever, only now Balebe gets into them too! Look, there are the monkeys, they have some new babies that are so sweet!"

Cynthia smiled as she let Adiari help her down the steep embankment to the river. *And I was worried about using the wrong fork at dinner!*

David

"We'll see you both this evening." Mary began to roll up her car window against the morning mist, then spoke again. "Please be out here at five-thirty sharp, so we can be home on time, dear. That will go a long way to patch things up." She pulled the Citroen into the traffic streaming by the national museum.

Balebe said, "This way, past the main exhibit halls. We've only got four minutes to get to Pierce's office."

They trotted through a staff parking lot and up the main stairs of the museum office building. The main entry was blocked by heavy iron grating, with a door opening inward next to a small booth.

"God, do I have to show my passport?" Cynthia wisecracked under her breath as they approached.

"It does serve to screen visitors, both indigenous and foreign, who might otherwise troop into David's office and demand to be shown the fossils." Balebe bade good morning to the young woman at the reception desk, who wore a telephone headset over an elaborate braided hairdo. On seeing him, she broke into a warm smile and an animated greeting, which changed into a cool formality as Cynthia was introduced.

As they turned away and Balebe gestured toward an open stairway, Cynthia muttered, "Hmm, am I imagining things, or do I sense a little proprietary interest there, Bwana Thanatu?"

"Um, actually you're probably right. I did escort Elizabeth to a museum lecture once, and she's always been very friendly. It's awful here at the museum, Cyn, where I am deemed an especially fine catch. It's all very well for you to snicker, but I've been fending off eager young misses intent on a socially advantageous marriage since I was seventeen, by any means necessary. It really doesn't give one a lot of room for having fun. America has been a real vacation from that kind of pressure! Here we are . . ."

They had reached the third floor. A sign stating "Palaeontology Department" pointed to their right, and another indicated the director's office on the left. Balebe opened a heavy wooden door, and a dignified African woman in a royal blue dress looked up from her desk.

"Ah, right on the hour, Balebe! Welcome, Miss Cavallo, my name is Anna Manyanga. I will tell Mr. Pierce you are here. She pressed a button on her telephone console and said, "Mr. Thanatu, Junior, and Miss Cavallo are here." At a word from the speaker, she bade them go in the door behind her desk.

As they entered, David Pierce was sitting at his desk. On the wall behind him hung a large color photograph of snowcapped Mount Ruba. Windows to the left overlooked the towers of downtown Wangara.

Pierce rose from his chair and fixed Cynthia with a look that combined cordiality with frank appraisal. Leaning forward and extending his hand, he said, "I'm very pleased to meet you Miss Cavallo. Do have a seat."

He settled himself back into his chair, made a little tent of his fingers, and smiled. "When this young man proffered me your resumé and lauded your field experience, he neglected to mention that you were quite ornamental as well." His dark eyes continued to hold hers with an intensity that was not entirely domineering, nor entirely playful.

Piqued by the man's attitude, Cynthia responded with some sharpness, "I hope this won't detract from my usefulness to your team—half my plane fare is a steep price for a Third World country to pay for a mere ornament."

"Why, not at all, my dear young lady," Pierce laughed, leaned back in his swivel chair, and began to replenish his pipe. "People in such restricted financial circumstances as we Asalians prefer the, ah, multipurpose instrument to those which serve only one function." He cocked a quizzical eyebrow at her while lighting his pipe.

"Oh, give it a rest, David," Balebe cut in, embarrassed. He turned to Cynthia. "He likes to see if he can unsettle the girls with all this talk, but he's really quite harmless."

"Don't say anything that I might take as a challenge, young man. You know how we Pierces can get about having our way," Pierce said, waving his pipe at Balebe in obvious good humor.

"You mustn't take any of this too seriously, Miss Cavallo," Pierce said. "This young fellow is angling for my job, and I try to keep him in his place as long as I can. I have to keep a sharp eye about me— he's rather smart, and very well connected, you know."

"This job you can keep, David," Balebe rejoined. "I'm afraid I'm not as deft at walking the tightrope as you."

"Yes, to tell the truth, it's a constant headache, a constant one.

Mark my words, you'd best be careful, or despite your efforts you'll be sitting in this chair within the next five years . . . and I shall be footloose and fancy free in the field again! Now, let's have some coffee, shall we?" Pierce buzzed Anna and requested refreshments.

He returned his attention to Cynthia, but in a more subdued, businesslike tone. "Actually, I'm delighted to have you with us. We have sorely needed someone with good excavation skills as well as some background in taphonomy. Juma's team needs further training in these areas." He picked up a pipe from his desk and inspected the bowl.

"They're first-rate fossil hunters and know every species and bone imaginable—Juma's always had a better eye than I have for species identification. However, we've had to depend on outside help for documentation of the sedimentological context of the materials. Even though I can excavate adequately, I haven't the microstratigraphic expertise, nor can I go running out to the field every time they need something taken out."

He squinted at them and gestured with his pipe. "Our aim, ultimately, is to have an Asalian field team with at the very least A-levels in zoology and a good background in geology. In the meantime, your tutoring will enhance the team's present ability to take on recovery of *in situ* fossil materials, independent of foreign teams."

Relieved to have the talk turn to shop, Cynthia said, "I hope I'll be able to provide the level of expertise you're looking for. I'm certainly not that experienced an excavator."

"I've read your vita, and I think that a total of twelve digs is quite impressive for someone in their mid-twenties. You'll do," Pierce said, raising an eyebrow and reviving a bit of the appraising smile.

The coffee, carried by a man in a faded gray cotton uniform, arrived and was placed on Pierce's desk.

As he poured, Pierce said to Balebe, "Juma's been downtown this morning buying supplies. He isn't likely to be back in his office until after lunch. So perhaps you'd give Miss Cavallo a tour of the paleontological collections this morning."

Turning to her, Pierce said, "I'm terribly sorry that I won't be able to give you a personal tour of the fossil hominids today. I've a group of Japanese computer people coming in a quarter hour. They're quite keen to see the materials and are likely to donate some much-needed equipment to the museum." He smiled and drew on his pipe. "I sometimes feel I wasted my time getting a doctorate at all. It seems I spend most of my time wining and dining potential donors and autographing various documents Anna offers me."

"Ah, the sad plight of the administrator . . ." Balebe began in a mocking tone.

"Right, young man, enough of that, or I'll appoint *you* acting head of the museum and *I'll* go out to Ruba with Juma and Miss Cavallo." Pierce glanced at the two of them significantly while drawing on his pipe.

Balebe raised his hands in laughing capitulation and said, "No, no, I'm going and you're staying! Speaking of going, what's the story on Michel? Will he be able to get out here? It'll be a lot harder for us to zero in on likely localities if he can't come."

Pierce nodded. "Mm, just had a telex from him this morning. He's feeling much better, he says, and wants to come out for at least a week to get you orientated to the regional stratigraphy. I'm actually quite concerned about him. His health hasn't been good all winter, from what I hear from van de Hoven. If he *can* get into the field with you, it'd be invaluable. At any rate, he's sending copies of his field notes from last season by fax, and you'll be able to start with those. Should have them by tomorrow."

"Good," Balebe said, "now, let's go over what time-indicator species you think Cynthia and I should review in the collections this week. I assume we'd better look over all the fossil pigs from Anthea's localities . . ."

Opening a drawer, Pierce withdrew a pad of lined paper and slapped it on the table. "Right, and mind you don't omit the equids and Hippopotamidae." He took an expensive pen from the pocket of his jacket and began scribbling on the sheet in front of him. "You'd best start with old *Nyanzachoerus* and work forward through the modern genera—I don't suppose you've had much chance to look at African suids, Miss Cavallo?" Cynthia shook her head.

"Yes, well, do get their dentitions down by the time you go to the field. We've a fine collection just down the hall."

Still hunched over the notepad, he bit on the end of his pen in a schoolboyish fit of concentration. "*Hexaprotodon,* Thanatu, as well as the various true hippos, and don't leave out *Hyaena* versus *Crocuta.* One never knows when one will run into a carnivore or two . . . *Deinofalis,* too—I take it you've never seen sabre-toothed cats, Miss Cavallo?"

"As a matter of fact, I have seen *Homotherium* in North American collections, as well as *Smilodon,* of course," Cynthia replied, a bit dizzy from the shower of genus names.

"Ah, yes, the La Brea Tar Pits cat, very nice creature," Pierce said, in a semidistracted tone. "Yes, well, I think this should do for a start. The Bovidae are a whole world unto themselves, and I'm not sure you'll be able to assimilate enough to make it worthwhile before going into the field—but do try, if you have time. Balebe can help you get acquainted with the dentitions of the major antelope tribes, the buffaloes, and so forth." He tore the sheet off his pad and passed it to Balebe.

He leaned forward on his elbows and looked up at them with a glint of excitement in his eyes and smiled. "I truly envy you both this season. I've no doubt, based on last year's reconnaissance, that we've got really old Pliocene deposits out there—maybe even late Miocene. I have a feeling you'll be making some really exciting discoveries out there this year."

The intercom on his desk sounded. "I'm afraid I must excuse myself now. I'm off to the board room to meet the Takasakiyama group. Miss Cavallo, it's been a pleasure. Thanatu, I trust you with this young lady's safekeeping!" He rose and walked with them out the door and headed down the stairway.

"So that's David Pierce in person—you two seem to be on pretty good terms," Cynthia said as they stood outside his office door.

"Hmm, yes, David's been very supportive of my career." Cynthia waited for Balebe to continue, but he remained silent, staring in the general direction of the paleontology collections.

Strange, again that same kind of noncommittal response that he gives when asked about Shafer . . . what is going on here?

"Well, would you like to have a quick walk-through of the collections before lunch? We'll have to wait until this afternoon, or maybe tomorrow, to really get down to work."

"I thought you'd never ask! This is the moment of a lifetime for someone like me—do you think Pierce will really show me the hominids, too?"

"Oh yes, he wasn't just being polite. He values your skills a lot, and this is a little way of thanking you. Besides, he does have an eye for attractive women." Balebe waggled his eyebrows suggestively.

"Oh, give me a break!" Cynthia replied. "I haven't got anything to worry about, do I?" she added.

"Truthfully, no, Cyn. I know it's a sore subject with you after McIntyre, but you needn't worry. David only teases a bit but never takes it further unless some sincere interest is evinced by the other party. He's told me some quite extraordinary tales about his fundraising tours, though. It seems that there are some, ah, fossil groupies, one might say, on the lecture circuit," Balebe smiled.

"Uh-huh, I've heard the same. We even had one in our department for a while. Remember Stephanie?"

Balebe beamed. "Of *course* I remember Stephanie! She reminded me a bit of the girls here at home—except that, refreshingly, she wasn't keen to marry."

"Ah so, Mr. Thanatu, I was wondering whether there was something going on between the two of you before she transferred to Berkeley last year!"

"Well, actually, she dropped me after a rather intense three weeks. I was quite crushed at first, until good old Tom Weller patiently explained that it was the level of my reputation as a paleoanthropologist rather than any other, ah, qualifications which dictated her attention span."

"Mm, so someone like David or Bob Shafer might have had a longer run of popularity? Fascinating!"

"Lord knows, maybe they have! But David told me that it can get to be quite a delicate matter for him during these lecture tours. Some of the, ah, interested parties are quite affluent, and to further complicate matters, some are quite married. I offered him my profoundest commiseration."

"And he threatened you with his job!" Cynthia grinned.

Balebe shook his head. "I fear that I might be a bit too novel to take up every aspect of David's role. I think that, should I ever acquire his job, I'd keep him on the lecture circuit. I haven't the nerves nor the right color skin to do so well as he."

Cynthia looked at him sharply, but his expression held nothing but amusement. "Look, this is the real world, Cyn, and some very nice people who love fossils still aren't quite ready to welcome a black African, even a fair-skinned sort, into their homes and hearts. David can raise more money for Asalia than I can, and I've not the slightest bitterness about it." He smiled mischievously. "Besides, I can't picture myself sitting around after dinner trying to sort out whether to take some millionaire's wife up on her offer of extra hospitality!"

"Phew! Hominids, money, and sex! All we need now for a best-seller is violence!" She laughed.

"Perhaps we already have that, Cyn. Bob Shafer's never been found, you know," Balebe replied, suddenly serious.

"You're right." She fell silent for a moment. "Although I can't help wondering if this isn't just another Shafer scam. You know, like, suddenly he'll emerge from the Batchilok beds, Lawrence of Arabia style, with some amazing find, a tale of adventure, and a guaranteed seat on every American talk show until the end of the century."

"Perhaps, it would be in character," Balebe agreed. "Well, let's go see some of the fossil pigs, eh? Then we can make pigs of ourselves at lunch with impunity!"

Juma

Balebe grabbed Cynthia's elbow as she was about to step off the curb. "Look *left,* dear lady, *left!*"

She gasped as a car whizzed past them from the left, close enough to touch. "God, I would have stepped right into that one!"

"Yes, and if you knew Asalian drivers better, you'd be looking left *and* right, as well as up, before crossing the street!" Balebe laughed. "Now, let's go quickly!"

They walked away from Taifa Avenue, along a street lined with blooming mimosa trees, pink and lovely despite a thin coating of red dust. Around them, people of all sorts jostled for headway on the crowded sidewalk.

Distracted by the incredible variety of humanity, Cynthia had a hard time paying attention to making her way through the crowd. Dozens of men in dusty, threadbare suits walked down the avenue. In this section of town, African women in light cotton dresses, some with a colorful *khanga* cloth wrapped over them, outnumbered the elegantly attired black women of the city center. An older white man in shirt, shorts, and knee socks skirted around two African nuns without seeming to notice them, striding through the crowd with a military swing. Cynthia suddenly had to dodge an oncoming trio of chatting youths whose clothes seemed to randomly sample the extremes of the last twenty years' styles.

Balebe followed her stare at one young man's orange and purple bellbottoms, polyester tennis sweater, and patent cowboy boots. "Let me put you onto another kind of Third World dumping, Cyn. Not only pesticides and medicines outlawed in developed countries, but also all the most toxic fashions end up here, at prices we can't refuse," he muttered.

She shook her head, trying to clear it. "You know, I feel a little dizzy. I don't know if it's the altitude, the buzz from that strong coffee you people brew, or sensory overload."

"Do you want to sit down? There's a little cafe just ahead where we could stop for a moment. I'm sorry to have pushed you so much.

You're also jet-lagged as well, and I really should have thought a bit more before scheduling in a lunch with Dhanni and Ben." He gestured for her to step into the darkness of a coffee shop and guided her back to a free table.

She sat down gratefully. "No, it's okay. I believe in getting into the swing of things, but I think I just need a breather. It's three a.m., my time," she said, glancing at her watch. "But shouldn't we get back to the museum to meet Juma Nane?"

Balebe shook his head. "Not to worry. Juma operates on African time. You know, go with the flow and all that. Half an hour either way won't make the slightest difference to him. He may well not be back himself, knowing the time it takes to get provisions in bulk in this town. I take it you don't want another coffee right now? How about a mango juice? It's fresh, you know."

"I don't know where I'll put it after the lunch we had, but I never can resist a chance to have a mango," she said.

Balebe went to the counter in the back of the cafe to get the juice, and Cynthia glanced at the occupants of other tables. The crowd was thinning quickly with the beginning of the afternoon work period, but two young women were intently conversing at a nearby table, eyed by a couple of lounging youths who were obviously university students. One of them cast an appraising eye at Cynthia, then glanced away.

"Here we are, fresh from the blender." Balebe set down an icy glass in front of her. "What did you think of Dhanni and Ben?"

"They're just great! He's so funny, and she's such a talented woman. I'm glad we had time to see some of her photos."

"Yes, Ben hadn't seen any of the big prints himself, and our visit gave him the pretext of getting in the door without arousing any suspicion about his motives." Balebe took a sip of his juice and sighed. "It's not in me to condemn anyone in this matter, Cynthia. I know how the respective families think and feel too well for that. I just wish that it could be easier."

She looked down at her drink for a moment. "Do you think that once they get together openly there's any possibility the families will come around?"

"Who knows, I certainly don't. I'd hazard a guess that if a child is born, at least Ben's family will. We had a major uproar in our own home when Semira Nyau wanted to marry a Mchacha, and it all turned out okay in the end. But that was two African ethnic groups, and Ben's and Dhanni's communities have been so separate, even in day-to-day social life. It's not only racial, it's religious, and a matter of lifestyle. I personally think that intermarriage is the only path toward true racial harmony—but then, I would, wouldn't I?"

She stared silently into her drink again. *And whom do you want to marry? Or do you? This is a complex world you live in here, what are your goals, and why are you so interested, Ms. Cavallo?* She looked up to find his eyes on her, an unfathomable expression on his face.

"Tell me about Juma Nane," she said, a little lamely.

"He's a remarkable man," Balebe said. "Very little in the way of formal schooling, unlike some of the younger members of his team, who are actually in the university, or about to enter. But incredibly well-versed in fossils—David wasn't being coy when he said that Juma outclassed him in that area. The man's a natural paleontologist, and a real leader, too.

"How did he and David get together?" she asked.

"That's a very interesting story. Juma's father worked for Anthea as an excavator and began taking Juma out with him, in a kind of apprenticeship, when he was just a boy. David's parents were sending him out to Anthea's, too, during school holidays. Although Juma was never allowed near Anthea's lab or table, the two boys started running together during the day.

"I must say that David's father and mother really differed from Anthea in taking a nonracialist view of Africans, and the friendship came quite easily. They learnt together, with David siphoning off his readings about fossils to Juma, and Juma and his father teaching David excavation techniques and bushcraft.

"Later, when David started doing his own prospecting, it was natural for him to hire Juma as his lieutenant, as it were—that's 'lootenant' to you," he said, smiling. "But their bond goes a lot deeper. I really believe that they're each the other's best friend."

"Boy, this is really a day for introductions for me. Maybe we'd better go meet him now?" she asked.

Once back on the museum grounds, they headed past the main office and collections building. Down a hill stood a set of identical one-story buildings with red tile roofs.

"These are the old office and collections buildings. Anthea still works down here, in that one over there, when she's in town. Colin Jones, the archaeologist, is using her lab right now to analyze the Ruba stone tools."

"Wow, I'd love to meet him, too! But that might be too much for one day . . ." Cynthia laughed.

"Let's see if we have any time once we've seen Juma. Colin heads for the bars at four-thirty like clockwork, so we may be too late to catch him today. Here's Juma's office."

The gray-painted door stood open. Balebe called, "*Hodi,*" the standard Swahili request to enter.

"*Karibu,*" responded a voice from within the room. They stepped into the darker space of the room, where two young men were at a battered desk, poring over computer output and what looked to Cynthia like a field catalogue. At a table next to the window opposite the door, an older man was working on a fossil antelope skull with a dental pick and brush. All smiled at the visitors silently for a moment.

One of the young men spoke. "Good afternoon, Bwana Nane is inside his office." He gestured to a door on their right. "Just go on in. We'll save our introductions for later."

They knocked on the door. A deep voice called "*Karibu,*" and they stepped into a room sparsely furnished with a desk and a small bookcase. However, the presence of the man behind the desk filled the room.

Cynthia was struck by the massiveness of his head, especially when he rose, and she could see its contrast with a slender, almost boyish body. For a moment his face remained impassive, and she felt a bit intimidated by this man's aura of personal power, which seemed even more profound than Ezekiel Thanatu's.

As Balebe presented her, Juma Nane extended his hand with a

self-contained and dignified smile. "I am most pleased to meet you, Miss Cavallo. We look forward to learning new methods from you for our fieldwork."

Cynthia was suddenly appalled and abashed by her situation. *My God, what presumption for me to be here to teach this man anything. What has Balebe got me into? Did David shove this down Nane's throat?*

"I hope that I can be of some use. I have a lot to learn about African paleontology and fieldwork, too," she said, feeling at a loss for words.

"Not to worry, Miss Cavallo, I am sure that we shall have a good exchange of skills. David has shown me your resumé, and I think it is a very good thing that you have come to help us. Have a seat now, and let me introduce my team members to you."

He raised his voice and called for the men in the outer room to come in. The older man, Maleti Musoma, was introduced first. Nane switched momentarily to Swahili while speaking to him, then back to English. "Maleti's English is not so good, but he understands a lot," he said to Cynthia.

She replied in Swahili, "Well, I hope he can help me with my Kiswahili." Nane raised his eyebrows in a mild expression of surprise. "Ah, you have learned a little of our national language, that's very good, very good."

Cynthia let go of some of her concern.

"This young man is Elias Nyondo," Nane continued with the introductions. "He is right now on break from our university, where he is studying prehistory and geology."

Ah, this is the one who's co-authored a paper with Pierce. Nane's successor, or maybe Pierce's? Balebe's competitor?

The young man grasped her hand with a self-assured smile. "Welcome, I am very pleased to meet you. My former classmate has told me so much about you," he said, gesturing at Balebe with a smile.

Andrew Kacha, the other young man, was introduced as having just completed his A-levels in biology and as bound for the university in the next academic year. "I am especially interested in archaeology," he said eagerly. "So please give me any instructions you can in the field. Later on, I hope to continue some of the excavations in the Asoka localities, using newer techniques . . ."

Cynthia smiled. "Well, I'll try to be helpful, although I hope you know that I've mainly dug sites much more recent than the Lower Pleistocene, and I suspect that not everything I've learned myself will be useful for these kinds of sites."

Nane interjected, "Just you teach us what you know, then we shall adapt it. This is what these university boys call SAS." The rest of the men chuckled.

Elias said, "Standard Asalian Strategy, a little in-joke with us. Like those *matatu* taxi vans you see on the road—a foreign idea, adapted to our own ways and means."

Andrew laughed. "Yes, with *matatu,* we kept the chassis and engine, but got rid of the brakes!"

Cynthia laughed with the rest of them. *They're sure trying to put me at ease, maybe this will even be fun!*

Nane looked at Balebe and said, "These young men have not been working hard enough for me, and I fear we shall not be able to get away from town until Friday. Can you find something to do with yourselves until then?"

Balebe smiled sardonically. "David gave us the charge of reviewing half the fossil and modern genera in the museum before going into the field. I'd say we'll keep busy."

"Well, you had better get started, then, and don't forget to show Miss Cavallo some of the stone tools from Ruba. We can never be too careful, even when searching exposures people think are too old for stone tools. This boy Andrew keeps bothering me about it. I think he wants to discover some Miocene archaeological site and be as famous as Louis Leakey!"

Over Andrew's laughing protests, Balebe said, "Yes, I'll see if we can catch Colin before he leaves. Perhaps we can arrange an afternoon going over the lithics in Anthea's lab." He glanced at his watch. "We'd better go if we want to catch him—Colin's pretty religious about his appointments with the bar."

Nane smiled. "Yes, you had better go along and find him. I suppose David told you that Michel will be joining us briefly after we are in the field? It is a shame he has been ill this spring, but even if he has to make a short visit, he will help us very much."

Balebe nodded. "Yes, David said he's due out in about a fortnight—that should give us time to get settled, at least. Look, we really should go see Colin. I'll look in again tomorrow morning."

After a round of handshakes, they trotted out the doors and up a few steps to a covered sidewalk that led to another long, low laboratory building. They hurried down toward the far end, where a door stood open and the voice of Placido Domingo was drifting out.

"Almost as big an opera buff as a beer drinker," Balebe muttered as he ushered Cynthia through the door.

Jones was sitting on a stool, hunched over a trestle table covered with bits of flaked lava. A high-intensity gooseneck lamp formed a pool in which his hands were fitting and unfitting some of the pieces of stone. He pressed a bit of plasticene from a lump on the tabletop on one flake, fitted another against it, and then tried to stick on a third. As he did, the first flake fell back onto the table.

"Oh, bugger! Damn them, damn them, why wasn't length and breadth and thickness good enough for the compulsive sods who invented core refitting. Oh, damn it all!"

He glanced up to see the two young people staring at him and continued on his tirade, only at a pitch more in competition with Domingo. "Oh, hello, Thanatu, what brings you here. I'd like to throttle the bastards who thought up this trendy new core reduction technol—well, *hello!*"

He'd stopped in midstream with a classic double-take, now turning on his stool to give Cynthia full, head-to-toe scrutiny and a winning smile.

Oh no, another idol shattered. Colin Jones is just another sexist pig. Now, remember, Cyn, try to make allowances for culture. Cynthia strove to maintain a polite expression.

Balebe interposed, "Colin, I'd like you to meet Cynthia Cavallo, my classmate from the States. She's the one who'll be going out with Juma and company this year."

Jones turned off his cassette player and hopped off his stool, hand extended. "Delighted to meet you, Miss Cavallo. I rather mistook you for a film star at first, but I see that you're much too serious a young woman for that. It's that slightly reproving line about the mouth. Besides, the film stars only come to see David."

She smiled despite herself. "How do you do, sorry to have disturbed you."

"Not at all, not at all. You'll have to forgive my use of the Queen's English, but I've been given to understand that if I don't include more of this 'core reduction technology' blather in my article for *Current Anthropology,* they won't put it in! What a bother, trying to fit the damned cores back together. It used to be that a good archaeologist just measured the stuff and compared it with some other assemblages, threw in a few nice illustrations, and that was that. I tell you, the field's in the hands of the anal compulsives."

"I rather like refitting, Colin," Balebe said, laughing. "Perhaps we could work a deal. You set out the Ruba type collection and some debitage for us to look at later this week, and we'll play jigsaw puzzle with your sample."

"Splendid! I've always been hopeless at jigsaw puzzles. Now I can't tell whether I've got a site from which most of the cores have been removed, or if I'm simply being bloody incompetent instead."

Jones glanced at his watch. "Look, it's just about time to pack it in for the day. What say we hit the Hibiscus Bar and make some plans for later in the week?"

"We'd love to, Colin, but my mum's coming to pick us up at five-thirty, so we'll have to take a rain check for some afternoon when I've got the car. Shall we drop in, say, Wednesday afternoon?"

"Super, I'll have it all laid out for you by then. Nice meeting you, Miss Cavallo, until later!"

As they retraced their steps up the hill toward the main building, Placido Domingo was cut off in midstream, and the door to Jones's lab slammed shut. Balebe turned back to watch the archaeologist lock his door and head downhill toward the staff parking lot. He checked his watch. "Four-thirty, right on time, no matter what."

"What a strange guy, BT. Every bit the stereotype of the colonial

Brit, but underneath very sharp and self-mocking. Not what I'd expected at all."

"No, Colin isn't. He was born out here, you know, and although he holds a British passport, I think the only way they'd ever get him back to England is in a box. He's seen a lot come and go. Raised on a tea plantation a hundred miles north of Wangara, inspired by what Anthea Pierce was doing, and by the Leakeys in Kenya, got a degree by submitting an independent thesis at Oxford, and came back out as fast as he could after its defense. He lives on a shoestring, in a shabby little flat near the Asian cinema, sustains himself on curries and beer, and does first-rate fieldwork. He's really been very kind to us young Africans, even though we'll probably end up taking away what little job he's got, through the process of 'Africanisation' of employment. I think most of us want to see him stay on, somehow."

He glanced at his watch and again shifted topics. "We really haven't enough time to do anything worthwhile with the collections today. How about a visit to the Museum gift shop before it closes? It's really rather nice." She nodded, and they headed toward the main exhibition hall.

As they reached the door to the gift shop, he said, "Look, I'm truly sorry about what happened last night. You've been an excellent sport all day, not bringing it up. It's been awful since I got home this year, Cyn. My father and I haven't seen eye to eye on politics and so many other things for years, but these disappearances have really set us at each other. I'm trying to believe that he's got nothing to do with them. But sometimes I fail. One of the people who's missing was a classmate of mine at university who decided to go into politics in his home district."

Cynthia turned and stared him in the face, unable to frame a response.

"You needn't say anything, Cyn. I just want you to know that at my mother's behest, I went and patched things up with my father last night, and we shouldn't have any more scenes at dinner. She also made him promise not to interrogate you from soup to nuts, either."

"Thank God," she said, turning again into the doorway of the gift shop. "The food was great, but the inquisition was a bit much, BT."

Balebe chuckled. "Yes, to paraphrase an old 'Monty Python' skit, nobody ever expects the Asalian Inquisition."

"Uh-oh, is this another SAS coming on?" she smiled at him.

His face grew troubled again. "For us here, possibly so, I'm afraid to say . . . but look, you have to buy this red and black soapstone baboon for Tom!"

She laughed aloud at the thought of presenting the ugly little statue to their serious friend, but the weight of Balebe's words did not entirely lift off her. *So much intrigue and danger under the pleasant surface, and his family so involved. And Malama said they'd also fought about Shafer. What was that about?*

She reached into her purse for her wallet, trying to still her sense of apprehension.

Journey to Ruba

Juma Nana shifted the Land Rover down into second gear again, slowing as they approached what seemed like the hundredth little dry channel cut into the desert floor. The Rover rocked violently through the runnel, and everyone but the man holding the wheel swayed from side to side. Nane shifted up again to third, accelerating across the open space for about a thousand yards, then shifted down and braked for the next channel.

In a heat-induced haze, Cynthia watched Nane's mahogany arm as he moved the gearshift. *Forward, to the right, and forward, the move of the knight in chess . . . it's endless.* Cynthia began to nod in the hot cab. She sat between Nane and Balebe, straddling the gearbox. The midday air was searingly hot, and the gearbox added another ten degrees of its own. The windows were open, and the fine white powder of the desert floor swirled in. She felt it settling in her nostrils, gathering an acrid, alkaline sensation somewhere between a scent and a taste and decidedly unpleasant. She coughed to clear her throat.

Despite the open windows, the cab reeked of sweat and gasoline fumes. A huge black plastic barrel of spare petrol was wedged into one side of the rear cargo space, with a smaller gray plastic barrel of water on the other, the space between padded with their small packets of personal gear. The petrol sloshed ominously at every bump and dip, and as the day had progressed its fumes had become more obtrusive.

They had set out from Wangara at five in the morning, heading west for the Ruba region well before the morning traffic began. Dawn had broken as the road began to switchback its way down into the Rift.

"We'll be descending three steps, uplift blocks, geologically, on our way down to the bottom of the Rift," Balebe said. "The first two are well-watered enough for farming, Pakyu lands, mostly. In fact, Andrew's grandparents live out this way, don't they?" He looked back at Andrew wedged into the back seat.

Andrew nodded. "Yes, about a hundred kilometers south, on the first step."

Balebe went on. "The lowest step of the escarpment is agriculturally marginal and has traditionally been used by the M'posas for their cattle. These days, however, landless farmers are colonizing out that way, with considerable tensions resulting. The floor of the Rift Valley here is Shurr country. Only camels and goats can find enough to eat out where we're headed."

Cynthia had been charmed by the small Pakyu homesteads, their terraced household gardens shining brightly against the red earth. Dense lines of silver-green sisal plants defined each homestead's perimeters.

"Those plants look like maguey!" she exclaimed.

"It's the same general family, Cyn, only here they make rope rather than booze from them."

"Someone makes liquor from sisal?" Nane questioned.

The three then launched into a lively discussion of the uses of the *Sanseveria* clan, attended to silently but intently by the four men sandwiched into the rear seat of the Land Rover. Andrew, Elias, and Maleti, plus their cook, Mupiki, were squashed into the back seat, while Cynthia and Balebe shared the front with Nane. They would remain squeezed into one vehicle until they reached Anthea Pierce's base camp, where they would pick up a second Land Rover, a truck, and their field gear. The trip would take until after nightfall.

At first Cynthia had pitied the men in the back seat. Although each was slender, they could barely fit into the space. However, as they bumped, rocked, and swayed over the unimproved roads of the Asalian back country, she began to envy their snug fit. The Rover had no seat belts, and without a door frame to hang onto, she had to exert the strength of back and leg to keep from smashing into Nane or Balebe when the car rocked wildly.

Now, the sun hung directly overhead. Even wearing dark sunglasses, she found the light reflected from the white floor of the Bara Desert blindingly bright. Ahead and to their left mirages filled the basin with water that expanded, shifted, and vanished as they sped onward. They had entered the desert about two hours before. Balebe had pointed out their route to her on his road map. Nane consulted no maps.

"Only the Shurr nomads travel here on foot," Balebe explained. "Their camels can make the trip from the eastern side to Watta in two days, unless there's a dust storm, and they have to stop until it's over. This road is an old Shurr trading route. It curves around the northern side of the Bara Basin."

"Why not cut through the middle? It seems like that would be a more direct route to Watta."

"Two reasons," Nane broke in. "First, in case of dust storms, one can find the higher ground by the touch of one's feet and so does not become totally lost. Second, if there is a rainstorm somewhere in the area, one is not suddenly in quicksand in the middle of the basin." He glanced sideways at her, his face as usual impassive but an eyebrow possibly a bit higher than normal.

"Ah," Cynthia said.

They settled into a stolid, enduring silence as the Rover began to encounter the tiny drainages that cut down through the shoulder of the basin. Cynthia found herself sinking deeper into a mute stupor, harboring her energies to withstand the jolting and increasing heat.

Nane pointed ahead to a camel skeleton lying near the side of the road. "We'll take some more petrol here, but let us wait until Watta Mission before having lunch." He slowed the vehicle and stopped a bit off the track. "Cynthia, if you want to go to the *choo,* go to that side of the Rover."

Cynthia nodded, noting the cross-cultural irony of Nane's referring her in Swahili to the nonexistent bathroom.

Nane, Balebe, and the rest of the crew piled out and went on a careful inspection of the camel skeleton while she retreated to the other side of the Land Rover. Squatting down, she again worried about the awkwardness of being the only—the first—woman on one of Nane's expeditions. Nane himself was cordial and correct, almost courtly in his manners, and each of the other men was unfailingly polite. Yet this was a man's world, doubly so. There was the Western realm of intrepid male fossil hunters, for whom fieldwork is an exercise in machismo. That one, at least, she was used to, from her own experiences and from some of Melanie's accounts of Shafer and others. This second world, the world of African men, some not steeped in European manners, was new to her. She feared making a serious blunder without knowing it, offending or discomfiting without meaning to. She was thankful that Balebe was inclined to coach her.

Walking around the back of the Rover toward the huddle around the camel bones, she was struck by the utter silence. The soft rushing of the wind and the ticking of the cooling Rover engine were the only sounds. As she approached the group, Andrew, Maleti, Mupiki, and Elias moved off somewhat sheepishly around the back of the Land Rover themselves, followed by a grinning Balebe.

She smiled at Nane. "I hope that you can manage the inconvenience of having me along."

"Whatever inconveniences we may suffer are recompensed by the advantages of your presence." Again, an impassive face, per-

103

haps a hint of amusement. He pivoted on his heel and headed for the other side of the vehicle.

Cynthia nodded and moved closer to inspect the camel's skull. It was a male, with the enormous canines typical of its sex. Balebe strolled back from the other side of the Rover and joined her.

"No herbivore should be allowed to have teeth like that," she said.

"Agreed, the world is full of rude enough shocks without having one's arm removed by a browser. I've heard that unrestrained males can actually kill each other during their rut. Speaking of camels, we must load up on water ourselves here. It's quite possible to get uncomfortably dehydrated just sitting in one of these cars without doing a thing. The awkward thing is that the first couple of days, if you don't drink enough water, you're liable to feel as if you've a bladder infection."

"Whew, show me the water bag! I don't feel thirsty, but I'll down an extra quart to avoid that." They walked over to where the rest of the group was drinking from the four water bags dangling from the rear mirror struts. Elias and Mupiki were simply catching the streams in their mouths in mid-air.

Balebe reached inside the cab for a battered enameled cup, filled it, and handed it to Cynthia. "Yes, it's not an experience to be sought after. The first time I went out with David and Juma, I didn't heed their advice, since I was used to running cross-country up in the highlands and thought I knew how much water I needed. Sure enough, I had a damned uncomfortable couple of days. Of course, I wasn't about to tell Pierce . . . I should think he guessed something as I was downing my twentieth cup of water on day two! The other side of it is that all one does the first few days back in town is pee, regardless of whether one's been drinking anything!"

She smiled. "Isn't physiology wonderful? It all takes care of itself, with only minor lags. More, please!"

Maleti had opened the rear door of the Land Rover and was gingerly unscrewing the top of the petrol barrel. A high-pitched rush of fumes escaped as he did. While Andrew and Elias unscrewed the braces holding two battered jerrycans on the outside of the cab, Maleti pulled out a length of rubber tubing from somewhere in the recesses of the tightly packed back of the car. Mupiki called out something in Kichacha and laughed uproariously. The others snorted a bit in sympathy with Elias, who was putting one end of the hosing into the petrol barrel.

"Mupiki asked him whether he hadn't got enough to drink that he has to drink petrol now—he's only told that joke every time anybody's done this siphoning since the Year One," Balebe explained in a low voice.

As Elias held one jerrycan near, Maleti sucked mightily on the hosing and leaped away spitting as the petrol surged out of the tube. Elias deftly brought the jerrycan up to the hose so that scarcely a drop was lost. Andrew stood ready with the second can, and the switch was made again with a minimum of waste. Maleti continued to spit.

"Efficient, but not healthy," Cynthia muttered.

"Standards are different here, Cyn. Maleti has a permanent job and is glad of it. Perhaps the next time you come you could bring one of those fancy bulb-pump siphons I saw in your tropical fish store, if you're so concerned."

Cynthia looked Balebe in the eye, a bit stunned by the obvious irritation in his voice. He stared back at her for a moment, then looked away. Again, a casual remark had triggered a sharp reply where she'd expected none, again in defense of the situation of his countrymen.

"I'm sorry, BT, I meant no harm, but I take your meaning," she said.

His face relaxed into a rueful smile. "It's I who should be sorry, Cyn, lecturing you when you're trying so hard to be a good guest. It's just my touchiness, as my mum calls it, probably from my having all the advantages while so many of my countrymen have next to nothing—and me not knowing what to do about it."

She wanted to take his hand but dared not in front of the group. "It's all right, I learn something every time you do get cranky, as well as when you're nice." They smiled a bit awkwardly and turned back to watch the men fill the Rover's two gas tanks from the

105

jerrycans, repeatedly filling them from the hose until the two full cans were set back into their brackets and bolted in.

"Last gas for two thousand kilometers, ma'am," Balebe said, attempting the San Felipe twang. She smiled back, but at the same time remained faintly troubled. *Is it me, or us? Or your father and these disappearances? Or does it have something to do with Shafer?*

They finally piled back into the Rover. Mupiki, whom Cynthia estimated to be in his fifties, went on in complaining tones in Kichacha to the two young men on either side of him, and Elias climbed out to give him a place next to the window. Cynthia glanced questioningly at Balebe.

"He's demanding his rights as an elder," Balebe muttered under his breath, as the old man continued to complain.

"I thought the thing about cooks always having grumpy dispositions was a myth," Cynthia muttered back, smirking.

" 'Myth collapses time and space,' " Balebe pontificated, giving a reasonable imitation of Professor Jarvis.

"Ah." She smiled.

All settled, Nane started the engine and rolled on through the glaring white landscape.

An hour and a quarter later they overtook a lean Shurr man in a wraparound cloth leading two loaded camels down the road. The man skillfully moved the animals off the road, prodding them lightly with the butt of his long spear. Nane slowed and leaned out of the cab, greeting the man in simple Swahili. The man smiled and gestured further down the road, calling something out over the roar of the engine.

"Did you catch that?" Balebe asked. Cynthia shook her head. The rough "upcountry" Swahili was a far cry from the elementary lessons she had taken in San Felipe with a suave Tanzanian graduate student. Consequently, she often found herself lost amidst a conversation such as this.

"He wants us to give his family in Watta the news that he is almost home," Balebe said. "It's a dangerous trip he's just made, by himself. The Shurr are pretty secure here, but in the part of their territory where we're headed, there's still raiding between them

106

and the Minka. Even here, a well-laden camel is a great temptation to the enterprising bandit."

"So you see that we still have our Wild West here in Asalia," Nane said. "Even this boy's father has not been able to stop the Shurr and the Minka from trying to kill one another and to steal camels. But unless we are very stupid, we have nothing to fear. They only want to kill one another."

She nodded. *Real life, Asalia-style. Well, there are worse situations. . . .* Unaccountably, the face of Bob Shafer, smiling so condescendingly that day at the physical anthropology meetings, flashed before her eyes. *Maybe a lot worse, for some . . .*

Anthea

"Almost there now." Nane's voice roused her from her fitful sleep slumped in the seat of the Rover. She checked her watch in the glow of the dashboard: half past eight. Night had fallen nearly two hours before, restricting their vision to a cone of dusty light that waved wildly as the Rover bucked over the ruts in the road. At first there had been the occasional dim light of a campfire or a kerosene lantern shining in the otherwise uniform darkness. Now the landscape was utterly dark. The gearbox kept the evening cool at bay.

How does he know we're close? I suppose if you've made the trip enough, you get to know the pattern of bumps and turns. Cynthia glanced at Balebe, who was blinking to clear his eyes and rubbing his face with his hand.

He returned her glance and smiled wryly. "Pleasant dreams?"

"More like the Worst of Stream of Consciousness . . ."

"As in, 'Don't wait, send $12.95 today for . . . ?'"

"You got it," she replied, sighing.

Nane downshifted and proceeded more slowly, searching the right-hand side of the track ahead.

"The road to Miss Pierce's camp is near here. Look out for some

107

stones piled up in a cairn. The camp is a few kilometers from this road."

"*Kuna maui ya kampi,*" called Mupiki from the back seat, indicating the stones.

They turned and proceeded slowly through the darkness. The headlights picked up red eye-shine in three pairs of eyes ahead, then caught the tawny outlines of three spotted hyenas, one smaller than the other two. They loped off into the darkness as the Rover approached.

"My first wild hyenas," Cynthia whispered. Balebe nodded.

They rocked slowly down the track for another twenty minutes, and then a point of intense light appeared slightly off to their right. As they drove ahead, another dimmer set of lights winked in the same direction. One detached itself and began bobbing rhythmically toward them in the darkness. As they approached, the lights of the Rover revealed a slender black man in a light shirt, worn pair of shorts, and tire-tread sandals, walking toward them with a kerosene lantern. He halted and opened the gate of a thorn fence.

Nane rolled up to the gate and leaned out to call a greeting over the racket of the engine. The man smiled and waved them through, closing the wood and wire gate behind them. He walked up to Nane's window, looked in, and whistled, muttering in Swahili with a smile, "No room for me in here—hello, hello, welcome."

Nane said, "Where is Memsahib Pierce?"

The man gestured toward the structure with the bright light. "There in the big *banda.*"

This memsahib stuff is so weird, Cynthia thought. *It reeks of colonial times, and yet here we are, twenty years after, still memsahib'ing the big mamas . . . I'll have to talk with Balebe about this later . . .*

Nane rolled the Rover to a stop a respectful ten meters from the thatch building bathed in the blazing light of a Coleman lamp. As they climbed out of the Rover, a figure rose from a chair within the structure and walked stiffly to the open doorway. Silhouetted against the light, the details of the face were lost. Only the cut of the mid-calf-length skirt, the walking stick, the slightly stooped shoulders stood out.

Anthea Pierce, in person, at last . . . the famous Recluse of Ruba, the woman we "girls" are always warned about turning into if we take our work too seriously . . . a little thinner, frailer, than I expected from the photos in the books, but God, some of them are probably ten years old. The woman must be somewhere in her late sixties now . . .

Balebe and Juma were already approaching the banda, and Cynthia fell in with them. The rest of the group followed, but at a distance.

"Greetings, Juma, how was the trip? Good, good. Hullo, Balebe! Is your mother well? I'm sure your father is, or we should have heard about it, even out here. And you are Cynthia Cavallo, welcome to Ruba. Survive the trip? You American girls can be quite tough . . . Melanie certainly was."

Before any of them could reply to this onslaught, the men behind Cynthia murmured, almost in unison, "*Jambo,* Memsahib Pierce."

Anthea raised her chin a bit more to peer into the night at them. "Yes, yes, *jambo sana* to you all too. Cook has something for you in the kitchen. Off you go, now!"

Returning her attention to Nane, Balebe, and Cynthia, she said, "I assume you've not dined this evening? Yes, well, do go get washed up, and I'll have Matthew bring us some chop. Balebe, I've put Miss Cavallo in the next banda over from mine, do show her the way. You and Juma will share the one on the other side."

Without waiting for a reply, she raised her voice and shouted into the darkness to their right, "Matthew, *letee chakula, haraka, haraka!*"

Cynthia cringed at the crudeness of the language as Balebe took her elbow and guided her to their left, using a flashlight she hadn't even seen him take out of the Rover.

"Whew, that's literally kitchen Swahili, ain't it?" she muttered. "Is she always so rude to her staff?"

"Well, she has her own style, Cyn, and anyone who can't put up with it left a long time ago. All the same, she pays good wages, she's fair, and she'll look after peoples' families if things go wrong."

"Where have the rest of the guys gone? Aren't they going to eat with us?"

"Remember when I was telling you about David and Juma? Ordinary Africans don't share table with Anthea. Juma and I are exceptions, as will be Elias when he gets his degree, and Andrew, and any other college-educated African who should show up."

"I can't believe this! Asalia's been independent for over twenty years!"

Balebe sighed as he halted her at the wooden Dutch door of a small thatch hut. The top half was open, and he leaned through and shined his flashlight thoroughly around the floor before opening the door. "Just a precaution. These inner walls of fiberboard keep most crawlies out, but one can never be too careful. Do remember to check under your bed, as well as on it, before sitting down and to use caution when standing up in the morning. *And* dump out your desert boots."

"Yeah, I know the drill, I've worked in the tropics before," she replied, still upset over the dinner situation.

"Yes, good. You'll find some water in that plastic pitcher, and that's a washstand there. Don't take more than ten minutes. Matthew will have dinner on the table quickly, and drinks are obligatory beforehand. And about Anthea, don't judge her by your standards. It's as much a matter of class as race—not that *that* answer will make you happy either." He chuckled.

"Look, we Asalians are more tolerant of old colonialists like her than you Americans might be. She's coming to the end of her days, and she's basically goodhearted, despite her attitudes. Besides, ultimately, we know it's our country now, and these are just the empty gestures of a bygone era. If a younger foreigner came here acting like her, he'd be out of the country within a couple of days, but with people like Anthea—we see no reason to humiliate these old folks to make a point."

He paused and shined the light around the door stoop. "And you have to remember that the older men here in the camp probably wouldn't *want* to dine with her, coming as they do from a group where men and women traditionally eat apart. Moreover, consider that Juma himself used to dine alone when in his field camp, until uppity college kids like us came along . . ." With that, he handed over his flashlight, turned on his heel, and walked off into the night.

Cynthia compulsively shone the light under her bed, then all around the room again. *Easy does it, Cavallo, this is arid East Africa, nothing to compare with the fer-de-lance country of Belize! God, I don't know what to make of this colonial stuff, the ethnic stuff. I know I need to have a little cultural relativism here, but this machinist's kid just can't stomach the class distinctions . . . oh, wash your face!*

A few minutes later, hands and face clean and hair in better repair, Cynthia made her way back to the main banda, noting now that the camp was set among a thin grove of thorn acacia trees. From beyond Anthea's brightly lit work and dining room, she could hear the rattle of pans, murmurs, and laughter. Juma and Balebe were already seated on canvas camp chairs inside the main banda, sipping beers from frosted glass mugs. Anthea was sitting in a smudged overstuffed chair. On a small table beside her stood a bottle of scotch and a half-full glass tumbler.

"Ah, Miss Cavallo, what will you have? There are cold beers in the fridge, also makings for gin and tonic—or you can have some of this, if you'd like," she said, waving the tumbler amiably at her bottle.

"A beer will be fine," Cynthia replied. *Guess the stories about the evening whiskeys Melanie told are true. The woman's been at it for the better part of thirty years now . . . she must have the constitution of an ox!*

"Balebe, do get it for her, there's a good fellow," Anthea said from her chair. "This damn hip has been plaguing me all season, and I'd rather move only when absolutely necessary."

Cynthia accepted the cold beer gratefully and fought the desire to drain the half-pint mug in one long draught. She took a healthy gulp anyway.

"Don't be shy, my dear, there's more where that came from," Anthea barked jovially. "The trip out here builds a dreadful thirst, and I know better than anyone!"

She shifted slightly in her chair and grimaced. "Now, Balebe, tell me about this last year and a half with Melanie. Has it been better than the one with that loathsome man Shafer?"

Balebe laughed, "Dear me, Anthea, how am I supposed to answer when you put it that way? It *has* been very good, working with Melanie and her students. But I did learn some useful things working with Bob as well."

"Yes, I imagine you did, though I hope that you didn't learn any of his nasty tricks." Anthea poured herself another half tumbler of liquor. "I know one's not supposed to speak ill of the dead—and most of us think Bob *is* dead, for why ever would a man like that miss a chance to publicly humiliate David or me. But he was a hateful character, and good riddance, I say, if he is dead!"

She took another drink. "You must think me a dreadful old witch, Miss Cavallo, saying such things. But it wasn't just Shafer's feud with David, or those shocking things he said to that journalist about me. He was an utter scoundrel to Melanie, you know, and for that alone he deserved a bad end. I mean, jilting her was reprehensible enough, after romancing her out here for two years, but starting all those rumors about her spying in Barbore! The man was completely beyond the pale. How *is* the dear girl these days?"

Cynthia froze open-mouthed for a moment, trying to match the phrase "dear girl" with Melanie's cool professional manner and apparently invulnerable personality. *So much must have changed since those days with Shafer . . . there's that picture on her wall of her out here, grinning at the camera, almost mugging.*

"Um, she's quite well. Did you know that she was invited to join the Russell team in Zaire this year? She was really excited about getting back into the field after eight years of lab work."

"Yes, yes, she told me about all that in her Christmas letter. But how is she *personally?* Is she happy? Has she got a boyfriend or whatever you Americans call them these days?"

Cynthia took another gulp of beer. *Where is dinner, anyway?*

"Well, she doesn't really let her students too much into her personal life. Um, she seems pretty upbeat about her work, and goes out to the local opera and theater. I don't know if there's anyone special." *And I doubt there would be, from the general impersonality with which she deals with most people.*

Mercifully, a man with a very full tray came rattling into the banda at that point, murmuring, "Food is ready!" in Swahili and laying out dishes on the table.

Anthea rose, leaning on her walking stick, and led the way to the table. She seated herself at the head and gestured to Juma to sit at her right, Cynthia to her left. Balebe slid in next to Cynthia.

"Roast gazelle," Anthea said, shoving the roast toward Juma to carve up. "The Game Scouts come through here every few months and bring me some haunches they 'shot outside park boundaries.' I don't believe it for a second. Oh well, they can't kill them all, and they do a reasonable job of stopping everyone else from poaching in the park. Do have some potatoes, my dear, there's none better than roasted over a fire."

Matthew returned with another tray.

"Ah, Matthew's *pièce de resistance,* Yorkshire pudding!" Anthea exclaimed. "You old devil! You didn't tell me you were making this tonight!" Matthew just giggled and walked swiftly back to his kitchen.

They all fell silent for some time savoring the meal. Cynthia found gazelle meat surprisingly tender and took a second helping from Juma.

"Have you been across the Ruba recently?" Juma asked Anthea, as he began picking reflectively at his third helping of everything.

"No, only down to the ford once. This damned hip has kept me to the easier exposures on this side and in the lab. As much as I hate to admit it, I'm not far away from my last field season, Juma. Do bring me my bottle, please. Thank you."

She sighed. "I'm dreadfully afraid of falling and breaking a leg out here, you know. So I'm being very careful. I want to do a deal with the Game Scouts to come shoot me if I do break something.

Five hundred diyanis, and no questions asked." She took another drink from her glass.

"I mean," she went on, "whatever is humane about letting some poor old crone with a bum leg sit around the Mudaka Club for the balance of her days, barely able to get about and making less and less sense daily? Huh! I'd rather a clean head shot and to the hyenas with the carcass . . . they don't leave much, you know."

She glanced significantly at Cynthia. "We had a lion go into a local goat pen one night recently and take off the young Shurr goatherd sleeping there. Just leapt in, lifted him up, and leapt back out. Two days later there was just the cranium and a few bits of humerus—looked just like our old *Australopithecus* from Asoka Locality Three."

Balebe glanced sideways at Cynthia and smiled as he addressed himself to his food.

Anthea took another drink. "However, Juma, you're in real luck as far as the crossing goes. The Ruba's low, and the point bar will get you two-thirds of the way across. I envy you the prospecting. I've known there was material out there, but I never suspected that it would be so much older than this side. Otherwise, I would have beat my damn nephew to them years ago!"

Juma nodded. "Yes, good. Could we have the lorry, your driver, and his helper out with us for two days? The place I propose to camp will take us most of the day to reach, and it would be better for the men to spend the night with us, rather than try the crossing back in the dark."

Anthea grunted assent. "You're sure you only want to have the four field crew with you? I could easily loan you a couple of my chaps, we're so slowed down this season."

"Thank you very much, Anthea, but I think we're better off with a smaller camp. However, there is one favor. If you could have Matthew ask the local Shurr headman to send over a couple of boys to help Mupiki with the kitchen work, that will be fine. Simply to help with wood, water, and washing. We'll pay the usual wages."

"As you wish, and have you heard from Michel? Will he be coming out?"

Juma patted his mouth with his cloth napkin. "Yes, we have heard from him by telex that he will join us in about a week, flying out. I suppose he will land here first to pay a visit, so if there is anything needed for the camp, do radiophone David, so he can arrange for Michel to bring it."

Anthea crossed her cutlery on her plate and leaned back. "Good, it will be wonderful to see him again. I do hope his health is on the mend now." Leaning to Cynthia, she said, "Foreigners like yourself must be very careful out here. We've plenty of very nasty bugs to lay you low—and the doctors don't know the half of them! Those of us who've grown up out here are a bit tougher. Right, Juma?"

Matthew returned with a bowl of tinned peaches, a gravy boat of custard, and wonderful-smelling coffee, and the conversation lapsed as they ate dessert. Finishing her second beer with dinner, Cynthia felt her relaxation sliding swiftly into total exhaustion. As much as she wanted to follow Nane's and Anthea's planning for the next day, she began to drowse in her seat.

"Now, look at us, Juma, we're keeping these young people up!" Anthea barked out with a laugh. "You've all had a really hard day. Please don't stay up to humor me. Go on to bed!"

Balebe rose from the table. "Come get your gear from the Rover, Cynthia." As they walked out to the vehicle, he added, "Don't forget the bottle for Anthea. This is an opportune time to present it. Take one of these lanterns Matthew's set out, too, to light your way back to your sleeping banda."

Anthea had settled back down into her armchair with her bottle and a pack of cigarettes when they returned from the Rover. Accepting the bottles of Laphraoig with relish, she said, "I've got to stay up to outlast the hip. When I get tireder than it hurts, I go to bed."

After bidding Anthea goodnight, Cynthia joined Balebe at the line of lanterns set out in front of the main banda. "Breakfast's at seven sharp," he said.

"Mm, thanks for letting me know. Uh, where's the choo?" she asked.

"You'll use Anthea's, out a path that starts between your two bandas."

After dumping her backpack and bag in her banda, Cynthia took her flashlight and cautiously moved down the path toward the small thatched outhouse. As she rose after using the toilet and turned to replace the wooden lid over the hole, she froze. Something glinted silvery green in the indirect ray of her flashlight, less than ten feet down the hole. *Eye shine! Christ, what is it?*

She hesitated, caught between the urge to flee and raise an alarm and the urge to a closer look. *Wait a minute, Cavallo, wait a minute . . . very few animals, even African ones, can leap ten feet straight up, so have another peek . . .* Heart pounding, she leaned forward gingerly and shone the full beam of her torch into the hole.

There below lay an almost solid mass of whiskey bottles, glinting in the rays of her flashlight. She quietly replaced the lid and walked back to her bed.

Field Camp

The sound of Mupiki coughing pulled Cynthia out of a dream of fitting bits of a *Pelorovis* skull back together, trying to make a hominid. She opened her eyes, looked into the grayness of her tent wall in the faint predawn light. She sat up, yawning, unzipped her flight bag, and pulled out a fresh T-shirt, underwear, and socks, pulling them and yesterday's field shorts on, and added a long-sleeved work shirt. Shaking out her boots to dislodge unwelcome bugs, she quickly laced them up and squinted at the face of her watch in the dim light: 5:30 a.m. Time to start the day.

Unzipping the flap of her tent, she stepped out into the chill early morning wind. The camp stood on the tapering end of a headland overlooking the deeply eroded badlands they'd been prospecting for five days. Although the wind blew unremittingly, the vista from the campsite was stunning. Far in the west stood a range of tall mountains, marking Asalia's western boundary. Elias had told her that the peaks were heavily forested and had many animal species now rare in other parts of the country. From here, at nearly all hours of the day, they remained deep purple. However, just now, as the sun rose in the east, it picked out the tan stone of their peaks and the deep green of their lower slopes. From those slopes to this place lay dry land, deeply dissected by seasonal streams feeding into the Ruba, the only river to flow year-round, fed by springs in the far-off mountains.

Cynthia walked past the store tent and the awning under which they ate their meals, over to Mupiki at the fire. The old man was attending a huge blackened kettle set on three stones in one end of the hearth and an aluminum cooking pot without handles—a *sufuria*—on a second stone tripod. His young Shurr assistants, wrapped in their burlap cloaks against the early morning cold, were chopping branches into usable lengths at the wood pile.

"*Hujambo,* Cynthia, *habari yako?*" the old man said, greeting her with outstretched hand.

"*Mzuri,* Mupiki, *habari yako?*" she replied, shaking his hand with some ceremony and, as she did every morning, reporting that her news was good and inquiring of his in their common tongue. Like Maleti, Mupiki understood English but insisted upon conversing in Swahili and maintaining at least the minimum of African civilities—a decent greeting in the morning, complete with handshake and eye contact, and a lack of rush, no matter the hour, time for recognition of the other.

"*Wewe nataka maji moto?*" Do you want hot water? he said, using the cruder upcountry form of the region's lingua franca.

"Yes, please," Cynthia replied in Swahili.

"*Ayah,*" he replied and turned to his array of cooking equipment set out to dry on an excavator's screen near the fire. With some muttering, he withdrew a plastic tub from the stack. He poured in a little cool water from a large water bag suspended from the tree adjacent to his hearth. Using a scrap of paper from a maize meal bag as a potholder, he added boiling water from the kettle. Testing the water with his finger, he pronounced, "*Sawa,*" and handed the tub to Cynthia.

Mupiki says "fine," and it's probably twenty degrees too hot for me, but it'll cool! She carefully negotiated the full tub back past her tent to the near-bare thorn acacia where stood the ingenious tub stand Maleti had rigged for her from three saplings and a little twine. Her canteen and mug hung in the tree, along with her plastic toiletries bag.

Screened from her campmates' view by the side of her tent, Cynthia listened to a horned lark's liquid notes rising from the gully below as she washed up. She reached into her bag for the sunscreen. *First dose of the day . . . feels like I've been doing this my whole life. Hard to believe it was awkward and alien a week ago. Funny how humans always manage to make the extraordinary into the commonplace and customary.*

Firmly securing her tent zippers against vermin, she returned to the dining area, where the rest of the crew were now gathered, drinking tea. *God, what I'd give for an espresso! Or even a good cup of Guatemalan café negro!*

"Still pining for that morning coffee?" Balebe smiled over his cup of tea.

"Am I that transparent?"

"There's always this tiny flicker of disappointment that lasts for just an instant . . ."

She shook her head. "I wish you people'd been colonized by the Portuguese, or by someone else who knew how to start the day right!"

Andrew interjected. "Ah, but if we'd been colonized by those guys, our economy would be in a shambles, nothing would work, and we certainly wouldn't be out here looking for fossils!"

"Yeah, but you'd know how to samba!" she shot back, grinning. "Now, leave me alone until this tinted milk settles my nerves!" She took a cup and sank into a canvas chair. *We're really becoming a working group, now. The young guys joke with me, like Balebe does, Mupiki's beginning to grouse at me as much as he does with any of the others, and Juma treats me pretty much the same way he treats Balebe. Fieldwork is such a strange process, creating a social*

118

unit from disparate parts . . . like a new nation, sometimes it works,
sometimes it doesn't.

Juma was poring over some aerial photos, checking them against
an overlay map of geological formations drawn by Michel Laporteau during the field season last year.

Balebe had been reading a copy of one of Laporteau's field notebooks from that season. He held one up. "These are really valuable,
but I'll be glad to see Michel get off the plane today. Even though
most of his notes are in English, it's so technical that I can't be sure
I'm getting full value from them—and the geological abbreviations!"

Juma glanced at the sun in the east, and then at his watch. "If the
sky in Wangara was clear at daybreak, he should be here by eight-
thirty. I hope your questions will wait until then, Thanatu. In the
meantime, go ahead and make the final inventory of our finds up to
today, so that we can consult with Michel about the localities."

Balebe nodded and called to Elias to join him in extracting cartons from the store tent. "Cyn, get your sketchbook, will you? I
want to be sure we've got the right genera and tribes for the bovid
teeth, and to check the suids again."

An hour and a half later, Andrew said, "A plane is coming. Do
you hear?"

Nane barked out to Mupiki to stop his rattling of pans by the
hearth, and everyone around the work table fell silent.

Cynthia strained her ears. For a moment, she couldn't hear anything, then, far off, came a tenor hum, growing into the recognizable
drone of an engine within a minute. They stood, searching the
eastern sky, until they picked up the plane as a speck at four o'clock.
It came on, changing course slightly to pass directly over the camp
with a deafening roar, only thirty feet off the ground. Just beyond
the camp, the plane banked steeply and came back over, waggling
its wings.

"Christ!" exclaimed Balebe. "Does he always fly like that?"

Nane laughed as he rose and headed toward his Land Rover.
"Yes, Michel is very exciting to fly with! Now, let's go meet him at
the airstrip!"

Fifteen minutes later, when they bounced over the lip of the dry

119

lake bed that served as a landing place, they found the twin-engine plane pulled up near the tattered windsock. A figure emerged from behind the wing and walked toward them.

"My God!" Balebe whispered to Cynthia as Nane strode ahead of them to grasp the man's hand. "He's lost at least forty pounds since I saw him last year—the man's really been ill, Cyn." They walked up to Laporteau, and Balebe reached out to grasp his hand. "Welcome, Michel, allow me to present Cynthia Cavallo, and I guess you know Andrew from last year at the conference."

Laporteau took Cynthia's hand in his. "Ah, Miss Cavallo, I look forward to spending the field season with you." His hazel eyes twinkled as he released her hand and turned to Andrew.

Cynthia was struck by his gauntness, and by the pallor underlying his naturally dark complexion. *Balebe's right, this guy's been really sick . . . no wonder he's been delayed.*

"Now, Juma, what do you say we unload the plane?" Laporteau resumed, after greeting Andrew. "David has sent some, ah, treats for the field crew, as well as a decent meal for tonight at least. I must confess, I do not look forward to these dinners of maize and tinned beef which you consume out here. Everything is in the hold." He reached into his chest pocket and extracted a cigarette.

As they moved toward the plane, Michel looked sidelong at Cynthia with a little smile. "I assume that you find the field life amusing, Miss Cavallo? Yes, David told me of your long record of excavation projects. Myself, I would enjoy it more if we were able to maintain a better standard at the table. But unfortunately, the most desirable fossil beds are seldom near the best markets, eh?"

Cynthia nodded as she reached to take a carton of fresh vegetables from Andrew, who was handing out cargo from the hold of the plane.

Laporteau reached into the cockpit, removing a flight bag and unzipping the top compartment. "Here is your mail, everybody," he said, waving a manila envelope aloft. "I know you have been too polite to ask if I brought it. Juma, you divide it up, yes?"

Juma distributed the eagerly sought-after mail on the way back to the Land Rover. Cynthia had the largest stack and quickly sorted through the envelopes as they drove back to camp. *The folks, Nona, the folks, uh-oh, the registrar, looks like Melanie's mail code on the department address, Millie and Roberto . . .* "Hey, BT, here's a letter from Weller! Let's see what he's up to!"

Balebe looked up from squinting at a handwritten page. "Right, but let's wait 'til we get back to camp. I'm going seasick, trying to read Mum's letter in this vehicle."

Michel

As they piled out of Nane's Land Rover, an amazing melange of smells came drifting from Mupiki's hearth. The old man was loading a huge pot of hot coffee and a pile of golden, aromatic scones onto a carrying tray held by one of his Shurr assistants. Over his shoulder, he shouted for everyone to wash their hands and come drink coffee. Balebe glanced dumbfounded at Cynthia as they headed for their washbasins, muttering, "You'd think we had visiting royalty!" Returning to the table, Cynthia noted that Mupiki had produced from somewhere a jar of honey and some tinned butter. Even Nane registered surprise at this apparition, muttering, "This old man is always going and hiding food, always, always," as he reached for one of the scones.

Laporteau was standing aside with Mupiki, engaged in an animated conversation in French-accented but fluent Swahili. Finally he reached into his flight bag and withdrew a bulging plastic bag labeled "Bruxelles Duty Free." Watching the exchange sidelong from the table, Cynthia began to smile, *Oh ho, should have figured as much. No, wait! That's not booze! What the hell is all that stuff, it looks like pastry equipment! Well, I'll be damned, this Michel's serious about his food.*

Mupiki was by now chuckling with delight, and ended the conversation by seizing one of Laporteau's arms and pinching it, complaining that he was much too thin and that he needed to stay here for a while to get fat again. With that, he turned away and hurried off to his bed in the store tent, poking through the plastic bag as he went.

Laporteau watched him go for a moment and then seated himself at the table, a small smile on his face. Leaning back in his canvas chair after the first sip of coffee, he sighed. "Ah, the old man has not lost his touch. Even Anthea's cook cannot rise to the same heights in a field camp!"

He looked across the table at Balebe and smiled while buttering a scone. "Mupiki and I have a relationship of nearly twenty years, Balebe, and we share a common respect for fine food. This man is an artist. Juma, you are wise to choose him for your team, but you really should provide him with better materials for his art!"

Nane smiled at the Belgian. "Ah, Michel, we have had this conversation before! You know that I am running these field works on a shoestring. If you want your fancy European food, tell your government to send us money! In the meantime, we will stick to the basics."

Andrew chuckled and chimed in, "Juma's four food groups: maize meal, potatoes, onions, and tea!"

Nane amiably waved him into silence and leaned toward Laporteau. "Well, we are fortunate to have you come out here for a few days. We have been making a reconnaissance of several areas, collecting fossil specimens and reading the copies of your field notes that you mailed to David, but we really need you yourself to help us evaluate the different areas' potentials."

The Belgian gave Nane a little smile. "And am I to presume that you wish us to begin immediately? Yes, of course. You know, Juma, you have been around these English colonialists too long. Always hurrying to the next task, without enjoying the sweetness of the moment." He lit a Gauloise. "Oh well," he said with a shrug, "let's see your specimens. I will get out my original notebooks. I never intended that my notes be used by anyone else, so I am sure I have much to explain to you."

As he exhaled, he was struck by a violent fit of coughing, which went on for over a half minute. Balebe and Cynthia exchanged glances, and Nane half rose from his chair. Laporteau finally recovered himself and waved Nane back into his seat.

His face still a congested purple shade, he rasped, "Don't concern yourself, Juma, I am fit enough to do fieldwork. It is just the remnant of the illness."

Nane paused for a second and then said, "Michel, you are smoking too much, and you should really stop the cigarettes until you are well!"

Laporteau cleared his throat and grimaced at Nane. "My friend, life is too short to give up its pleasures. Now let's see the maps and specimens."

Ten minutes later, the top of the table was covered with a large map of the area, aerial photographs, and several open notebooks. Andrew and Maleti were rummaging in cartons, handing out specimens from the several locales they had sampled before Laporteau's arrival.

Nane spoke from his end of the table. "Michel, what do you think of this quadrant Balebe and Elias sampled over in eastern Area 14? Is it worth focusing our efforts there? I am concerned that nearly all we've found in Area 8 has been scrappy postcranial materials of mammals and lots of reptiles and fish. The deposits are old enough, but the material is too poor."

Laporteau looked up from a page in his notebook that he and Elias were reading through together. "Area 14? In the east? I don't think so, Juma. The mammal fossils are in better shape there, I agree, but I am convinced that the deposits are higher stratigraphically than the ones in Areas 8 or 11. This means that they are as young—or even younger—than the ones on the other side of the river in East Ruba."

Balebe looked puzzled. "But that's odd, Michel, I must confess that I didn't get that at all from your field notes. It seemed that the eastern Area 14 materials were at least as old as those from Area 8."

The Belgian lit another cigarette, inhaled deeply, and looked up at the flysheet above them for a moment before replying. "Ah, yes, I suppose you could have interpreted that from my notes on the area. But as I said, my friend, these notes were never meant for anyone else to read as reference materials. Besides, I have given some thought to the matter since leaving the field last summer."

Balebe pressed on, "But don't you agree that the nature of the bones from that eastern Area 8 indicates a more promising locale? The western side seems to have too much in the way of large-scale floodplain deposits, which don't seem to favor preserving terrestrial fauna—maybe too-long intervals between major floods. The sediments I've seen so far in the eastern side look more diverse, and the encounter rate for land mammals has been five to ten times what we had in the east."

Laporteau shifted in his chair and replied with an air of slightly strained patience. "I congratulate you on your taphonomic observations on the fossils, Balebe. We are in complete agreement on the nature of the sedimentary regimes in the two areas. The eastern side does have a more swamplike set of depositional environments, with higher potential for covering fossils quickly. Therefore, the mammals are indeed better preserved. Nonetheless, I must urge you not to waste your time there, because of the age." He leaned across the table and gestured with his cigarette. "Tell me, have you found any species from the eastern area that would indicate greater age?"

Balebe shook his head. "But then, we only collected two days out there, and we didn't get anything very diagnostic of time."

Laporteau nodded and leaned back in his chair. Glancing at Nane, he said, "Instead of Area 14, I would advise that you put your crews in Area 11, where the preservation is nearly equally good and the deposits are older. I am convinced that when the potassium-argon datations of the volcanic deposits are complete, my chronology of the deposits will be supported."

Cynthia had been scrutinizing the aerial photos while listening to the discussion. "Well, if we're not going to go into Area 14, please satisfy my curiosity about one thing, Michel." She looked up to find the Belgian's hazel eyes fixed intently on her. "Please tell me if I'm correct in assuming these features out on this little spit between the two channels are man-made?"

Laporteau glanced down at the aerial photo to which she was

pointing and smiled. "Ah, the archaeologist's sharp eyes! Indeed, you are correct, Cynthia. Those are, ah, what do you call those conical piles of stones in English? Yes, cairns! They are made today by the Shurr, to bury their important men, but some of these are also rather old. I have seen microlithic stone tools eroding from some of them, so they must go back at least a thousand years." He smiled at her. "Now, do you have any questions about Area 11?"

Nane said, "Yes, Michel, I am convinced by your arguments. We will work in Area 11. It is very fortunate for us that you were able to come out so early in our season, so that we did not waste time elsewhere. Now, show us the best localities within that zone."

Farewell

Two days later, Balebe manhandled the wheel of the Rover as they rocked up the steep incline toward the camp. Cynthia and Elias swayed and bumped shoulders constantly as they negotiated the hill.

Elias groaned. "Ten hours in the hellish heat, and then we are being beaten to death on the way home. I'd rather be hoeing my grandmother's *shamba*—at least she always had a little treat for me at the end of the day!"

Cynthia chuckled. "What's the matter, don't you think lukewarm lemonade's a treat? Myself, I can't wait to drink a gallon or two of Mupiki's finest!"

Elias groaned even more eloquently and lapsed into silence. As they topped the headland where their camp lay, Balebe stopped for a moment. They were facing west, and the sun was beginning to dip toward the mountains on the horizon. The wind whipping relentlessly through the cab of the aged Land Rover was cooler, and shadows lengthened across the lowlands in the distance.

"My favorite time in the desert," Cynthia said softly. "Makes it all worthwhile."

Elias gave her an amused glance. "Some persons have very odd tastes indeed. Are all Americans like her, Balebe?"

"No, only those who have been out in the sun too much!" he replied, putting the Rover into gear again and rolling toward camp.

As they piled out of their vehicle, Nane rose from his chair and approached them. He cut short their account of the day with a gesture, and spoke in an undertone. "Michel is not well. He fainted today when we were walking through the exposures down by the lower Memlolo. We brought him back to camp immediately, and he has been resting ever since. I am very concerned about him."

"Oh God, how are we going to get him out of here? We none of us can fly the plane," Balebe said.

Nane nodded. "Michel is being very obstinate. I said I would radio for the Flying Doctors, or at least to David, to get his advice, but he insists that he will be fine tomorrow. He has taken some medicines, and Mupiki has made some soup with the bones from the roast. We agree that if he is well enough, he will leave tomorrow."

They all looked toward the tent the Belgian was sharing with Nane as Laporteau's racking cough rose and continued for a long while.

Nane shifted from foot to foot and stared at the ground. "This man is very ill. He should never have come out here to help us. I am concerned David will blame me if I don't radiophone him, but Michel insists I should not. I am afraid that if I go against his wishes, this will upset him and make him more ill." He sighed.

"Can't you simply phone in the morning if Michel goes, after he leaves, to let David know that he is coming, and to meet him at the airport?" Elias asked.

"Good idea—I can also alert David to perhaps have someone fly out to check on his progress back to Wangara. I fear he will faint again in the air and crash. Now, you all need to get something to drink and then tell me about your day."

It was a subdued group around the dinner table that night. Mupiki served them rather summarily and spent most of his time in the tent with Laporteau, proffering him broth and various hidden delicacies.

After another awkward silence, Cynthia spoke up. "Juma, how was your collecting today? Did you have better luck than the first time out?"

Nane toyed with his food, then pushed his plate away. "Only a little better. Of course, we stopped around eleven o'clock. We did find some mammal bones in pretty good condition. But they are scattered, very scattered."

She leaned her elbows on the table. "That's my impression of our part of the area, too. The materials very thinly dispersed, no real pockets of density. Well, we'll just have to keep looking."

Nane nodded. "Let us be patient and persist. Michel assures me there will be areas of greater density further back from the river."

After a moment of silence, he rose. "Now, I think we will have to get up early tomorrow to see if Michel is able to travel and to help him get ready. So I am going to bed now. Thanatu, you are okay in the Rover for another night?"

Balebe smiled wanly. "My back can handle the strain one more time, and it's better than fighting it out with Mupiki for room to put my bed in the store tent!"

Nane chuckled. "Yes, the *mzee* is very fierce about defending his control there! I myself will bring my bed over to sleep here by the table. Michel will probably rest better on his own tonight. Andrew, come help me carry the bed. The rest of you get ready for bed—we are all tired, these days."

In the predawn grayness of the next morning, Cynthia peered down to the dining area to see if Nane had already arisen. She saw him sipping tea by the light of the kerosene lamp Mupiki had set on one of the poles supporting the flysheet.

"Ah, *habari za asubuhi,* Cynthia?" Nane said as she approached. "It is still cold. Come drink some *chai.*"

"Thanks," she said, pouring herself a cup of the milky liquid and warming her hands on the tin cup. "Do you know how Michel is this morning?" she said in an undertone.

"Michel is very well, indeed," said a voice from right behind her.

Laporteau was standing there, an ironic smile on his face but a twinkle in his eyes. "Permit me to apologize for my lapse of health yesterday. I am not so recovered as I had supposed. I have decided to take Juma's advice and return to the capital to rest. Perhaps when you return, I will be well enough to escort you to one of my favorite clubs in the city—I assure you that you are safe with me."

Cynthia smiled. *If the stories I've heard about him are true, perhaps not totally "safe," but he's a decent fellow.* "That would be nice. I'm afraid we were too busy before coming out here to check out the nightlife of Wangara."

Laporteau shook his head. "Ah, the British colonial mentality! Or should I say, the American, too? Work, work, work. No, how do you say these days in the States, 'quality of life'?" He turned toward Mupiki, who carried a small pot of coffee to the table. "Excellent! The decent way to start the morning! *Asante sana, mzee!*"

Mupiki grunted and fixed Cynthia with a penetrating glance. "This coffee is for Bwana Michel, you drink tea!" he declared in Swahili, then turned and stalked back to supervise his minions at the fire.

Cynthia shook her head ruefully. "Well, I've been put in my place!"

Laporteau gestured toward the coffee pot and said in a solicitous undertone, "Yes, but I can dispose of 'my coffee' as I please, and it would please me greatly to provide you with a cup of it. Quick, throw away that awful stuff and let me pour you some of this!"

Cynthia smiled as she settled down in a chair next to Laporteau with a half-full mug of coffee. *He seems pretty well recovered from yesterday, but the guy's obviously been really sick. I wonder if he's really over it . . . God, I hope so, he's such a fine geologist, and a real mensch, too.*

After breakfast, Laporteau said to Nane, "*Bien,* Juma, I will pack my little bag and be ready to go. I suppose most of you have mail to be taken back to Wangara?"

They all handed over envelopes. Andrew went down to check with Mupiki to see if he had any correspondence, returning after a few moments with a piece of folded paper, to which he added a few lines with his pen. He then handed it to Michel. "Mupiki wants you to give this to his nephew in the botany department of the museum. He will carry it to Mupiki's wife."

"Certainly." Laporteau added the letter to his stack. Encompassing them all in an amused look, he said, "Have no fear, I will not crash on the way, taking your cherished communications to oblivion."

They all laughed, embarrassed that he had named their thoughts.

Laporteau rose. "Now, Juma, let me get my bag, and then we can go."

"Um, Michel," Balebe said with some hesitation, "would you mind leaving us your actual field notebooks? The pencil sketches of the sections are so much clearer in the originals than in the faxes. We could do a swap. You would have the copies with you . . ."

Laporteau stood, letters in his hand, for several seconds before answering. Then he shrugged. "Why not, I see your point. But please be very careful with them. I have still not written up much that is in them."

Forty-five minutes later, the entire camp crew, including Mupiki, stood at the edge of the dry lake bed as Laporteau taxied the plane down to the western end and faced it into the rising wind. The engines rose to an ear-shattering pitch as the aircraft began to roll, picking up speed quickly as it passed them on its way toward the east rim of the playa. They all sighed with relief as it rose into the air about twenty meters from the end of the lake bed.

Laporteau banked the Cessna gracefully, still gaining altitude, and flew back over them, waggling the wings as he passed over. Beyond the playa, he banked again and headed east toward Wangara. In a minute the plane was out of sight, and in another its sound faded into nothing.

Nane turned and said, "Okay, let's go. I will radiophone David about Michel, and you three," gesturing to Elias, Cynthia, and Balebe, "need to get on your way to the exposures."

"No rest for the weary," muttered Balebe to Cynthia as they squeezed into the back of Nane's Land Rover.

"Nor for the wicked and lazy, Thanatu," Nane said from the driver's seat. "I will stay in camp today to take a call from David that Michel has arrived safely, but Andrew and Maleti will also go out in this *gari*. We cannot afford to lose time when the finds are so few."

Memlolo

Five days after Michel's safe landing in Wangara, the crew sat around the work and dining table as the equatorial dusk swiftly turned to dark. Though they'd washed up after coming in from a long day's prospecting the exposures, their desultory conversations and tired postures reflected the physical exhaustion wrought by heat and wind. Cynthia joined them a little later than normal, having tried to give herself a more thorough sponge bath than usual with the scant water Juma rationed out for washing. Andrew offered her a glass of lemonade, which she gratefully accepted. *Can't believe how much water I drink out here . . . even more than when I worked at that hellhole with McIntyre . . .*

Balebe gestured for her to sit beside him. As the conversation resumed among Elias, Andrew, and Maleti, he said in an undertone, "I've found another of those funny passages in French, down at the bottom of a sketch of a geological section in Area 7."

Cynthia leaned toward him and said, equally quietly, "Do you think we should be reading these? I mean, Michel was good enough to leave these with us when he left, and I feel like we're taking advantage of him in his absence, reading the other stuff. I mean, he wrote the actual field notes in English, and these personal notes in French, so just because you and I read French, should we be snooping?"

Balebe sighed and looked out across the camp. "I hear you, and clearly there were some things he didn't want us to see, with the razored-out pages in the Area 12 notes, but I'm afraid I've already read this, and I think you should see it." He turned the pages back to a spot he'd marked with a paper clip and slid the notebook over to her. "Down there, just a few lines up from the bottom, you'll see the next page has been torn out."

Cynthia nodded, straining to decipher both the language and Michel's tiny, precise script, translating aloud as she read.

"I am troubled by Anthea's state of mind. She is of course very tense about the arrangements for the excursion. But I believe there are deeper matters with which she is preoccupied. Last night, when visiting the camp, I observed that she is drinking even more than is her custom. She was very depressed in her conversation after dinner, saying her life was, in the end, worth little, that perhaps Shafer had reason to say she was incompetent. I myself am very uneasy with such emotional circumstances, but I made an effort to cheer her. I am sure that I heard her weeping in her banda after we had retired. She is the last person on the whole earth I have thought that I would pity. It is difficult to imagine . . ."

Cynthia looked up at Balebe. "Not the woman we saw a few weeks ago, I'd say. So, what's bugging you?"

He glanced down the table at Juma and muttered, "If Bob's really dead, then there are suspects . . . sounds as if she was really more devastated by Shafer's attacks, and the Barbore find, than I thought."

Cynthia nodded. *Suspects! And Anthea and David Pierce are two of them . . . but what happened out there in Barbore with you and Bob? God, why can't I shake this feeling that there's a link between Shafer's death and all the people I've met here?*

Juma looked up from his end of the table. "Thanatu, what do you think of that quadrant you and Elias have been searching in Area 11? Is it worth taking a second crew into it? I am concerned that all we've continued to find are very scattered mammal remains in both areas we've surveyed so far. The deposits are old enough, but the materials are too few."

Balebe sighed. "It's the same in our quadrant, really thin." He paused for a moment, then visibly gathered himself together to address Nane.

"Juma, Cynthia and I were talking over Michel's field notes last night, and we agree that the western side of Area 14—even if Michel says it's too young to bother with—seems to have much more potential for yielding mammal fossils than anything we've seen so far. Remember, we had really high rates of recovery there in the two days we prospected, and the bones were in great condition. I think it's a lot more promising, Juma. I'd say, let's switch."

Nane took a sip of his water. "Yes, I, too, am concerned that we are wasting our time in Area 11. Not only are we failing to locate primates, but we have not yet found any locality worth trying a test excavation for training. The deposits may be older than in Area 14, but if we find nothing in them, they are worthless in any case. I have also been considering switching."

The others nodded in agreement.

He was silent for a moment and then continued, "I think David will support the move. Even if we bring back finds of the same age as East Ruba, that is better than nothing at all, and we need to begin an excavation soon."

He glanced at the sun, then at his watch. "I think, too, that it will be best for us to move camp, to be closer to those exposures. I remember seeing a rather nice place along the Memlolo, not too far from Area 14. So, let us break camp and move down there. There is no time to lose."

By ten the next morning they had driven both heavily laden vehicles down to the spot Juma remembered.

The site lay some twenty meters from the banks of the Memlolo, a large dry stream lined by huge thorn acacias with leaves that remained green year-round, fed by subsurface waters. While Elias and Maleti went back in the two cars to fetch the rest of the supplies, Juma set them to pitching the tents. The thorn trees where they set up camp were shorter and sparser, providing less shade than the huge ones along the riverbanks. Juma and Mupiki had vetoed camping any closer to the river, in case of rainstorms and flash flooding. Debris from former floods indicated that the waters had not transgressed this far back from the banks for many years, if ever, and Juma had deemed it safe.

The trees did provide lots of storage space for materials they wished to keep out of the reach of jackals and hyenas. As she helped secure the tents' ropes, Cynthia delighted in the bird sounds along the river course. The gurgling coo of Namaqua doves, the twittering of weaverbirds, the liquid notes of the horned lark, all combined in a dense and calming pattern.

"*Chai!*" Mupiki called from his new fireplace, and they all joined him and his busy assistants around the hearth. Still awaiting the camp furniture, they took their tea standing up and surveyed the layout of the tents.

"A good camp," declared Juma. "Less wind here than up on the headland, and closer to water."

"The birds are wonderful, too," Cynthia said.

Juma chuckled. "Yes, and if you dig a little waterhole for them in the sand, many, many will come. Ah, here come Elias and Maleti with the rest of the camp gear. Let us hurry and get the camp set up, so that we can make plans for our next surveys." He gave orders to the Shurr assistants in simple Swahili and headed for the vehicle.

It was twilight and the camp lamps were set before they had gathered at the dining table to look over the area map and air photos.

Juma pointed at the aerial photograph showing the stretch of the Memlolo upstream from their campsite. "Cynthia, I want you and Elias to survey this western side upstream. Balebe, you take the east with Maleti. You can share the same vehicle for going up the riverbed. Balebe, drop off Elias and Cynthia here, then continue on until you reach this big canyon. Then both of you survey it as far up as you can make it by midday," he said. "Andrew and I will go down the river to check the exposures along here." He pointed at another aerial photo.

He looked up. "Elias, I want you and Cynthia to go inland here, over this ridge and up onto the lava cap about two kilometers north. Then take these two drainages and work down from the lava cap. Michel's notes say that this is probably the same lava that is on top of Anthea's oldest deposits in the Asoka Formation. So if we find anything in these underlying beds, David will be happy."

He swept up the photos and maps as Mupiki approached, calling, "*Chakula tayari!*" With his hands swathed in dish towels, the old man carried a huge aluminum cook pot of steamed cornmeal to the table, muttering, "Watch out, watch out!" to no one in particular. He flipped it over and set it down on its flat oversized lid with a resounding thump. With a little shake, Mupiki lifted the pot off, revealing a solid mass of white corn meal, molded in the shape of the pot. Handing a large knife to Juma, he hurried away, ordering his young helpers to bring the plates and stew.

Juma cut the *ugali* into large wedges, placed them on the plates supplied him, and passed them down the table. Cynthia took hers, adding a couple of large spoonfuls of stew on the side, and followed African custom of taking the *ugali* in her right hand and using it to scoop up the stew.

Everyone settled to the business of filling their stomachs. Nane took the knife to serve out seconds. "Cynthia, more of this African polenta, as you call it?"

"Sure, Juma, but just a little slice, okay?"

A few minutes later, Nane burped quietly and continued his earlier conversation. "To maximize our speed in covering this area, I want Elias and Cynthia each to take one of these drainages. They are hard to stray from, and they come together about six kilometers from the lava. I don't think you will have any trouble keeping to the course, will you, Cynthia?"

She shook her head. *First time solo in this country. Can't say I'm thrilled . . . there are hyenas in the exposures and the occasional lion. But I had better get on with it.* She craned her neck to get a better look at the air photos that covered the drainage. *Ah, there are the cairns, right above where my little drainage comes together with Elias's!*

Juma swiveled the air photos around for her to see. "You see, here is the airstrip we used last year—not so far away, really, and over here will be Balebe's and Maleti's area. The drainages I want you two to look at come together right here. You have only about six kilometers on your own. Then, another two kilometers downstream together you meet the Memlolo. Balebe and Maleti can pick you up on the way down from their area. Be ready to meet around one o'clock. And be sure to take extra water, all of you."

Cynthia caught Balebe staring at her with concern in his eyes. She met his glance with a calm smile. After they'd finished their meal, most of the crew moved off to their tents, eager to rest from the day's exertions and to organize their field gear for tomorrow. Cynthia remained at the table, studying the air photos. Balebe also hung behind. When they were alone, he said, "Look, you're sure you'll be all right tomorrow? It's not too late to just tell Juma you want a little more time to get the hang of things—or to ask if you can take one of the Shurr kitchen boys with you. They know the country."

"No, I'm fine. Don't worry so much—I've prospected alone before, in some pretty rough country, too."

"Yes, but this is different. Most of the places you've worked didn't have animals that could eat you as an appetizer!"

"No, only guerrillas with anti-Yankee outlooks! Look, it'll be just fine. And I wouldn't press you so hard to back out if it was you on solo survey today."

He sighed. "There you go again, being such a bloody stiff-necked feminist! I know you're just as good in the field as I am. In fact, I know you're better. It's just that I worry—and what would I tell Melanie if you were eaten by a lion?"

"How about, 'Can I have her desk in your lab?'" she laughed, rising and moving toward her tent. "I know you've coveted that spot near the window all year and would probably be delighted if I pulled a Bob Shafer and never came back!"

He tried to hide a sudden grimness with a smile. "I'd miss you a lot more than I miss Bob," Balebe said quietly. "Do be careful!"

"Don't worry, BT, no carnivore capers planned," she replied and turned toward her tent, in a less self-assured mood than she showed Balebe.

Another Find

The sun was vertical over the widening gully as Cynthia stopped to remove her cowboy hat and wipe the sweat off her forehead. She ran her bandanna down around the back of her neck, catching the drops that ran down from her hairline. *God! It's hot! I can't believe it can get this hot! I can't believe I thought this was a good idea! And now, no wind.* She'd slipped off her T-shirt and stuffed it in her pack an hour ago. Now she unbuttoned her long-sleeved shirt and flapped its sides, trying to dry her damp skin.

She began to button it again, then muttered, "Screw it, who's gonna see the bare-chested female paleoanthropologist, huh?" and trudged on, scanning the ground and walls of the wash.

The lava stones, polished by years of exposure to the elements, glistened in the intense sun. Thin crusts of alkaline sediments, cemented in the last rain to run down this channel, crunched under her boots. She veered left to poke at a little scatter of disintegrating mammal bone. *Nah, too far gone, and the wrong shape for hominid or primate . . . probably pig, anyway.*

Her heart gave a leap at the sight of a grayish-brown arc of bone sticking out of the wall of the wash about a meter ahead. She rushed forward. *Cranium! Look at that curve, the suture, no wait, the suture's weird—damn! Turtle shell again! If I don't stop having heart attacks over carapaces, I'll never make it.* She trudged on.

As she walked, the small cache of fossils in her collecting bag, each swaddled in toilet paper, thudded against her leg. She muttered under her breath as she panted, "At least we've got some decent index fossil material in this area, and if this maxilla's really Mr. Pliocene Porker like I think it is, these exposures are a good five hundred thousand years older than Michel estimated they'd be."

Suddenly, the gully turned right, toward the northeast, affording her a little shade on its western side. She checked the shadowed wall for unhealthy creatures, kicked a large stone to dislodge any lurking scorpions, and lowered herself onto it with a sigh. For a moment she just sat panting, gazing at the opposite wall of the wash. She pulled out her neckerchief again and mopped her neck and sweaty chest, under her arms and breasts. "Shit, it's hot!" she pronounced.

After a long swig of hot water from her canteen, she pulled her clipboard with aerial photos out of her backpack. "Where am I, and how much longer does this water have to last?" She removed her sunglasses and leaned forward to scrutinize the photo. "Let's see, sharp northwest turn, that's here, and there's the confluence with the little stream where I'm supposed to meet Elias. Wow! I've really covered some ground! Looks like only about a click and I'm there. Twelve-fifteen now, meeting him around one, and then down to the main river by one-thirty. That gives me a little more time than I thought. Let's see, looks like the arroyo widens out in just another half kilometer. Okay, now where are those cairns? Oh yeah, here they are! Well, I think I'll just waltz on down there and do a little archaeological survey in my spare time!"

She stuffed her clipboard back in her pack and rose. "That is, if I don't find *Homo erectus* in the Pliocene in the next thousand meters and make my day!"

As the gully broadened, Cynthia cast her eyes left to the adjacent upland, looking for a way up to the crest, which lay about ten meters above the bed of the wash. She said, "Aha!" and made for a small feeder channel cut into the side of the main wash. After three minutes of scrambling around loose volcanic boulders, she made the top of the table land. She immediately looked north, scanning the distance. "Aha again! Behold, the confluence! Three hundred meters, thirty minutes to spare, piece of cake!"

She then turned her attention to the tableland on which she stood. It was strewn with the same volcanic boulders and cobbles over which she'd just climbed. Between the stones lay fine-grained beige sediments, bare of vegetation. In the distance stood a single thorn acacia, its upside-down umbrella shape devoid of leaves. About ten meters from her stood a cone-shaped pile of stones, nearly four meters tall at its peak. Wispy stalks of dried grass grew out of the spaces between the stones. Three other cairns stood beyond that, further up the tableland.

She walked toward the first. *Michel said that some of these appear to be Late Stone Age, with stone tools and ostrich eggshell beads eroding out of the sides, others may be made by the Shurr. They bury their prominent men this way today . . .*

She slowly walked around the first one, scanning the ground for artifacts. A single chalcedony flake lay in a tiny alluvial fan opening out on the southern side. She picked it up. *Desert varnish, exposed some time, looks like simple percussion flaking, nothing real fancy . . .* She dropped the flake back on the little fan, checked her watch, hesitated a moment, and then walked quickly toward the next cairn. "Just one more, said the closet archaeologist!"

As she approached the second cairn, a fat ground squirrel climbed out from a gap in its stones, bounded over to the third cairn, and dove in. Cynthia chuckled, "Sorry to disturb you, pal!"

The moment she began her transit around the cairn, she noticed something different. The western side had an unusual bulge, created by the addition of more stones, imperceptible from her original vantage point. She stood a moment, examining it with a practiced eye, then moved in closer.

Hey, these rocks look like they've been added recently! There and there, these ones have lighter, reddish surfaces showing, that's where they were facedown on the ground and protected from weathering, while the stones on the older part of the cairn are all uniformly weathered. Must be a recent Shurr burial . . . funny they didn't make a new cairn, or open all the way into the center, just slapped on some extras on this side—sloppy.

"Whoa! Sloppy indeed!" she muttered. A couple of stones had fallen or been pushed off and bone was showing. She moved in and squatted to scrutinize the bones.

"Distal radius and ulna, carpals still in sinew, must be pretty recent. Phalanges gone and the metacarpals chewed up by some carnivore. Looks like a hyena tried to get the body out. Phew! No matter how many human skeletons I look at, I always get the creeps. He must have been an important guy to bury in a cairn, but why just slap him on the side of an old one like this?"

She shifted her weight slightly to her other foot. The sun glinted on something in a crack between the stones to her left. She could see the dim outlines of bones just under the rocks. Moving her head, she caught the glint again. *What is that? It's so bright! Would they have buried him with jewelry? It's too far up to be a bracelet on the upper arm, it is his head? This is weird. I should be going.*

She rose, glanced at her watch, and scanned the confluence of the two washes. No Elias. She turned again to the cairn. *Cynthia, let the dead rest in peace, haven't you ever learned to leave well enough alone? No, there's something about this that's strange . . .*

As if in a dream, she reached out with both hands and lifted off one of the rocks blocking her view of the bones. She gazed down into the not-quite-empty eye sockets of a skull, tilted back at a crazy angle, with a neat hole only slightly left of center in the bone between the brows. Hairline cracks radiated out into the bone from the hole. As she gazed, a thick brown spider scuttled across the jaw. The creeping malaise that always held her when she was with recently dead human remains grew into horror.

"Shot!" she exclaimed. "Murdered! Poor devil, for God's sake, Cavallo, put the rock back and let him rest! Bad enough to be shot in the face and stuffed into somebody else's grave, without you coming along disturbing him. Huh!" She shuddered and began to replace the rock.

She froze in mid-gesture. The sun was glinting again, glinting as she leaned forward to put back the stone, allowing the light to fall once again on the skull, glinting on metal, silvery stainless steel, on four little plates of stainless steel on the backs of each of the corpse's upper incisors. She dropped the stone, chilled from head to toe.

"Oh God, oh Holy Mother, this isn't a Shurr, this is somebody with capped teeth!" Unable to control herself, she began to shake from head to toe.

Urged by some instinct, she whirled around and stared toward the confluence of the streams. She saw a dark figure moving toward her. Abject fear struck her. *Who is that? Is it Elias? Or is it the killer? Has he been watching me discover this?* "Oh, GOD, why did I ever come up here?" she cried.

"Cynthia! Cynthia!" the figure called out and waved. It was Elias!

"Elias! Come here! I've found something!"

The young man broke into a run, calling excitedly and grinning.

"No," Cynthia spoke softly to herself, "it's not the fossil we came for, Elias. It's something terrible, something we never wanted to find."

Deathwatch

Cynthia sat in her canvas chair, drinking her third lemonade and wishing it were rum. She stared at the sunset clouds, which were unusually lovely tonight, cloaking the sun in the west in shifting golden-pink. *Huh! Just like nature to rub it in, making like "The Sound of Music" or something . . . the sound of music that radiotelephone is not. More like the soundtrack from hell. Oh God, why did I have to find him?*

She glanced around the camp. Mupiki was occupied at his cook fire with the two camp helpers, and Maleti sat on a log near him, conversing softly in Kichacha. Andrew and Elias were seated in camp chairs, a little way off from her and Balebe. Balebe had been mute for nearly an hour, sunk in his own thoughts and unwilling or unable to talk with her. Juma was still trying to raise David Pierce, as he had been for the two hours since they returned from the cairns.

"Wangara control, Wangara control, this is 33905, do you read, over," Nane said for the hundredth time, switching back to the distorted metallic howls of radio conversation. Cynthia tried to follow scraps of conversation as they rose and fell in tone and volume, tangled strands of Swahili and English, punctuated by "Ovah" again and again.

As the bad-dream noise of the radio continued, she went back over the afternoon, for what seemed the thousandth time.

Staring with Elias at the gaping skull, his startled "Allah!" when he saw the teeth. "*Mzungu,* it's a European!" he had said, turning to her.

"Yes," she said. *A white person, very dead, out here . . .*

"Elias, we shouldn't touch anything," she said, feeling inane the moment she had. *Sure! Big detective! Should have told that to whatever chewed off his hand . . .*

Elias backed away, shaking his head. "This is bad, Cynthia, a very bad affair."

"Yes, I couldn't agree more," she said, at a loss for words.

Elias shook his head. "Balebe will be here soon, and we'll have to get Juma out here as soon as we can. He'll decide what to do."

"Yes, I guess we should go on down to the river to meet him. It's almost twelve-thirty . . . Oh God, how could I have been so stupid, I have my camera! At least I can take some pictures!" She reached into her pack.

"Save them, Cynthia, we need to go to meet Balebe. This one will not go away while we are gone."

She had nodded and repacked her camera, following Elias down the little gully and onward down toward the Memlolo.

Balebe and Maleti had listened to their account in shock, and Balebe drove to the camp at breakneck speed. Nane emerged from the shade of the flysheet as they sped up to the camp, a look of annoyance at their battering of the old vehicle rapidly changing to grim concern as they told him of the find.

After a moment's reflection, he asked, "How far up can we drive the *gari?*"

"All the way," Elias replied.

"Get in," he ordered. "I will see this now. Maleti, Balebe, bring extra water."

They had driven up the little drainage in silence, with only a few quiet directions from Elias. As they approached the tablelands, Juma halted the Rover. He turned to Cynthia. "You have your camera with you?"

"Yes," she said.

"Good, I also have the Polaroid. We will document this completely and then radio to David in Wangara. He will contact the police."

They dismounted from the Rover. Juma insisted that they retrace their steps to the other side of the headland and mount it by the path they'd taken earlier. "It is probably a useless precaution, but there may be some traces elsewhere which we would not want to damage," he said. On the tableland, they also walked in their earlier footprints.

Standing in Cynthia's tracks, Juma gazed down at the exposed

141

bones. After a long silence, he sighed and turned to Elias. "It is Shafer," he said quietly.

Elias nodded.

Cynthia stirred. "How can you tell it's Shafer? Is it just because he's missing?"

"No, Cynthia, it's the teeth. I remember this time when Bob took me out to dinner at the Meateater right before he disappeared, after he had made those first finds in Barbore and his new book was selling well. He was drinking lots of beers that night, and quite happy. He was boasting to Elias—don't you remember—how he had never had to use the dentist, just like we Africans. No tooth problems, ever, he said.

"But he told us that he had recently gone to have one of these dentists put covers on his front teeth, so they would look better. They had been crooked, he said, although I never noticed so much. He was smiling and asking us if we could tell that they were covered."

"Capped, yes. It sounds like something he'd do . . ." *Lord, Cynthia, speak well of the dead, at least at the graveside . . .*

"Your camera, Cynthia? Elias, give me the meter stick for scale."

They had spent a half hour carefully documenting the cairn and its exposed contents from all angles. Juma insisted on leaving the rest of the stones as they were, until after they had talked with Pierce. Finally, their Polaroid film exhausted, they packed their cameras away.

"Cynthia, can you remember how that stone was set in the cairn?" said Juma, gesturing at the rock she had dropped on the ground several hours before.

"Yes, I remember," she replied.

"Good, put it back in place. We don't want the hyenas to do any more damage than they already have."

Cynthia shivered now in the cool evening breeze and glanced again at Balebe.

He caught her eye and tried a weak smile. "Sorry, Cyn, it's just that I've been thinking all these months that he really wasn't dead, and instead was really pulling a publicity stunt, or some such. And I've got quite a few mixed emotions right now."

"Yes, I guess so," she said, feeling it was a lame thing to say. *What emotions, precisely? Could gladness be one of them? What did go on between the two of you anyway?*

Balebe opened his mouth to say something more when the radio emitted a new, hollowed out female voice that said, "33905, this is Wangara control, do you read, over."

"Wangara control, this is 33905, confirmed, we read you, over," Juma immediately replied. He rapidly put through a call to Pierce's home number. After an interval, a horribly distorted version of Pierce's voice came on the line.

"David, this is Juma, we have a bad situation, over."

"I read you, Juma, what is the matter, over."

"We have found Shafer, repeat, we have found Shafer. He is dead, over."

There was a silence for a few seconds on the other end, and the screeching of the airwaves rose in the interval. "I read you, Juma. How did you find him, over."

"Cynthia Cavallo found him near the Memlolo, under some stones against one of the cairns, repeat, in one of the cairns, over."

"I read you, in one of the old cairns. How do you know it is Shafer, over."

"By the cappings on his teeth, David, his incisors have caps with steel bases. I am sure this is Shafer, over."

"I read you, Juma. Are there signs of violence, over."

"Yes, repeat, affirmative. Gunshot wound to the head."

They heard a muffled "Christ!" at the other end, then, "Right, I read gunshot wound to the head. Have you moved the body, over."

Juma glanced at Cynthia. "Negative, repeat, negative. We photographed it and left it in place, over."

"Good work. Stand by at nine p.m., repeat, twenty-one hundred hours tonight, for my call. I will phone the attorney general and give him the news. I will advise you, do you read, over."

"Affirmative, David, we will stand by at twenty-one hundred hours tonight. Signing out, over."

"Signing out, Juma, good-bye."

Juma cut off the roar of the radio with the flick of the switch. The silence was nearly as disquieting as the noise. He turned in his chair to face the five people staring at him. He looked directly at Balebe. "I think David is right to call your father. The case is under his direct supervision, is it not?"

Balebe nodded, without a word. The rest of the men averted their stares from him, but Cynthia felt a subtle separation, unlike any she had noted before in the camp, between Balebe and the rest of the crew. In the wake of this realization, she felt separate too, doubly the foreigner, for having found Shafer's body and for not knowing what to make of the new social currents in the camp.

Juma rose from his chair, stretched, and, as if he too sensed the unease and separation among them, said, "Now, it is only seven-thirty, and we have to wait until David calls us back before we know what to do. Let us at least try to eat this meal that Mupiki has made for us. It will not help anything for us to go hungry!" He called to Mupiki to bring the food and motioned for the rest of them to assemble around the table.

At eight forty-five, Juma turned on the radio again, leaving it set on receive, and patiently awaited the call. At about nine-fifteen, they picked up the voice of Wangara control, who told them to stand by. Pierce came on the radio and in turn asked them to stand by.

"This is Ezekiel Thanatu, do you read me, over," came the unmistakable accents.

"Yes, I read you, Attorney General Thanatu, over."

"Let us dispense with formalities, Nane. I will tell you what we have decided to do. Are you reading, over?"

"Affirmative, we read, sir, over."

"David Pierce will fly me, my chief criminal investigator on the case, and one of our CID medical examiners out to your airstrip tomorrow morning. We will accompany you to the death site. Do you read, over."

"Affirmative, you arrive tomorrow morning, over."

"Dr. Pierce confirms that Miss Cavallo is an expert at archaeological excavation. She will supervise your crew in uncovering the bones. I am convinced your team can do as good a job as the forensic people in the CID, so long as the doctor and Inspector Malongo oversee their work."

Juma glanced at Cynthia, who had the arms of her chair in a white-knuckle grip. "Roger, Miss Cavallo will supervise the exhumation. Our crew will be ready to assist, over."

"Good. Give my greetings to Miss Cavallo and my son. Dr. Pierce wishes to speak with you again."

After a few muffled sounds, Pierce said, "Juma, plan for arrival as usual. Stay in camp until we buzz you, over."

"We read you, David, we will wait for you here, signing off, over."

"Right, try to get some rest. I'll bring lunches out for the entire group, so don't bother with camp preparations. Do you need anything pressing? Over."

Juma glanced at the group briefly, then spoke into the microphone. "Some fresh meat and vegetables would be very nice, over"

"Roger, Juma, will do," Pierce replied. "See you tomorrow, signing off."

The silence that followed stretched for several minutes. Cynthia sat staring at Juma, unable to speak. Balebe sighed but said nothing.

Finally Juma spoke. "Okay, Cynthia, you will make a plan for the excavation with Balebe, then check it with me, and we will work out the equipment and men needed. We will have plenty of time to go over this in the morning. David cannot take off until at least six a.m., and the flight takes about an hour and a half. Tonight, I think we all need to rest well."

Nane added, "David will also be bringing us new rations tomorrow. So, let us all have a good night drink. You all go and take your chairs to Mupiki's fire!" Calling in Kichacha to the old man, Nane rose and went into his tent and soon returned with a bottle of liquor. He went around the group, pouring healthy dollops into everyone's tin cups. As he came to her, Cynthia was able to make out the label in the dim firelight. It was a liter of Courvoisier. She stared at Nane, too dumbfounded by the appearance of this expensive bottle of booze amidst all the other events to formulate a clear thought.

As he bent to pour into Cynthia's cup, Nane caught her eye and said, "Heathrow, duty free," in a stage whisper, with a wicked little smile. Several men gagged on their cognac, trying mightily not to spill the precious liquid while giggling at his remark.

Cynthia burst out laughing, suddenly feeling giddy without taking a drop. "Not from Bob Shafer, by any chance?" she bantered recklessly.

"As a matter of fact, yes!" Nane laughed, throwing up his arms in mock surprise. In the silence that followed instantly, he pivoted toward the rest of the group, raised his cup, "To Shafer!"

They all stood, spontaneously, if a little self-consciously, murmuring Shafer's name and drinking his last liquor. Before they'd all finished drinking, Nane cracked a joke in Swahili that had everyone but Cynthia convulsed. Andrew was gasping and wiping tears from his eyes, having sneezed the cognac up into his nose.

As Maleti and Elias were comforting him, Cynthia whispered to Balebe, "What did he say? I couldn't follow that at all!"

Balebe moaned and muttered, "I'm not sure I'd like to try to translate that, it's a rather naughty pun on a common toast. While not anatomically impossible, what Juma suggested would at the very least be uncomfortable!"

Cynthia was puzzled. *What's going on, here we are with a dead anthropologist on our hands, and Nane's turned into a comedian? Maybe there's a method in his madness.*

Pouring a second, larger dollop into Mupiki's cup, he cajoled the cook to sing a Wachacha song. Mupiki started out with a light song about a girl who kept running off to dances instead of helping her parents in the fields. As Balebe translated to Cynthia, the rest of the men took up the refrain. Andrew brought his precious guitar back from his tent and strummed the chords of the songs. The young Shurr boys, as usual, squatted on their haunches at the outer rim of the firelight, tonight muttering uneasily to each other in their own language.

By the fourth verse, the rest were giggling at the old man's lyrics, which, Balebe explained with increasing embarrassment, were departing from established forms in cleverly salacious ways.

After nearly a half hour of singing and replenishments from Nane's bottle, there came a pause as Mupiki mournfully examined his empty cup and Nane gestured that there was no more. Then, in the moment at which the reality of their situation began to intrude again, Nane began to sing softly in his deep voice, a slow tune, entirely different from the ones that came before.

There was an almost inaudible gasp from Elias and Maleti as Mupiki took up the words in his higher, plaintive voice. "It's the Wachacha song for the dead, for the first period of mourning," Balebe whispered to Cynthia. A moment later, the younger men took up the tune, and Balebe joined in. Elias, though not himself Chacha, began humming the tune. After another few moments, Cynthia had caught the melody and began humming it, too.

As she drew herself deeper and deeper into the cadences of the song, she raised her head and looked across the fire. Nane's eyes met hers, holding them for as long as she cared to look back, as they shared the song.

Balebe did not translate, and she was glad, in a way, because it allowed her to pour her own imaginings into the song, which in its higher solo lines and deeper choral backing so fully evoked for her the solitude and unity of sorrow. She found herself remembering her grandfather, and Mike Hill, accidentally shot by another sixth-grade boy in her hometown. Her tears began welling up. Glancing at Balebe, she saw that he, too, was in the grip of sorrows that probably had little to do with Shafer. As the music went on and on, she reached a state of calm. The coming day still disturbed her, but she was viewing it from a different vantage point.

What a master this man is, what a leader, she thought. *And this is the best wake that Bob Shafer is likely to get.*

At last, near midnight, with a misshapen last-quarter moon low in the sky, Juma spoke. "Ever since we worked together at Lake Logo, this man Shafer was generous to me. He always brought me expensive liquor, and one time a tape player, from the Duty Free. When my children needed school fees and my farm was not paying well, he gave me the money for them. I know some speak against him, but he was good to me and my family."

"*Ayah,*" replied the rest of the men.

Elias spoke. "Shafer was kind to me, also. Even when I was still going for the A-levels, just nobody, he brought me a book on physical anthropology from America, so I could study it. He never asked for anything back."

Andrew nodded, swallowing. "The same for me, an expensive book, that not even the university library could afford."

Maleti spoke in Swahili. "When we worked at Logo, he helped me with shoes for the children, and then gave me some books for them to learn English."

"*Ayah.*" Mupiki cleared his throat. "I didn't know him, he was never where I was cooking, but I heard he was good to African people, friendly. He spoke good Swahili."

There was a long silence. Cynthia suddenly thought, *Christ! They're waiting for Balebe and me to say something! What the hell good can either of us say about this guy . . .*

She took a breath to begin to speak, but Balebe spoke first. "Shafer was very hard sometimes, very ambitious, but he was generous to people here, and whatever else, he was not a racialist." He lapsed into silence, staring at the ground.

That leaves me . . . well, he was *a sexist, so what can I say? Here goes . . .* "I didn't know Shafer, and I only know what I have heard about him. Before I have heard some bad things. Tonight I have heard good things. He made a big contribution to paleoanthropology." She stopped, not knowing what else to say.

"*Ayah,*" said a few of the others. After an interval Nane stood up. "Now, let's go to sleep, tomorrow we will have to rise early."

Research Design

She awoke at 5:15, pulled instantly into consciousness by the cold weight of the day's purpose. She sat up and pulled new clothes from her bag, thinking over Nane's masterful management of his demoralized crew the evening before. Now, as she stood up and emerged from her tent, the plan of the day began to form in her mind. She washed up and combed her hair in the dim predawn light, trying to assure that her collar and scarf weren't askew for Ezekiel's arrival.

Moving down toward the breakfast table with her flashlight, she saw that Nane was already up, sitting with Mupiki at the fire and sipping tea. Balebe was just carrying a cup and a glowing kerosene lantern back toward the table.

She smiled at Balebe as she approached. "Good morning, how'd you sleep?"

"Need I say, rottenly. How about you?" he replied.

"Oh, so-so, I kept thinking about the Command Performance today, not too conducive to deep sleep."

"Mm, I know what you mean. This is even worse than field school with Miriam Grady!" He smiled, obviously trying to lighten her mood. Before coming home to attend the paleoanthropological congress last summer, Balebe had spent six weeks with one of the most notorious martinets in Southwestern archaeology. It was said that if one survived one of Grady's digs, one was set for a lifetime in terms of field methods. But the attrition rate was high.

"How *did* you do at Big House Ruins, anyway? You never talk much about it."

He grinned. "I've also had an appendectomy, but I don't talk much about that, either. Actually, I did rather well, once I'd sussed out the game. My boyhood experiences with the old colonial memsahibs came in quite handy, you know. *Chai?*" he said, reaching for a cup and gesturing toward the fire.

"Yeah, please. Then we'd better get to work. I've got some ideas, but I really need to bounce them off you before talking to Juma."

He nodded. "Be right back."

She opened her small field notebook and a larger three-ring binder. Leafing through the larger one past drawings of various animals' dentitions and horns, she reached a section of blank sheets. She nodded thanks to Balebe as he handed her a steaming cup of tea and gestured for him to sit beside her.

"Okay, first, let's go over the notes I made in my notebook yesterday on the situation of the cairn, the bones, and all that. Get familiar with the data, and then let's figure out what will work. Why don't you read it over and look for anything that strikes you as worth following up." She started to make an outline on the notebook, then stopped, turning to Balebe.

"You know, I'll bet every archaeologist has been told that the standard for care in excavation and documentation of finds should be criminal forensics—good enough to stand up in a court of law and all that. Remember Don Smith quoting Augustus Pitt-Rivers in that history of archaeology course? Boy, I never thought we'd have to put it to the test!" She laughed ruefully.

Balebe didn't laugh back but looked into her eyes. "Cyn, we can do the job. You, at least, wouldn't have been out here in the first place unless you had the excavation skills it will take to do what we have to today. Let's just treat it as another human burial to be excavated with all due care and respect. David and my father have confidence that this approach will be successful. So let's get on with it." She nodded and went back to her outline.

After a few minutes, Balebe looked up from her notebook. "Excellent documentation, right up to Grady standards! Tell me how you want to approach it."

"Well, the first question for me is whether there's anything in the immediate area of the cairn that needs to be documented. I'll leave the initial surface survey of that and other areas to your dad's criminal investigator. Then I want to lay out a grid around the cairn for about five meters, or whatever they think is appropriate, and carefully scrape and screen the sediments. They're loose and could have trapped a cartridge case or some other clue. We'll plot in anything interesting as we recover it."

Balebe took a sip of tea. "Hmm. Come to think of it, they may bring out a metal detector to look for the cartridge cases, but we will still need to go over the area for nonmetal items. Do you want a rectangular grid, since that will be time-consuming to set up, with the cairn in the middle? I could shoot one in with the transit, I suppose, but have you considered the "leash sample" approach from Binford's old paper on research strategy? It's circular, and we could use a cord from a pole set into the top of the cairn as our center. It's a little unorthodox, but quick, and we could still sub-divide the circle into successive concentric rings, each of which could have quadrants, giving us the control over provenance we need."

"The leash sample idea's interesting—but how should we document the materials on a master map?"

Balebe bent over a piece of scrap paper. "It would work—let's see, if the cairn's five meters across and you want to go out another five around it—yes, it should, if we make it a one-to-fifty scale." He thought for a moment, then added, "Look, let's leave the quad versus circle approach up to my father and the CID. They may get nervous with anything that isn't rectangular, in terms of evidence for the courtroom. Perhaps I could convince my pater that round is more African?" He cocked an eyebrow at her and grinned.

Cynthia laughed out loud. "God, you're incorrigible! Here we are, about to dig up your former advisor, and you're making jokes! Look, I have an idea about the stones, too. I think we should docu-ment them with color film, in place and then as we take them off. We'll clearly mark what used to be the down-side before they were added to the cairn, but I have a hunch that color photos will pro-vide strong back-up documentation."

"Right," Balebe said, checking his watch, "we'll just have to burn off all that Agfa we brought in case we found a hominid—um, I guess we have, actually. I suppose the CID can reimburse the mu-seum. Should we number the stones as we remove them?"

"Why should we do that?" she asked. "To reconstruct the order they were put on? I'm not sure that will give us any clues, unless the police want to know the sequence of events that closely. Too bad we can't try taking them off as fast as we can—it might give an estimate of the amount of time the killer spent putting them up—but would that matter? Let's ask them when they get here, and get out the white paint, just in case."

She glanced at him. "Why are you looking like that? Another idea?"

He shook his head. "I was just thinking how implicated David is—his fossil area, the means to get out here quickly by plane, it doesn't look good. Perhaps my father's having him bring them out to keep an eye on him. Anyone with a light plane can readily skip the country."

Cynthia nodded. "Yes, but it's just *too* obvious! I can't imagine David doing it in a way that makes him the prime suspect. What if someone's trying to frame him . . ."

"I've thought of that, too," he said. "Then I remembered that other French passage in Michel's notebook."

Cynthia glanced around the camp and whispered, "Oh, God, I'd forgotten that, about how angry Juma was at Bob for the tone he was taking in his comments about David after the Ruba find . . ." She was suddenly distressed by this new line of thought. What *if Juma did it, and David covered it up, out of friendship, you're trying to say . . . and it almost was never discovered. But Juma, would he kill someone? What was that "funeral" all about, anyway . . .*

"Cynthia!" Balebe said. "Snap out of it! We've got a job at hand, and the best contribution we can make here is to do a good job. We've enough white marking paint to put on numbers to show up in photos, if the police want. Who should be in charge of that?"

She shook herself a little and glanced at Balebe. "Ask Andrew to, he's got great handwriting."

They looked up as Nane sat down across the table from them. "You have a plan developing?" He eyed their notes.

Cynthia nodded. "Yes, and there are some things we need to check with you. We'll need as many fine-mesh screens as we have. In fact, perhaps you can get Maleti and Elias to tear out the coarser mesh from those other two this morning and put in some of the spare fine screening we brought with us. Balebe can help them. We'll need Andrew to check the white paint supply, since we may number the stones from the new part of the cairn, if the police want us to."

"What about the body itself?" Juma asked.

Cynthia sighed. "God, I know how I'd do it if it were a prehistoric burial, but we'll just have to defer to the medical examiner on that.

We should probably expose the body, photo document it in Polaroid, black-and-white negative, and color, then I'd like to get a sketch map of the bones, too, if there's time. You often see things while drawing that you don't taking pictures. Then we lift it."

She raised her eyes to Juma's. "I don't know what shape the body's in, and whether it'll all come out in one piece. You could see that there was considerable tissue left on the parts we could see. In its mummified state, the ligaments and what's left of the muscles could hold most of the bones together. Clearly, the jaw's already off the cranium, and I'll bet there's been a cervical detachment, probably at the atlas or axis, so we'll have to lift the head separately." A chill ran down her back as she imagined lifting out Shafer 's head.

"What about screening under the body, Cyn?" Balebe interjected. "There may be pieces of bone under it, or other clues."

"Yes, we'll have to do that—this is where a small grid plot of the bones themselves and then a clear plastic overlay for the substrate will come in handy. I'll set that up."

She looked at Juma again. "If all those mystery stories I read on airplanes are right, there should be a larger exit wound in the back of Shafer 's head. Depending on the caliber of the gun, the bullet type, and range, I guess the back of his head could be completely blown off." She paused, recalling Shafer's smiling face, his slightly predatory eyes. "We definitely should excavate with brushes to see if we can recover fragments from under the body or around the cairn."

"Ah yes, if we can't find them, it could mean Shafer was shot elsewhere," Nane said.

She nodded and hunched over her sheets. "Yes, but of course the medical examiner may have different ideas, and it's his case. Anyway, here's a list of gear we'll need, and . . ."

The rattling of crockery on trays interrupted her. Mupiki set breakfast down with a bang, declaring that Bwana David would be here soon and they had better eat now, while they had the chance.

As Nane began dishing up the cornmeal porridge, Balebe leaned over to Cynthia and whispered, "Take heart, this may be your last *uji* for several days. David detests the stuff, and he'll surely be bringing bacon and eggs to improve camp morale!"

At the end of their brief meal, Nane rose to go check the gas, oil, and water in the two vehicles. Andrew went off to check on paint supplies. Maleti, Elias, and Balebe hauled out the wood-frame screens for refitting with fine mesh. Cynthia huddled over her notes again at one end of the table, making a detailed list of materials needed for the day.

A few moments later, Nane returned to the table. "Are you ready to get the materials you need? I believe that David will be coming soon, and we really should be prepared to go into the field straightaway."

"Uh, I suppose so. Let's go to the supply tent, and maybe anything else we need will occur to me." She and Nane went into the tent behind the flysheet and she began reading off items, which he took out and stacked on the table or placed in a carton on the floor of the tent.

"Surveyor's stakes—all of them. String, one ball should do—no, let's take two, it's a long way back to camp. Um, have we got something like a very long wooden pole that we could secure a string to so that it would rotate—yeah, that's it! Andrew can pound the top of a stake in? Good. Plane table, alidade, stadia rod, the big roll of graph paper—if you've got extra pencils, great! Where's the masking tape? Okay, and the box of tacks? Right. Now, I think we should take as may clipboards as possible into the field, so that everyone can have one to work with. Empty notebooks? Fine! That's all I can think of, okay . . ."

As they continued down the list, the sound of hammering rose from outside as Balebe, Elias, and Maleti prepared the screens. Juma checked his watch. "It is now eight, and we must be prepared to move out by eight-thirty. Is there anything else?"

She shook her head. "I don't think so, I'll double-check as we pack it into the vehicles."

"Have Andrew help you put it in the pickup. We will have to carry David and Attorney General Thanatu in the other *gari*." She nodded and headed out the door in search of Andrew and the paint.

Excavation

Cynthia and Andrew were just wedging the last of the cartons into
the back of one Land Rover when he stopped and said, "Listen . . .
it's the plane."

Far off she heard the engine, swiftly increasing as it came on
toward the camp. Pierce's green-and-white twin engine passed
over, banked, and headed back toward the landing strip.

"*Twende!* Let's go, hurry!" Nane shouted, as they all trotted to the
Land Rovers and piled in. Mupiki stood by the store tent, waving as
they pulled quickly out of camp and headed in the direction of the
airstrip. Juma drove the larger vehicle, with Cynthia, Maleti, and
Balebe inside, while Elias and Andrew had the pickup.

Ten minutes later they crested the low lava hill that formed the
lip of the dry lake bed landing strip. Pierce's Cessna was pulled into
the scant shade of a tall acacia about two hundred meters down the
dry pan. Four figures stood in the shade near the plane's wing.

Juma drove down to the plane, with Elias following behind him.
Juma, Balebe, and Cynthia got out of the Rover and stood waiting
for someone in the other party to make the first move. David Pierce
came forward to meet Juma, dark hair tucked under a beret, eyes
grave. Ezekiel Thanatu remained near the plane. His son went to
greet him and shook hands with his two associates, another African man in a police uniform and an older man of Indian ancestry in
a safari outfit considerably more rumpled than the elder Thanatu's.

*Wow, Ezekiel looks like he just got that safari suit from the dry
cleaners, and the desert boots straight from the Bata Shoe Store,*
Cynthia thought.

David nodded to her and the rest of the crew, but addressed
Juma. "There's a carton of boxed lunches and a cooler of drinks in
the cargo hold which will go with us. I assume you have all the gear
you'll need? Good. Dr. Deep has his kit and a body bag, and Inspector Malongo has his outfit as well." Malongo was occupied with
working a battered-looking metal detector out of the plane's small
cargo compartment.

"The gear can go in the back of the pickup, David," Juma responded. "The CID people can get in this *gari*. You can either ride with us or go in the other Rover."

David nodded. "I shall ride here, and Miss Cavallo should stay with us, so that we can go over the circumstances of the initial discovery with her. You drive us. The rest can pile into the back of the pickup. Now, let me perform the introductions."

He turned to lead them toward the group by the plane, then turned back. "Oh, you'll all want to know, Michel flew home last Sunday, after a stint in Wangara Hospital. He's not at all a well man." Without waiting for a reply, he led them on to where Ezekiel Thanatu stood.

Ten minutes later, they were jouncing down the road toward the Memlolo drainage. All four visitors were listening intently to Cynthia's account of her visit to the cairns, and how she made the discovery.

"And it was apparent right away from the teeth that the skeleton was not local—Juma was the one who figured out it was Shafer," she concluded.

There was a short silence as she waited for Ezekiel or Inspector Malongo to ask further questions. The silence lengthened. Cynthia's unease increased.

At last Ezekiel Thanatu said, "That's a very good, concise description, Miss Cavallo. I commend you on your level-headedness. Of course, we shall need to make an official confirmation of the body's identity. We shall probably have more questions once we get to the site."

She nodded. Ezekiel then continued, "Now, please let us know how you propose to extract the body from the cairn. We will want to see if it suits our documentary requirements."

Cynthia saw Juma give her a sideways glance as she took a deep breath and began outlining their strategy.

After arriving at the site, the investigation team proceeded with Cynthia up the path taken the day before. The rest of the crew, including Pierce, waited until they'd made their preliminary reconnaissance.

Ezekiel held a brief conference with his companions, then turned to Cynthia and said, "Tell the others they may come up, but not to approach the cairn too closely as yet. Inspector Malongo wants to make some photographs."

Cynthia and Balebe hung together in the group. "Ten-thirty already," he muttered. "If we don't start excavating soon, we mayn't finish by nightfall, even if we do work through the heat of the day." She nodded.

A few minutes later, Ezekiel came over to Cynthia. "Miss Cavallo, Inspector Malongo wishes you to get up your grid, prior to his sweeping the area with the metal detector."

By 11:15, Malongo was systematically quartering the rectangles demarcated by lines of twine shot in by Cynthia and Balebe with the surveying equipment. He and Ezekiel had insisted on a rectangular grid. The rest of the party sat on the edge of the little tableland, watching the uniformed man, whose cap balanced awkwardly atop the large earphones, as the time extended.

Ezekiel leaned over to Cynthia and said quietly, "British Army surplus, a bit antiquated but a great savings to us—managed to get twenty for the cost of getting them over from a base in the Maldives." Cynthia nodded and was about to reply when Malongo froze and then bent over a patch of ground, blowing on the sediments to clear them from something.

Straightening, he turned to Ezekiel. "I seem to have a bullet, sir. Have someone bring a marker while I continue sweeping."

A murmur ran through the group as Ezekiel nodded to Balebe to take out a flagged stake to where Malongo was working. Twenty minutes later, Malongo stopped and took off his headphones. "All clear, sir."

"Right, Balebe, Miss Cavallo, bring the cameras, please. We'll need to document the find. Dr. Deep?" They converged on the area, the pathologist in the lead.

Bent over the stake, Dr. Deep took a small paintbrush and gently swept away a bit of earth. He leaned back. "This seems to be the place Shafer was actually shot."

Cynthia saw that for just an instant, Balebe's eyes locked with those of his father, then he looked away. *I wonder what that was all about.*

After photos had been taken, Inspector Malongo picked the bullet up. "Distorted, but medium caliber, possibly a .32. Consistent with the size of the entry wound, don't you think?" he said, inclining his head toward Dr. Deep.

Deep dusted his hands against his trouser legs and took the bullet. "I would agree that the entry wound is consonant with a medium-caliber weapon, but further lab work will be needed to be certain. The nature of the exit wound should offer us some clues."

Malongo nodded. "Always precise, you are, Deep!" He swept the area with his eyes. "We have not located the cartridge in this area, probably meaning that the killer took it with him. A common pattern." He turned to Cynthia. "Are you ready to begin the excavation now?"

David cut in, "It's just past twelve-thirty now. How long do you think this process will take? We really can't spare much more than three hours, cutting it very close for adequate flying time."

Cynthia looked to Dr. Deep. "It's hard to say, but I think we had better plan on working straight through." Deep nodded agreement.

"Right," David said. "Plan on taking lunch in shifts. I assume you'll want to get the stones off the cairn first?"

By 1:15 they were nearly done with removing the stones. Andrew speedily applied numbers to them during initial photography by Inspector Malongo, who watched closely and interjected questions and directions from time to time. As Andrew and Maleti withdrew the stones and set them beyond the limits of the grid, more and more of Shafer's body was exposed.

Dr. Deep and Ezekiel gazed down on the corpse, talking in low tones, as Cynthia and Balebe continued to amplify their respective plots of the overall excavation and the interior of the interment. "We'll see if bone fragments from the exit wound lie under the body—if it is a medium-caliber bullet, they should have been trapped in the scalp," Deep said quietly. Ezekiel nodded.

Cynthia sat cross-legged on a cushion pulled out of the Rover, closely documenting the disposition of bones. The clipboard behind her plot kept sticking to her knees with her sweat, and she had to brush away an increasingly bothersome swarm of flies.

Feh! The smell is faint, but it's there . . . like that naturally mummified corpse we found at Playa Salina . . . and Bob was always so well groomed!

She turned to Dr. Deep. "How do you think so much flesh was removed from the bones? Wouldn't the corpse mummify out here very quickly?"

"Yes, my dear young lady, we have just been discussing this point, actually. Of course the arm which was chewed by the hyena, as you saw from the tooth marks, is one thing, but what of the rest?" He hunkered back on his heels and went on.

"I believe I detect the presence of pupal cases of maggots on the soil around the body. Please be sure to collect them all in this vial when you begin your digging. If there were some rains quite soon after the decedent was placed in the cairn, it is possible that flies could have established enough of a colony to do a reasonable job of defleshing before the next dry season, leaving very little for other creatures."

He glanced at the clear blue sky. "Last year we had extraordinarily early and heavy rains in the highlands—just after your paleoanthropological congress—so it's possible that they fell even here. The AG will be checking rainfall reports for some adjacent stations."

He inclined his head toward her and went on. "It is possible as well that smaller carnivores in the area, which could enter through the gaps between the stones, were at work during that time."

Juma, who had been strolling around behind the cluster of onlookers, cleared his throat. "I have sometimes seen those little kinds of, what, mongoose, out here. They would be able to go between the stones."

Cynthia shook her head to clear away the picture of sharp little muzzles chewing on Shafer's flesh. "If it's okay, Inspector, we can check closely for small tooth marks on the bones."

159

Inspector Malongo nodded. "Just wait until after we have made our photographs, then you may move in more closely. Is that the last of the stones? Good."

Shafer lay in a kind of splayed fetal position, partly on his right side, partly with his back against the old wall of the cairn. His right arm was folded against his rib cage; the left, gnawed one, had now fallen against the ribs. His legs were drawn up in a flexed position, but not tightly so. At the ends of his feet, a few of the last toe bones had fallen off and lay scattered on the ground.

Cynthia again turned and gestured to Dr. Deep, who came and bent over her. Ezekiel followed and listened with interest. She said, "This amount of flexion in archaeological specimens usually means the body was still fleshed, and not tightly bound, as with cords."

Deep nodded. "Mm, yes, they do teach you a few useful things, don't they? Also," he said, turning to Ezekiel, "the flexion denotes lack of rigor mortis when the body was deposited."

"So, you think he was deposited soon after death?" Ezekiel queried.

"Well, that's hard to say. Of course one can wait until rigor passes off, but in this climate the body will become less and less pleasant to work with, if one does."

Looking at the backward-tilting head, imagining the well-groomed features and charming smile, Cynthia felt a wave of light-headedness. *No, Cavallo, don't start down that path, the last thing you need is to lose your nonexistent lunch out here . . . hey, what* are *we going to do for lunch?*

As if on cue, David sauntered up to the group. He'd kept himself to the periphery of the dig, seemingly unwilling to spend much time contemplating Shafer's corpse. Now he cleared his throat and said, "It may seem in frightfully poor taste, but the box lunches from the Neville aren't getting any younger. I suggest that the AG, Inspector Malongo, and the stones removal crew have a break to replenish their energies. You two, go ahead with the work with Dr. Deep, and have a break later."

Cynthia sighed as the sweat trickled down her back and glanced at Balebe, who was glaring at Pierce's back. "David, could we at least get some drinks out here?" He said somewhat testily.

David turned and favored them with a small smile. "But of course, Thanatu, coming right up." The rest of the party retreated to the scant shade of a flysheet Maleti and Pierce had rigged from a bare acacia. Seats from the two vehicles, plus a few large lava cobbles, had been laid out under it. Somewhat to Cynthia's surprise, it was Ezekiel who returned with the cool drinks and insisted on remaining with the excavation team.

Bent over the cavity in the cairn, Cynthia gratefully accepted a Coke.

Dr. Deep addressed Ezekiel. "I'm not sure you've noticed, sir, but the decedent was placed in the cairn nude. There are no traces of clothing, and at this remove from the time of death, there should be."

Ezekiel nodded, taking a drink of his Fanta.

They moved in on the corpse. As Dr. Deep jotted in his pocket notebook, Cynthia minutely inspected every bone they could see. The odor of dried flesh dominated the little cavity in the cairn, and they were constantly brushing away flies. She pointed to Shafer's left cheekbone. "There on the zygomatic—it looks like scratches, probably small carnivore tooth marks. That would make some sense, this is the origin point of the masseter, and something chewing it would ultimately come down on it . . ."

She glanced up to see Ezekiel looking faintly ill and Balebe staring at the ground.

"And what do you make of these marks along the radius?" Deep asked.

"Looks like rodent gnawing to me. Funny, I've always thought that they only chewed older, ungreasy bones. Anyway, that's what it says in the literature."

"Ah, but some rodents—in fact many—relish flesh. The marks may be incidental to its consumption," Dr. Deep said quietly.

Cynthia remembered the ground squirrel that had dived out of this cairn and run to the next. *Wuh! No wonder he looked so fat and sassy! Now look, Cavallo, here you are, all into ecology and na-*

ture's cycles, and you're grossed out by the little critters doing what comes naturally . . . and really, isn't this better than all that awful embalming? I mean, Shafer's now just cycled back into the environment. Oops! What did he say? She looked questioningly at Dr. Deep.

The older man gave her a patient smile. "I said, do you wish to record the location of the damage for me on this diagram, as I continue my examination?"

"Oh, yes, of course, sorry."

"Not at all, my dear young lady." Deep addressed himself once more to a close scrutiny of the skeleton. "Did you know Dr. Shafer?" he said over his shoulder.

"No, not really. I was introduced to him once at a professional meeting in the States, talked with him for about a minute . . ." *And he was obviously doing a cost-benefit analysis of the time it would take to chat up a good-looking woman student, to see if she was a likely devotee, and the time he'd lose in making important professional connections. And when he saw that San Felipe State on the name tag, it was all over . . .*

"Well, in any case, it is a bit unnerving to work with someone one knew in life, however superficially, is it not?" Dr. Deep pointed with his pen. "Ah, there's another cluster of carnivore tooth marks on the left acetabulum of the pelvis, closest to the origin of the rectus femoris—you know where that is? And here again on the left greater trochanter."

They continued on, documenting down the legs to the scattered toe bones. Dr. Deep turned and called to Inspector Malongo, "It's time for the bag now, would you be so kind as to fetch it, Inspector?"

Cynthia stood back as the two CID men opened a somewhat worn, heavy, blue zippered bag on the ground next to the cairn and, after a moment's conferral, began by lifting Shafer's head. There was a soft, collective intake of breath from the onlooking group as the head parted from the cervical vertebra. Cynthia caught Juma's eyes on her for a moment. *Detachment at the atlas-axis joint, as I'd suspected . . .*

Dr. Deep turned the cranium over in his hand. A jagged hole the size of a plum gaped in the right side of the occipital region. He nodded at Inspector Malongo, who took the cranium and lay it in the body bag. The mandible followed, after a cursory inspection. Dr. Deep went to the opposite end of the skeleton.

"Miss Cavallo, could you hand me one of those little zipper-lock bags? Yes, thank you very much. Just right for the phalanges. Right, Inspector, let us try and lift the rest of the body in one piece. Would you be so kind as to support the neck vertebrae and the middle of the back—just so, very good. Now I'll take the femora and feet, let's lift—ah, perfect!"

As he zipped the bag, Dr. Deep spoke over his shoulder to Cynthia. "Miss Cavallo, you may begin your excavation of the soil underneath now. I'm sure Inspector Malongo will want to advise you."

Balebe handed Cynthia the long nails and string they had ready to subdivide the area into halves, set up within their larger overall grid. As they did, he muttered, "The space is really too small for two people. I think you'd better do it all yourself. You're a much faster excavator than I am, anyhow."

She nodded, silently.

After a few quiet moments of tying the points into their existing lines, Cynthia picked up her trowel and a small paintbrush. Andrew handed Balebe the clipboard with the detailed plot of the body, over which he'd taped a plastic overlay to plot subsurface finds. Squatting beside Balebe with a dustpan and a big, bowl-like metal *karai* for transporting backdirt to the screen manned by Maleti, he smiled at Cynthia and nodded.

As she went down on her hands and knees to begin scraping the sediments, she glanced back over her shoulder. The two CID men, Ezekiel, Pierce, Elias, and Juma formed an intent semicircle behind Andrew and Balebe.

She rapidly lost herself in the familiar motions of hand excavation, trowel held sideways at an acute angle to the ground below, peeling off a thin layer of sediments with the leading edge, eyes scanning as she went. She worked on the end where Shafer's head had lain, scraping slowly across the area, back from the stones of the old cairn toward the former perimeter of the stones that had covered Shafer. She established a rhythm with Andrew, scooping the sandy soil she'd pulled off into the proffered dustpan, dumping it into the *karai,* returning to digging.

No bone fragments appeared on her first scrape. She paused and sat back on her heels. Addressing Ezekiel, she said, "I doubt we'll find the missing skull fragments here. It's best to widen the search." He nodded.

Cynthia turned to Balebe. "You and Andrew and Elias begin scraping around the cairn—nothing much is showing here, and Maleti can both carry and screen for me. Start from the other side and work out. You guys screen your own backdirt and be really careful to keep the sections separate, okay? I can document anything that comes up here."

Balebe nodded and began organizing the crew.

Almost immediately she saw a spray of white bone fragments, most not on the soil but scattered down the stones at the back of the cairn. "Dr. Deep, could you come look at this?" she called.

Pointing with her trowel, she said, "Are these connected with the exit wound?"

Deep bent over and gazed at the trail of fragments leading from midway up the cairn wall to the ground. "Ah, yes, I believe so. Would you be so kind as to hand me that large piece on the ground? Balebe, you have got that on your sketch map? Good."

The pathologist turned it over and inspected it briefly before handing it to Cynthia. "Yes, part of the occiput, you see, a section of the foramen magnum right there."

Cynthia saw the imprint of blood vessels on the inside of the fragment and swiftly handed it back to Deep. "So, how do you explain these here? Was he shot against the cairn?"

Deep shook his head. "No, my inference is that these fragments were in fact captured by the scalp—it's quite stout tissue, you know—after the decedent was shot over where we recovered the bullet. With the natural decomposition of the cranial tissues, the fragments would ultimately cascade down from the back of the skull area, as you see them there on the stones against which the back of the body was resting."

Cynthia swallowed hard and nodded, trying to exclude any visions to match Dr. Deep's narration. "So, do you want us to simply plot these and lift them?"

"Yes, but first let us get some documentary photographs. Do be so kind as to replace the occipital fragment where you found it. Afterwards, I think it best that you proceed with your excavation of the earth under the body. One never knows what unexpected things one may find."

About two minutes after resuming her work, Cynthia's trowel hit something with a tiny metallic ding. She carefully brushed around it, slowly exposing the object. A chert flake. She pivoted on her heels and showed it to the onlookers. "A stone flake, probably from the old burial here . . ."

Balebe seemed to be stifling a grin as he turned back to his work, and Cynthia duly noted the find on the plot.

Ten minutes later, after a second sweep over the area, she sat back. Looking at Ezekiel, she said, "Nothing here . . . I could go deeper, but we're already nearly five centimeters below the surface."

He shook his head. "No, leave it. It's clear that there's nothing connected with the burial here. Inspector, make a few more photos, and then prepare to pack up."

Cynthia stood up, dusting off her knees. The others were already moving away from the cairn.

Glancing at Balebe, Pierce said, "How much longer will it take to complete your documentation?"

"I'm basically done here, David." Balebe glanced at his watch. "Two-twenty. Do you think we can get some lunch now?"

David shook his head. "Afraid you'll have to tuck into it in the Rover, Thanatu. We need to be away from here by three-thirty, which gives us just over an hour to get back to the airstrip and another couple of hours' flight time to Aluyabi. That's cutting it a shade too close for dallying about here, since we'll only just get in by nightfall."

Balebe heaved himself to his feet with a sigh and for the second time today glared at Pierce's retreating back as the tall man hurried over to help Maleti take down the flysheet.

Cynthia hurriedly worked on packing up the excavation gear, with Andrew volunteering to act as beast of burden for most of the heavier equipment. After an intense ten minutes, Cynthia looked up to see what the others were doing.

Inspector Malongo had enlisted Pierce and Juma to help transport the body bag. Elias and Maleti were finishing folding the flysheet.

Balebe followed her gaze and muttered under his breath, "Malongo's right to get Pierce and Juma to carry the body, the others have too much traditional African distaste for corpses to want to get too close."

As he removed the plots from their backing boards and rolled them up, he said, "I guess we should turn these numbered stones face down, so they don't show. Just in case some curious Shurr would want to carry some of them off."

"Right, let's do it," Cynthia said, stooping to begin the job. "Why not scatter them around a little too, like they would be naturally."

She was surprised to find Ezekiel joining in with them. He glanced at her, still stooped. "Yes, Miss Cavallo, I am capable of manual labor," he said, with a small smile. "I used to engage in a considerable amount of it in my younger days. However, I was rather a fifth wheel today, with all you experts."

Cynthia smiled back, at a loss for words, and continued working. *"A time to cast away stones, a time to gather stones together." What an increasingly weird funeral ritual Shafer's being treated to, with the attorney general of the Republic of Asalia scattering his erstwhile tombstones!*

"Over there, Dad, get that one, would you?" Balebe said.

Ezekiel grunted and lifted the stone behind him into another location, turning the number side facedown. Balebe handed him two more stones from the pile nearest the cairn.

Cynthia watched unobtrusively as father and son worked together, nearly without speaking. *I wonder how often, in all their years together, they've had moments of working like this . . . per-haps this is another healing act.*

A few minutes later they stood, checking the area for numbered stones. Ezekiel broke the silence. "I think we can safely say that we've left no stone unturned in this investigation," he said dryly.

Both Cynthia and Balebe stared at him in amazement. He raised his brows and continued sardonically, "You needn't look so astounded. I do happen to be possessed of a sense of humor, though seldom does life present me with quite such an easy mark. Thank you, both, for a very educational day."

He turned and made for the edge of the uplands where the others were starting to descend to the waiting vehicles.

Discovery

As they watched Pierce's plane disappear into the eastern sky, no one seemed disposed to move. Finally Juma looked around at the rest of them and said, "All right, we are finished with that. Now, David and I were talking about what to do next. He advises us to continue with the field season."

He glanced at Balebe and Cynthia. "For one, it will keep us all out of the reach of the newspaper people until after the formal inquest, when the interest has died down." He smiled. "And David said he was damned if he would let Shafer sabotage his field season. So let us go back to camp and prepare for tomorrow!"

Cynthia smiled at the joke and turned toward the Rover. *It will also keep Juma out of reach of the press, and those of us who might have thought about his and David's involvement, too. God, what am I to think?*

The next two days saw more survey. Cynthia and Elias continued to reconnoiter in their study area while Balebe, Maleti, Andrew, and Juma checked eroded deposits closer to the Ruba River. Camp returned to a normal routine, buoyed up by continued high rates of finds of well-preserved mammal bone. Maleti found the jaw of a small baboon in one patch along the Ruba, and time-diagnostic pig specimens were numerous in the localities being worked by Elias and Cynthia.

At around five in the afternoon three days later, Balebe, Cynthia, Andrew, Elias, and Juma were seated at the table, sipping tea and going over all the pigs and other time-indicator species found so far. The specimens were spread out before them. Balebe and Elias pinpointed the locations of the finds on Michel's field maps while Cynthia and Andrew pored over a battered copy of *The Evolution of African Mammals,* verifying the ages of the pig species.

"Yeah, there's no doubt about it, Juma, these exposures we're working up beyond the cairns are at least a couple of hundred thousand years older than Michel guessed, maybe even five hundred thousand," she said.

Balebe chimed in, "It's odd he was so far off, Juma. I mean, had he known how old these exposures in Area 14 were, he'd not have advised us to give them a miss."

"Well," Cynthia replied, "in all fairness, I can see why he didn't hit it bang on. He was working with the geology rather than the fauna. And these exposures are so faulted and eroded that it must be pure hell to match up the formations. It's just like the problems they had with the East Lake Turkana stratigraphy—until they got the geochemical signatures of the tuffs worked out, it was a mess. God, I wish Michel were out here now, to help us sort out how the different sections in Area 14 fit together, with the ages the pigs are giving us."

"Mmmm, yes." Juma lit his pipe. "I miss Michel, too, it is a pity that he is so ill. David said that he had another letter from him saying he hoped to be fit enough for the next field season." He drew on his pipe and fell silent. Cynthia and Balebe glanced at each other, and Balebe shook his head imperceptibly.

Balebe sighed, toying with a pig molar. "It's frustrating, not knowing whether the Ruba or the Section 8 exposures are older, since they're both yielding so well. If we knew, we could decide where to spend the most time. But Michel's field notes just don't let us sort that out, and none of us can . . ." He glanced momentarily at Cynthia, then away.

Yes, we really got into detective work with Michel's Area 12 notebook last night, didn't we? Looking for clues to the murder got us nowhere but embarrassed. She recalled trying to recover the contents of one of pages that had been razored out, by lightly rubbing the succeeding page with pencil, to show up the imprint of Michel's ball-point.

The result was largely illegible, except toward the middle of the page, where he had pressed harder with the pen: " . . . feel so deeply for others. Not since my mother died have I felt these troublesome attachments, to persons so full of human frailties. I shit on myself!"

They'd looked at each other, guiltily, and without a word Balebe had picked up a gum eraser and carefully removed all the pencil markings. Cynthia was brought back to the present by Juma's voice.

"Yes, well, as we say in Kiswahili, *shauri ya Mungo,* it's God's affair, and we just have to live with it," he said. "I am content to keep both teams in the field right now, to maximize our chances. My other main concern is that we find a good excavation situation soon."

"Well, the partial *Nyanzachoerus* specimen Andrew found down in Section 10 will do nicely, if you want to go with that . . ." Cynthia said.

"Yes, it will, too bad it can't be a hominid," Juma said. He called to Mupiki, requesting the old man's presence for a moment. After a quiet discussion in Swahili, he said, "*Sawa,* we have enough food for another eight to ten days. We shall continue survey for three more, have our day off on Sunday, then work on the *Nyanzachoerus* site—unless one of us has found a hominid by then!"

Directing himself to Elias and Cynthia, Juma said, "Tomorrow I want you to move down to the exposures just up the river from us. Section 7." Pulling out some air photos, he said, "Elias, Cynthia, I want you to walk through these open exposures, just off the Memlolo. Do you think that you will be able to do that without becoming lost?"

Cynthia nodded. "I don't think they're so high that we can't keep the uplands on this side of the river in sight. If either of us gets disoriented in the badlands, we'll just plan to head for the river."

She heard Andrew repeat, "Badlands, badlands," under his breath, smiling. "What a nice word, Cynthia, is it American?"

"I guess it is . . . never thought about it before. I suppose it reflects the farmer's view of this kind of country."

Juma chuckled. "Hmm, even the Shurr don't bring their camels here too often. Except along the Ruba, the land *is* bad, for everyone but us!"

The next day began like any other. Juma instructed Elias and Cynthia to take the larger Rover, because it was more of a gas gobbler and their locality lay only four kilometers upstream from camp, as opposed to the ten-kilometer trip to the Ruba River beds.

The trip up the sand rivers was relatively smooth, and they followed older tire tracks most of the way up the Memlolo. Elias pulled the vehicle up near the mouth of a small gully that gave out onto the main sand river. Reaching for the air photos, he said, "If we walk a little upstream, then enter the exposures, it looks like we can end up here, following these little gullies."

"Yeah, I'll take this area, if you don't mind, then I'd be able to drop down into the gulch just around this lava bed here, right?"

"Yes, and I will meet the little *korongo* farther up, where it begins to cut down into the sediments. Let us meet at the *gari* at noon, okay?"

"Good, usual rules? If you're not at the Rover by twelve-thirty, I'll start up into your territory. Same for me, okay? And if you have trouble but can travel, or if you find something, come back to the car and start blowing the horn."

"Okay!" Elias grinned, shouldering his backpack. "*Bahati mzuri,* Cynthia!"

"Good luck to you, too, man!"

By ten a.m. it was unbearably hot in the glaring white badlands. Cynthia kept her long-sleeved shirt on, to guard her skin. "God, I'm beginning to regret going for these low exposures. no shade at all to speak of . . . and the uplands on the other side aren't as prominent as I'd thought. Already thought I was lost twice," she muttered.

She bent and poked at a curve of bone protruding from the ground on her left. It didn't move. She swung her backpack off and drew out her trowel. She began to gently flick away the earth from around the bone. *Big, whatever it is. First time I've used my trowel since Shafer, this is better. Rats! It looks like a really big mandible, suid? Nah, a little hippo. Only half. Goes with the fluviolacustrine nature of the sediments . . . a nice little marshy area, maybe, with a stream running in, great place for the hippo and the piggies. Better take it back to camp, could be a time-indicator.*

She hefted the jawbone out of the ground and dusted it off with a cloth collecting bag. She made a few notes on the situation of the find in her field notebook and then settled the bone into her backpack. It protruded out beyond the pack's zipper.

As Cynthia was swinging her pack onto her back, she caught a sound in the distance. Again. The horn of the Rover! "Oh, God, let it be a find! Don't let him be hurt. No snakes, please!"

She ran up a little hill to check her bearings, then headed toward the river as quickly as she could, skirting boulders and ducking around the bare branches of thorn trees. After two minutes, she was panting and a little dizzy. The horn was still sounding, much closer. *Just a little more, keep pressing, he may really need you there.*

She came out to the river on a high bank, about fifty meters upstream from the Rover. She shouted and waved, running along the bank, looking for a way down to the riverbed. Elias detached himself from the driver's side of the Rover and ran toward her, waving.

"A femur! A femur! I have found a femur! Cynthia, I have a hominid!"

She stopped and howled in happiness, at the same time struck by a pang of jealousy. *Why not me, dammit, I was so close! If only I'd chosen the other side of the exposures . . . oh, Cavallo, stop being such a shit!*

She leaped a meter down into the riverbed, instantly reminded of the hippo jaw as it hit the base of her skull. She saw stars and shook her head to clear her vision. Struggling through the pea gravel of the riverbed to Elias, she threw her arms around him.

"A femur? Complete? Everything? Yeah? Oh, wonderful!" She pumped his hand.

"I think it may be *Homo,* it looks different from the Ruba australopithecines! Come, you must see it!"

They jogged back down the riverbed to the car. Elias grabbed the meter stick for a photo scale while she ditched the hippo jaw in the back seat. Then they both set out at a blazing pace up the little *korongo.*

A kilometer later, she'd developed a stitch in her side and called a halt. "Uh, why are we running, anyway, the damn thing's not going to walk away, is it?"

Elias grinned back, sweat streaming from his face. "No, I guess not, especially since it is still partially embedded in the wall of the *korongo.* Let us walk. It is not far now . . ."

Five minutes later they encountered a piece of surveyor's tape on a metal stake. They approached the right side of the gully. "Here," he said, in a quiet voice. Her eyes followed his pointing finger toward a tan layer of sediments about a meter and a half above the level of the gully floor.

Her eye picked it out immediately, although it was nearly the same color as the encasing deposits. It lay slightly out of line with the set of the wall, so that more of the distal end of the bone was showing than the proximal. Half the length of the shaft and the head of the femur were still buried in the wall.

"Wow. It's hominid all right—look at that greater trochanter! And it's big! I think you're right about it being *Homo* rather than *Australopithecus*, from that alone, although we'll have to see the relationship to the head and the angle of the distal articulations." She turned to Elias, smiling. "Congratulations, Elias, this is a big find. You've really earned your spurs now!"

He grinned back. "Yes, this is much better than the radius fragment that David and I found two years ago!"

She leaned forward into the shadow still overhanging the bone. "It's in gorgeous shape. Doesn't seem to even have any hairline weathering cracks, and no visible post-depositional alterations. What a great color!"

"Yes, it seems that it was buried quickly, if the weathering stages can be a guide—and no one has been chewing on it, either!"

"Careful, we still haven't seen the head, and that might have been chewed, but if the third trochanter's untouched, I'm inclined to agree it's not been gnawed." *Uh! Can't shake that picture of Shafer being chewed by mongooses . . .*

"You know, with this quality of preservation, and the fineness of the sediments . . ." she began.

"Yes!" Elias snapped his fingers. "I have been thinking it, too! There's a good chance that there is something more in the wall—or eroded out down here. A perfect place for the excavation!"

She grinned. "Well, let's take some pictures and get back to camp! We won't have long to wait for Juma and crew—and I can't wait to see their faces!"

They bounced into camp, sounding the horn, at twelve-thirty. Mupiki came out from under the flysheet, looking concerned, but his face converted into a huge smile as Elias gave him the news. "*Sawa sawa!*" he chortled, pumping Elias's hand. "*Tutapiga ngoma!* Now we can have a big dance!"

Party, dance, drum . . . all the same word . . . so much meaning condensed into one word, Cynthia thought, as she poured lemon- ade mix into cups for Elias and herself. "Here, drink this," she said in Swahili. "Your tongue has been hanging out for an hour now, and you've probably lost a lot of water!"

Mupiki cackled and went into the back of the store tent, mutter- ing about a cake.

They had just about got settled in their chairs when they heard the sound of the other Rover laboring up the river. They raced out into the bed of the river and jumped up and down, waving their arms at the oncoming vehicle. When Juma pulled level with them, he was already smiling. Listening to Elias's hasty description, he said, "Get in, we'll see it now!" and called to Mupiki to hold lunch.

A half hour later, they all stood staring at the femur, silent for a long moment. Juma finally said in Swahili, "I think it is *Homo,* isn't it?" The rest of them quietly assented.

He turned to Elias, continuing in Swahili, "Man, you have found a very fine specimen, very fine. David will be very happy. Very."

Cynthia ventured into the language as well. "We could dig here. I think this is a good place to find more specimens, with the mud . . . Oh, I'll have to speak English! With the fine-grained sediments, low transport velocities, and the lack of carnivore damage to this bone, our chances are good to recover more."

Juma nodded. "Okay, today, just in case, we remove this bone. Then tomorrow, I want you, Balebe, and Maleti to begin to lay out the grid up here." He glanced at Elias, who was looking a bit disappointed. "Man, your luck is good right now, so I want you to come to the Ruba with us tomorrow. Maybe you'll find something there, too."

Is it that, or just making sure that he doesn't get too inflated an idea of his importance? Cynthia thought.

"Who has the camera? Good. And excavation tools? Okay." Nane turned to Maleti. "Go to the car and bring a *karai.* Hurry, we want to eat lunch before dark!"

Juma did most of the extraction of the specimen, as Cynthia and Balebe took notes on its orientation and sedimentary context. The two younger men and Maleti looked on with interest and asked numerous questions about the note-taking. At last the femur was resting in two cloth collecting bags, one drawn from each end of the bone toward the middle.

As they walked back down to the Rover, Cynthia fell in with Nane at the rear of the group. He inclined his head toward her a little and said, "I want you to train Maleti especially well. He is not so well-educated as the other two, but he will stay with this team when the others may leave. I need him to have the best skills he can develop."

Cynthia nodded. *Yes, Andrew and Elias are both bound for bachelor's degrees at the very least, and then what? Will they and Pierce have a need for you, once their training is complete? Probably, but it must be hard, to see these young ones having all the advantages you were denied.*

Juma radiophoned to David after lunch, and his congratulations came crackling over the airwaves. "I trust you'll share that bottle of Johnny Walker I gave you against this occasion, Juma, over."

"Affirmative, David, we'll have that and a special cake tonight, over."

"Tell everyone that it's a trip to the Meateater when they return, as well. Over and out."

After dinner, as they broke out the whiskey, Nane commanded, "Andrew, go fetch that guitar you pound on and let us have an *ngoma!* None of that reggae or American rock—good African music!" They danced and sang until well into the night, with Mupiki outdoing himself in dancing as well as lyrics.

Catching her breath in one of the chairs drawn near the fire, Cynthia watched the old man with a new respect. *He dances with such a grace and economy of movement. I wouldn't have believed that, from his usual bent-over walk . . .*

Juma leaned toward her. "You are watching Mupiki dance. Well, he used to be the dance leader in my home location. This was a very important post, and he is still very famous, in his retirement." He reached out and took her hand. "Now, you are doing us no good sitting there. Stand up and dance!"

She danced with everyone in turn, to the good-natured rhythms of the African songs Andrew picked out on his guitar. *Such a distinctive sound, a little delicate and plaintive, even in the joy of it,* she thought, two-stepping with an exuberant Elias.

"Another first experience in the bush, eh?" Balebe asked, taking her hand for the next tune.

"Yes, and quite a nice one, too," she replied.

"This is kind of a custom in David's camp, an *ngoma* after a find, or at the very least at the end of the season. This tops it all off beautifully, with the femur and the potential for excavation . . . puts an otherwise rotten season in a new light." He smiled down at her.

"Yeah, and I'll finally have a chance to do what I came out here to do."

"Mm, looks like clear sailing from here on," he said.

"Well, as we say in the Midwest, never count your chickens till they're hatched."

Flash Flood

By six-thirty the next morning, Maleti, Cynthia, and Balebe were heading up the dry sands of the Memlolo in the pickup. Picks, shovels, cartons of gear, stadia rod and legs for the surveyor's level, plus screens bounced in the bed of the Rover. Cynthia held the surveyor's level on her lap.

Balebe chuckled and said, "It was very kind of Elias to find the femur so close to camp, and so readily accessible by major highway, wasn't it?"

"Yeah, no packing the stuff in for two hours," Cynthia replied, "but these screens are still gonna get heavy going up that gully."

Balebe grunted, "But we only have to take them in once and leave them until the end of the excavation. That's a blessing, too."

Maleti pointed ahead to the far horizon, saying in Swahili, "Rain over there, the Shurr will be happy."

The other two nodded. Cynthia asked him if he thought any would come their way.

He shrugged. "I don't know, maybe. We will see."

Balebe parked the Rover in the streambed near the confluence of the little gully with the major watercourse. "All out for Korongo ya Paja," he intoned.

Cynthia grinned. "Femur Gulch. I still like Arroyo de la Pierna better."

"Fine, just you go and find a Pliocene hominid femur somewhere in the Greater Southwest and name your gully whatever you wish. This one stays African!" Balebe laughed, handing out a screen to Maleti. "And don't tell me, you want to carry the other one of these, don't you, Cyn? Well, go ahead, and have a shovel, too!

"Brother," he continued in Swahili to Maleti, "this woman wants to prove she's as strong as we are, so let her carry it." He cocked his head and smiled. "In fact, Cynthia, since you're in Africa now, we should let you carry *all* our gear. So you can learn African customs!"

Maleti laughed and grabbed a pick from the bed of the Rover.

Cynthia laughed as she reached into the pickup and grabbed a shovel and a duffel with survey instruments. "Careful, Thanatu, or I'll tell Melanie! You know she's pretty serious about gender equality—you're already in trouble for calling us 'ladies' last fall!"

Balebe moaned and they set off up the wash, each heavily laden with gear.

By ten-thirty they were just finishing laying out a grid to cover the floor of the gully downstream from the find, which tied in with the one they had established on top of the southern side. They would have to remove the top of the ravine to a depth of three feet to reach the level of the deposits in which the femur had lain, to search for more bones.

Balebe straightened up and looked at the southern face of the arroyo. "Well, unavoidably, here comes work. I don't much relish the prospect of picking our way through the caliche layer."

"At least it's not so hot today," Cynthia said. As they'd worked, she'd noticed that the wind was appreciably cooler than normal for this time of morning.

Maleti had straightened up, too, and looked intently up at the little ribbon of sky showing above the steep-sided arroyo. It showed a layer of high, hazy clouds. He muttered something about rain and scrambled up the south side of the gully. The other two watched him look east and exclaim, "Not good, rains are showing very close up the river."

Cynthia and Balebe struggled up to join him. They saw that the eastern sky was completely covered with blue-black clouds. Curtains of rain drifted across the exposures only a mile or two away from them.

"Leave it all," Maleti said, gesturing to the gear they'd deposited on the shoulder of the gully. "Let's just go." They scrambled down and began to trot back toward the car.

In this stretch, the walls of the gully rose steeply several feet above even Balebe's head, and Cynthia shuddered at the thought of being trapped in this narrow defile by a flash flood.

Without speaking, all three lengthened their strides even more, slowing only when the walls lowered and fell away as they reached the Memlolo. As one, they all turned east to check the sky. The rain clouds hung over the near distance, although the land around them was still dry. Balebe had turned to say something when Maleti spoke urgently.

"Listen! Water's coming, *mbaya sana*—very bad, very bad!"

Cynthia heard a faint hissing that rapidly became louder, acquiring a low, rumbling tone.

"Oh, my God, the car!" Balebe cried, running down the sand to where it was parked. Cynthia turned and began running with him.

Maleti shouted in Swahili, then in English, "No, leave it! It cannot pass! Cynthia, *kuja hapa!* Come here!" He gestured for her to return to the south bank of the stream.

But she was already at the door of the Rover before she grasped the meaning of his words. Balebe was frantically turning the key in the ignition and yanking on the choke.

"Don't flood the engine!" she cried.

The engine ground slowly, turned over once, and shook into silence. He hit it again, it turned over, caught, and died. "Oh *damn,*" he said in a low, intense voice. "Come on!"

Cynthia looked out the driver's window, saw that Maleti had climbed up the bank and was waving and shouting frantically. In the same glance she saw that the riverbanks on either side on them were steep, over a meter high. *That's what Maleti meant . . .*

The hiss had become a full roar, punctuated with little wet lapping sounds. Balebe cursed and said something inaudible, the engine caught, stuttered, and roared into life. In the same moment Balebe looked ahead and said, "Oh Christ."

Ahead of them, about four hundred meters up the river bed, a wall of water swung around the curve. Its frothy brown front was pushing a huge acacia tree and innumerable smaller branches before it. It moved with a mesmerizing speed over the undulating surface of the riverbed, sending up tall spouts of spray when it hit obstacles, advancing toward them steadily at a pace impossible to gauge. It was over a meter high.

"Quick," she shouted, "you have to go upstream, to that far bank, the banks are all too steep downstream!" Before she'd finished speaking, she was thrown back against the seat as he slammed his foot down on the accelerator and the car raced forward. She momentarily thought of the lunacy of speeding toward that monstrous wall of water as Balebe slewed frantically to the left.

She shouted over the roar of the engine and the water, "Go up on that point bar, the bank is lower beyond it!"

He grunted and slammed down into first gear, turning the nose of the car upstream as they jolted and slammed up onto the bar.

"Oh God, we're not gonna make it!" she screamed, as the hood of the Land Rover and the wall of water sped together.

Balebe wrenched the wheel hard left and the nose of the car rose up the bank. At that instant, the water hit the side of the car with a vicious jolt, tilting them wildly. The engine raced, then sputtered as water came shooting through the floorboards, caught again, and the vehicle leaped above the flood, front tires digging into the dry earth at the top of the bank. For a moment they held there, the force of the water slewing the rear end downstream, the engine screaming, then they moved forward up the bank, first imperceptibly, then in a lunge that put them over.

Balebe gunned the Rover through the dense thicket of brush along the bank. Thorny branches whipped into the cab through the windows, and Cynthia flinched away into the center of the seat. Balebe grimly hung onto the wheel, letting the spiny vegetation rake his right arm. As they cleared the brush, she leaned out the passenger window and looked back. They were at least twenty meters from the river.

"Stop, we're okay here," she said.

He braked and killed the engine, leaning back in the tattered seat. His shirt was soaking wet, his face shiny with sweat. They looked at each other, exchanged tremulous smiles, and Cynthia threw her arms around him. They held each other, trembling, for a long moment.

Without releasing her from his embrace, he murmured into her hair, "Oh Cynthia, forgive me, please. I very nearly killed us both." He rubbed her back with his hand. "I was so fixated on getting the damn Land Rover out, worrying what Nane would tell Pierce if I lost it—Christ!"

She drew away a bit and smiled. "BT, there's nothing to forgive. I was just as much a fool as you were, since I didn't get what Maleti was trying to tell us. And look, you got the Rover out when it seemed impossible, so it's really a great coup."

Uncontrollable tears of relief ran down her face, and she disengaged a hand to wipe them away, smiling. He smiled back down at her, looking her in the eye. They were so close, it was only a little bit closer to make it a deep, hungry kiss.

She tightened her arms around him. *Oh, God, this feels so good!* But after a moment, she pulled away. He looked at her, misgivings on his face.

She said, "Maleti! We have to go back to see if he's all right!" He nodded and let her go. They hopped out either side of the cab and ran back toward the roar of the river.

The sight as they pushed through the trees was staggering. The entire riverbed was full to within a few inches of the top with a brown, heaving flood that lapped onto the bank in little wavelets. Waves stood out a half meter above the main surface of the water downstream, covering where the Land Rover had been parked. Huge branches rafted past, occasionally snagging on the bank for a moment before wrenching loose.

They jumped back as a chunk of the bank near them was undercut by the current digging against it. Slightly downstream, a tree as tall as three men leaned, sagged lower, then fell headfirst into the current, its roots exposed by the racing water beneath it.

"Look! There he is!" Balebe pointed to a waving figure downstream from the junction of the gully they'd walked earlier.

Maleti raised both hands to head level and waved to them.

"He's okay," said Balebe.

Maleti then pointed and gestured downstream and made as if to run, pointing again.

"Oh God, I bet he means the camp," she said. "We picked the campsite so carefully, the old flood debris showed it was beyond high water—but what if this is the hundred-year flood? Mupiki's there all alone . . . and the fossils! And what about Juma, Andrew, and Elias, they're supposed to be working downstream!"

Balebe nodded. "Yes, I was just thinking. Look, we're on the same side of the river as the camp, let's drive down along the banks until we get there. Maleti will just have to walk." He waved to Maleti, pointing back into the bushes and miming driving at the wheel of a car, then pointing down toward the camp. Maleti nodded, turned, and ran downstream along the opposite bank.

They pushed back through the bushes, reaching the Land Rover in less than a minute. Climbing in, Balebe bowed to her. "Does Madam wish to drive?" he intoned, smiling.

"No way!" she replied. "I'm still a basket case after your recent carwash attempt!"

He started the car and turned it in the same direction the river ran, smile fading and lines of concern developing on his smooth face.

Glancing sideways, Cynthia saw the transition. She shivered as the wet wind blew in through the window. Large drops of rain began to slap against the windshield.

After thirty minutes they had negotiated their way through the brush along the river to a small watercourse only about two meters wide but raging full of water. "Damn!" Balebe exclaimed, jamming on the brakes. "We can't cross this in the car, and look how far inland it goes!"

Cynthia took his arm. "Hold on, this is the one that's only about a hundred meters upstream from camp, right? Remember where it's deeply incised near the main riverbank, and there was that big tree across it? We could try walking over there."

Balebe looked at her for a moment as if she were out of her mind, then said, "Okay, let's find some safe place to park this." He turned the Rover around, and they headed inland.

Having parked the vehicle on a little hillock above the general level of the land, they jogged back to the confluence of watercourses. As they approached the main river, Cynthia said, "Does it seem to you that the water's slacking off a bit?"

"No, yes, maybe. It still looks pretty heavy to me—and this little stream is certainly wild. Ah, there's the tree!"

The large acacia log on which they'd sat a few weeks before still lay across the little stream. Despite its size, it was rocking lightly. The surging current had risen enough to undercut the bank on their side, and the highest crests of the waves were nudging the trunk.

"Cyn, this looks pretty dicey to me. We'd have to balance on this thing while it's rocking, and if we fell on either side, it's right into the main channel!"

"Well, what else do you suggest?" she demanded. "hiking four miles upstream on this feeder? Waiting until the water dies down?"

Balebe glared at her. "Dammit, I don't know, but stop treating me as if I were a coward! How do we know it will do either Mupiki or Juma and company any good to get to camp, anyway? The damage may already be done!"

She nodded. "Yes, but we don't know that! I think we can get over safely. There's enough branches from this end to hang onto, except for that last meter or so, and we can just run for it . . ."

"Okay, let me go first . . ." He clambered up through the protruding branches and started across, holding onto the bases of other ones further along as he inched his way across the rocking log.

Cynthia was seized by doubts. *Doesn't look as stable as I thought! Jesus! There goes some more of the bank!* "Hang on!" she screamed as the tree heaved to the left, then stabilized again.

Balebe held fast, steadied himself, then began to inch forward again until he reached the span where the trunk was devoid of branches for handholds. He stood balancing for a second, then ran along the trunk and leaped down onto the ground on the other side of the flood. He turned and gestured her across, his words drowned out in the roar of the river.

"Oh, Cavallo, you thought this was a good idea," Cynthia muttered as she climbed up through the branches and stood on the tree trunk. It rocked rhythmically under her as she grasped for the nearest branches and picked her way out over the torrent.

She looked ahead to Balebe, who was hopping from foot to foot, gesturing wildly, *Shit! What was that?* The log jolted and tipped backward. Glancing back, she saw the bank behind her had been undercut more, and water was washing over the log, which seemed perilously close to swinging into the main channel. She heard Balebe screaming at her but didn't understand what he was saying.

I can smell the gouges in the bark . . . She dug her right foot into the rough bark a little ahead of her and took three huge strides down the rocking trunk. As her foot landed for her last leap, the base of the tree rose up in front of her and she started to slip. *God! It's going! I'm not all the way across!* She heard herself screaming as she threw herself sideways and forward off the rising log.

Her arms and face landed on muddy soil, and an instant later her legs hit the torrent. It tugged at her thighs strongly. She felt herself slip a little into the water, screaming, "No, no!"

Balebe was shouting something she couldn't understand. The water smelled of earth and broken vegetation. It pulled at her more strongly. Something hit her side, hard.

Balebe seized her under the arms and heaved her away from the current, so hard that she actually flew through the air and knocked him down, partly under her. They each scrambled to their hands and knees, frantically fleeing the bank of the stream. They rose and ran back through the bushes for a few meters.

Then she collapsed, sobbing, "Oh God, oh God, I thought I was going to die, it almost got me, I was really going to die!"

His hands were on her arms, around her. "You're okay, you're okay, you're okay," he kept repeating.

She pushed him away and looked at him. "You saved my life, it's the truth. Thank you, thank you." She saw tears pouring from his eyes. *You're crying* . . .

He tried a smile. "We've got to stop meeting like this . . ." and burst into sobs, drawing her close. "Oh, Cynthia, don't let's ever risk our lives again, I don't want to lose you, you're too important to me."

She pulled back from his embrace. "Look, I think we'd better get on with what we crossed the damned river for," she said, shakily.

"Oh, God, yes, let's get to camp!" They raced through the brush toward the campsite. Suddenly they could see the green of the store tent through the trees. They burst into the clearing where Mupiki's fire had stood. The hearth stones were totally submerged. Water was lapping at the side of the store tent.

"Our tent's gone," Balebe shouted. "The fossils! Damn it!"

"My tent's gone, too! My clothes! My Walkman!" *What an idiotic thing to say, Cavallo, where's Mupiki?*

Balebe was already calling Mupiki's name. They heard halloos from beyond the tent and ran to meet the old man, who was pulling his drying screen like a sledge, full of tins and dry goods, up through the brush, while his two Shurr assistants were hauling a drenched, collapsed tent inland from the river. Mupiki pointed and shouted to them in Swahili, "I am putting the food over that side, there up higher, go get more from the tent. Hurry, hurry!"

They dashed into the tent. Balebe yelled, "Pile up stuff in my arms, Cyn. There, all those cartons, yes, all of them!" She did as he said, and he staggered out of the tent. She looked around. *Jesus! There's the trunk with the hominid and the field notes! Mupiki got them this far!*

She seized the trunk by its handles and raced out of the tent. *Wow! This is unexpectedly heavy and it doesn't rattle at all. What's he got in here?* As she emerged, she saw the water was starting to lap under the canvas walls.

In the next five minutes they were able to salvage everything from the tent and take it to the higher ground Mupiki had found. The floodwaters now covered the tent floor and were beginning to tug at the walls of the tent.

"Leave it, Cyn, it probably won't go far," Balebe said, as she made a move to untie the ropes of the tent to drag it inland too.

They stood watching as the water rose another twenty inches, slowly pushed the tent over, and carried it downstream to snag in a tangle of brush a little further on.

As they continued to watch, Mupiki said, "The water is beginning to go back."

They stood, mesmerized by the brown waters, watching as they imperceptibly receded from where the tent had stood.

Aftermath

"Look!" Balebe pointed. The tops of Mupiki's hearth stones were emerging from the receding waters. Within another five minutes the stones were completely exposed, standing in brown mud the consistency of chocolate pudding. The five followed the retreating water through the trees, back toward the riverbed.

As they reached the trees along the bank, they saw Maleti on the other side, waving and shouting, a smile on his face.

"It'll be a while until he can get across," Balebe said. "At least he's safe."

Mupiki said in Swahili, "The water is going down now, he will cross soon. I pray God Bwana Juma and the boys had good luck."

Cynthia and Balebe nodded, somberly silent.

"*Ayah,* we have to look for the tents and other things now," Mupiki continued. Waving to Maleti, he called, "Look for things from the camp on your side!" Maleti nodded and began to search the banks downstream.

"Let's get the store tent back," Balebe said.

Two hours later, a thoroughly wet and muddy group of five stood back, panting, and surveyed their handiwork. The store tent was pitched again, on dry land beyond the flood zone. Managing the soaking wet canvas had been utterly exhausting, and as the sun sank lower in the west and the wind rose, Cynthia found herself shivering uncontrollably. "Oh no, not hypothermia in equatorial Africa!" she mumbled. The painfully thin Shurr boys were also shivering and coughing.

Mupiki looked at them with concern. He went over to the pile of goods they'd carried inland from the rising flood and rooted under the flysheet he'd thrown over it. Extracting three blankets and a cook pot with odds and ends of food in it, he returned.

"Put these on, and eat some food!" he ordered.

Cynthia gratefully wrapped herself in the blanket and chewed on the crust of bread with bully beef.

Mupiki handed a bit of bread and beef to Balebe and said, "Eat this, and then go get my fire stones. These boys are too cold now to help. I will make tea."

In a few minutes, Cynthia felt well enough to help Mupiki sort through the items under the flysheet and set up a new kitchen. Balebe made several grunting journeys between the old kitchen and the new, hauling the heavy rocks, and the Shurr boys joined him as the food took effect.

As they stood considering the matter of firewood, Maleti appeared through the brush, surprisingly clean. He grinned as he held up two soaking blankets and a ziplock bag with Cynthia's cassette tapes safely dry inside.

They surrounded him, laughing and pounding him on the back. Mupiki pointed at Cynthia and laughed, miming holding the tapes up to his ear. "We can have a dance tonight!"

She laughed, too, and asked Maleti, "Did you find my tent?"

"*Ndio,* yes. But it was too heavy for me to carry. We can bring it tomorrow. Balebe, you should try to bring the *gari* here now."

"Oh my God, I completely forgot about it!" Balebe exclaimed.

"You and Maleti go bring the *gari* here," Mupiki ordered, as he handed Maleti a sandwich, "and bring dry wood for the fire when you come. Cynthia will help me fix the camp things. Cynthia, grab this blanket and help me get the water out."

As Balebe and Maleti set off to get the Rover, Cynthia and the two Shurr assistants sorted through the gear and set it where Mupiki wished. She noticed that the boys' shyness of her was wearing off as they shared both the shivering misery of the cold and the common work of setting Mupiki's kitchen to rights. *The old man's keeping us going, making sure we're okay . . . has he eaten anything yet? And where are Juma, Andrew, Elias? Oh, God, let them be all right. This country will lose so much if they're not . . . Those young men, so promising, and Juma. No! Stop thinking like this, Cavallo. What's Mupiki saying?*

The old man was looking at her, an incipiently grumpy expression on his face. "Are you sleeping? Help me with this cloth. We will sleep on it tonight."

They heaved the flysheet into the store tent and unfolded it to cover the ground. Mupiki then ordered her to start carrying cartons of food into the tent.

As she did, she marveled at the amount that Mupiki and the two teenagers had been able to save from the flood. *Not only the contents of the store tent, plus blankets from Juma's and Balebe's tent,* and *the fossils, but also the camp chairs and the two folding tables.*

"You did so much work," she said to them in Swahili, gesturing to the pile of supplies.

Mupiki grunted and tugged at a huge bag of maize meal. "Huh, I saw the rain showing up the river, and we just started carrying things here. No one else to help, we just did it. Now, *you* carry this into the tent, you are young and have plenty of fat. Hurry up!"

Back to the old Mupiki, she thought, hefting a twenty-kilo bag of maize meal onto her shoulder.

When Balebe pulled the pickup truck into camp, the hearth was completely composed, awaiting the firewood. Kitchen gear stood on the drying screen, propped against a new tree stump, and chairs were unfolded around the fireplace.

Mupiki and Maleti began picking through the wood and laying the fire.

Mupiki turned to Balebe and the boys. "Now, go to the river and wash. Look for a sandy place, and be careful!"

Balebe looked at Cynthia. "Care to join us? We can use this blanket to dry off, I guess. Sorry we've no change of clothes."

"At least I've got my long-sleeved shirt in my backpack—it's still in the Rover, right? I can change into that while the T-shirt dries."

When they reached the riverbank, the scene had utterly changed. A moderate current flowed through the deepest part of the channel, gurgling like a respectable mountain stream. They leaped down to a sandy point bar and picked their way over to the flowing water, the boys trailing shyly behind and murmuring in Shurr.

"It's hard to believe this is the same stream that nearly killed us," she said, shaking her head.

"Yes, it certainly looks sweet and innocent now. Look, you go first. I'll stand guard with my back turned, madam, and make sure the boys don't peek either!"

She searched her mind for a wisecrack, found none, and felt a little of the personal disorientation of earlier in the day emerge again. *What* are *we becoming to each other? More than friends, but what precisely?*

The water was shockingly warm, not at all what she'd expected. She washed her clothes out and rinsed her shoes and socks. She stepped out of the water shivering and reached over Balebe's shoulder to take the blanket. Stacking her clothes atop her shoes, she wrapped herself up. "Your turn! It's actually rather warm."

As Balebe and the Shurr boys bathed and rinsed their clothes, she shuddered as she stepped back into wet shorts, then buttoned up the long-sleeved shirt, grateful for its dryness. She opted to put the wet shoes right back on her feet, without socks.

"I'll take that blanket now," he said from behind her. "Go on back to the fire and we will try to get dry. I don't much fancy putting these wet shorts back on!"

She smiled. "Yeah, it's a real thrill! But do we have enough blankets to go around?"

"Enough for the six of us . . ." he said somberly.

Her heart sank as she thought of the three downriver, and she walked silently back to the fireplace.

Ten minutes later they stood around a smoky but serviceable fire, as close as they could get, letting their clothes dry and soaking up the heat. Having made them tea, Mupiki had gone off for a wash in the river himself. A pot of water for *ugali* was coming to a boil over the cooking stones, and Maleti was chopping up onions for a stew at Mupiki's cooking table. The Shurr boys seemed content to stand and watch, excused from their usual duties by the day's emergencies. The night drew on.

Balebe wrapped himself tightly in a blanket, shivering. "I think I'll just make like a Chacha elder tonight and sit in my blanket by the fire!"

Cynthia broke a long silence. "What do you think has happened to Juma and the crew?"

"I don't know, Cyn," Balebe replied. "Juma has as much bush sense as anyone on the planet, so if anybody's likely to be safe, it's him and Andrew and Elias. On the other hand, they were farther away from the uplands, and maybe they didn't see the rain clouds so clearly. So I just don't know. I pray they're okay."

"Mm, it would be hard to bring the Rover back up the floodplain right now, too, so maybe their not getting back yet isn't a bad sign," she said.

By nine o'clock there was nothing else to do but try to sleep. Mupiki said he would sit by the fire a while and ordered the others into the store tent. "At least we'll all be warm, with the five of us crowded in among the maize meal and bully beef!" Balebe said in a joke that seemed to fall flat.

As she wrapped herself in her blanket and tried to get comfortable on the canvas floor, Cynthia thought again of Andrew and Elias. *Such promise, God, don't let it be snuffed out. It's the tragedy of developing countries, the loss of only a few can set back a field— a nation—for years. Look how easy it was to nearly wipe out the educated middle class in Uganda, and the consequences. If these two guys aren't here to take up paleoanthropology, who will?* She turned over, trying to shake off the gloom.

It seemed as if she hadn't slept at all, but suddenly Mupiki was in the tent whispering loudly, "Come out, wake up, someone is walking over there, with torches."

As they emerged and looked in the direction he indicated, they saw nothing for a moment. Then, Balebe said, "There!" and they all could see two dim lights weaving around in the distance.

"Do you think it's Juma?" Cynthia whispered.

"Probably," he said in a low voice. "Who else could it be? The Shurr or Minka certainly wouldn't go out to raid on a night like this. I think."

Mupiki whispered, "Wait a little, wait for their voices, then we will know. We must be careful." The Shurr boys were whispering nervously between themselves and peering into the darkness.

Cynthia shivered, only partly from the evening cool. *Great, all we need is to be overrun by raiding warriors! The end of a perfect day!*

They watched silently as the lights wove weirdly around, winking on and off. At last they could hear barely audible voices. They all strained to identify the language, the personal tones.

"It's Juma!" Balebe exclaimed. "Hullo, Juma! Over here! Come on, folks, start shouting so they know it's us!"

Mupiki returned from the hearth area with a kerosene lantern turned up high, waving it and calling in Kichacha.

An answering call in Juma's voice assured them, and the lights began to bob toward them, painfully slowly at first. Finally, three mud-coated figures emerged into the light of camp. Although they moved with the staggering pace of the totally exhausted, they all grinned and spoke at once, shaking hands all around.

Cynthia felt tears well up in her eyes, holding Andrew's hand in both of hers. She saw that he, too, was close to tears in the moment of relief and happiness.

"Where are your shoes?" she exclaimed.

Elias laughed. "We left them in the *gari.* Juma said we would only lose them walking in the mud. He was right—I nearly lost my feet a couple of times!"

"The *gari* is stuck down in the delta," Juma said. "We were too far from the edge of it to escape when the water came. Luckily, we had some high ground to stand on and the water was very dispersed and low when it reached us.

"We were very frightened for you," he said, nodding at Cynthia and Balebe. "I knew the water would have been high coming down the river so close to that korongo."

"Yes, we nearly lost the Rover," Balebe said, "but we managed to get out."

"I am surprised you got the *gari* out, that is very good. The other one will be free once the mud dries, but if this one had been caught in the flood up here, it would have been ruined."

Cynthia recalled the wall of water again, the huge trees tossing in the flood, and shuddered. "Mupiki and his assistants rescued the fossils!" she interposed, glad to change the subject.

"Ah, *vizuri kabisa!* Excellent! Let us go wash up and then we will celebrate!"

Around midnight they all were huddled around the fire, sipping hot cocoa with dark rum. Juma had unexpectedly produced yet another bottle, plus several dry sweatshirts, from his trunk. The red one he wore proclaimed "Stanford." Mupiki had been presented, with considerable ceremony, a blue Yale shirt, while Andrew sported one emblazoned with the logo of the Washington Redskins. Elias, Maleti, Balebe, Cynthia, and the Shurr boys contented themselves with blankets.

Juma smiled at the rest of them and said, "Now you all know that my liquor store is in the *sanduku,* and I thank Mupiki for rescuing it. But it won't help you too much to know this, since this rum is the last of it, until we can persuade David to come back out here!"

Balebe looked up quickly from his seat on a jerrycan. "Oh God, the radio—it's gone, isn't it?"

Nane grunted assent. "I fear so. But tomorrow we shall make a thorough exploration downstream, looking for the other tents and things from the camp. Perhaps we will be lucky. Even if not, I can drive to Anthea's camp to use her radio. We are expected there soon, in any case, to arrange for the lorry to come pick up our tents.

"Thanks to this old man and his helpers, we have our food, and I would like to stay for another few days, first to rescue and clean our camp gear, and then finally to excavate that femur locality. Thanatu, you didn't leave the excavation gear in the korongo, did you?"

Balebe shook his head. "No, thank heavens, we'd got all of it up to the top of the gully before we noticed the rain. I fear that the grid we laid out will be gone, but if that's the worst we have to contend with . . ."

"Indeed. Now, let's finish our drinks and get some sleep. Cynthia, perhaps you would be more comfortable on the seat in the *gari,* with your blanket. Balebe, escort her out there, please. Take this torch."

As they got to the Land Rover, Balebe broke their silence. "Look, Cyn, I need to clear the air a bit about today, and I'm feeling damned awkward. Please bear with me a moment." He paused and seemed to struggle for words. The silence lengthened.

"You don't have to say anything now, BT," she said softly, laying a hand on his arm. "It's been a wild day, and we've both been through the emotional mill. I'm not going to take anything that happened or was said between us seriously."

"That's just the problem, Cynthia!" he said with some heat. "I *did* mean what I said, I mean, to the extent that I was intelligible at all— oh, damn! I knew this was going to come out wrong." Again, the silence lengthened.

He took a deep breath and continued. "Here it is, as clearly as I can put it. I can't imagine spending my life with anyone else but you as a companion, and I know as well that I can't imagine spending my life anywhere else but here, in my own country. And I'm also painfully aware that I've no right to ask you to leave your country, your family, your plans for a career in the States . . . to take on being a white foreigner here."

He sighed and looked heavenward, then back at her. "And on top of all that, I haven't the faintest notion of whether you have any similar feelings for me, and whether I've just made an utter fool of myself, and I'd sooner die than lose your friendship!"

Cynthia stood leaning against the Rover door, stunned. "Well, that was sure a mouthful," she said, casting about for words. "You *are* one of my dearest friends ever, and a very attractive man, too. And the thought of being more than a friend with you *has* crossed my mind. But I'm not sure, either, of what I want, ultimately, or how to handle the present. Field situations can stir up feelings and actions that one regrets once back home."

She smiled in the darkness. "I just know that I don't want to mess up our friendship, either . . ."

Balebe spoke, more softly this time. "Cyn, I didn't say any of this in order to pressure you into an intimate relationship. In fact, I want to go slow, in any case. Your friendship and respect is not the sort of thing I'd want to risk by losing our heads. Oh, God, that sounds like the worst kind of nineteen-thirties cinema, doesn't it?"

"Well, there'd be only so much pressure you could exert before I'd simply deck you!" she said, laughing. "I guess that would just get us further into the nineteen-thirties battle of the sexes, huh? Look, I'm incredibly punchy right now. We both need some sleep.

Let's just put this stuff on hold for a while, while we rescue tents and excavate fossils, okay?"

"Gladly! But thanks for hearing me out." He put his warm hand on hers as it rested on the Rover's door handle, then abruptly turned and left.

"Oh, Cavallo, a fine pickle you're in now, the guy's as much as proposed marriage," she muttered, settling down across the Land Rover's front seat. "Never mind the culture, the politics, and the racial tensions . . . what about being a memsahib with parquet floors? Me, the machinist's kid from Topeka? The aspiring woman paleoanthropologist? How could I live this life here, would caring about him be enough to make up for all the differences—a white minority in a black nation, in a class situation I hate." She squirmed around, trying to find a comfortable position on the cracked vinyl seat. And she went to sleep.

Postmortem, Wangara

Cynthia gratefully accepted the cold glass of beer from Colin Jones. She was still readjusting to the uproar of city life, and the din in the bar of the New Hibiscus had been too much for her. Jones, seemingly intuiting her unease, had swiftly ushered her to a table in the garden terrace behind the building and plunged back into the fray for drinks.

"There, that ought to take the edge off a very wearying day, I should think," he said, brushing a hand over the thinning hair on top of his head and smiling brightly. He took a sip of his own beer and continued. "You've had quite the eventful field season, and I could see no sense in your being snagged by that revolting man from *Newsday*. I mean, let Pierce and Thanatu fend 'im off! It's their country, not yours!"

Cynthia took another sip and nodded. "Thanks so much for pulling me into your lab when I nearly walked into that mess! All the same, I feel guilty about Balebe having to deal with that reporter while I'm hiding out in a bar."

"Nonsense, the boy's got to learn some public presence, and David's there to steer things straight. Damned bloodhounds! I should have thought it was all blown over by now, with the inquest two weeks past. But this enterprising johnny was just lying in wait for your lot to get back from the field. I'd like to know who tipped him off. Well, there's plenty around the museum who could use an extra hundred diys. Waiter! Another, please!"

Jones turned to her again. "So, what are your plans now? Are you doing any more sightseeing?"

Cynthia shook her head. "Sadly, no. I'm due to be a teaching assistant for an introductory course in physical anthropology that starts in only ten days, and I promised my folks to come home for a visit before school begins, so I'll be leaving day after tomorrow."

"A pity, there are such lovely places in this country—I grew up in the north, you know, boyhood in the bush and all that? Well, you've dinner tonight with David at the Meateater, I'll bet! A well-worn custom, my dear, that's how I know. At any rate, you'll not need any animal protein for a month after a visit there."

She smiled. "Well, I am ready for something other than maize meal and stew."

He nodded. "Mm, quite so! I'm sorry I couldn't get you out to the Kashmir for a nice tandoori dinner. Michel and I used to frequent it quite regularly. Now, there's a chap who likes his nightlife! Never a dull evening in his company!"

Cynthia asked, "We heard that he was still very ill when he went home. Do you know any more about it?"

Jones looked down at his drink grimly. "As a matter of fact, I got a postal card from him about a week ago. Said he was on the mend now he's back with his own medicos. I hope he's not just trying to cheer an old friend. Saw him off at the airport, and he looked like death then. Dunno what it is, and he won't say. You can pick up a lot of very bad bugs out here, you know. But look, enough of gloomy topics. Tell me what you'd like to hear about!"

Cynthia nodded after having a sip of her beer. "Actually, I'd like to stay with the gloom for a minute. Did you follow the inquest on Shafer? All I've done is read the newspaper clippings that Balebe's mother saved for us."

Jones grimaced and nodded. "Yes, well, I did go so far as to attend the proceedings, and I must say that your documentation of the scene of the crime was most impressive. Actually, old Malongo played it up big, 'an expert in archaeological excavation,' and all that—don't cringe, it went down quite well. That's what probably pricked up the ears of this wretched *Newsday* fella."

He swirled the beer in his glass. "Well, you know the verdict, death by person or persons unknown, shot to the head with a .32 caliber revolver. Interesting fact came out from Dr. Deep's testimony: seems that Bob was shot at close range from above, while looking up, from the path the bullet took, as if his killer were standing above him on a higher spot—or as if he were down on his knees or crouching, and his killer standing."

"No other signs of foul play," Jones continued, "unless you count all the little postmortem nibblings. Oh, I say, I'm sorry, didn't mean to put you off dinner."

Cynthia smiled wryly. "It's okay, I've had to get used to it." She took a sip of her drink. "The terrain up there on the plateau was pretty flat, unless someone climbed up on a cairn, which is pretty much out of the question, so I guess he was crouched down . . . ."

She shuddered a little at the image of Schafer crouched before his killer and changed the subject. "You don't think this *Newsday* guy is going to try to catch me somewhere else, do you?"

Jones laughed. "Well, he'd be a bloody fool to go near the Thanatu residence, I'd say. So you're safe there. And I should think the museum will be safe tomorrow, once David and Balebe get rid of him. Do have another. Waiter!"

She shook her head. "No, thanks. But it's strange—even though I saw him dead, it's hard to believe that someone actually killed Bob Shafer!" She sipped at her beer again.

The waiter delivered another beer to Jones. "Ah, here we are, *asante sana, bwana*." He took a long drink and went on. "Well, it is rather shocking, but then so many people had good reason, and most of them were right here in Wangara when it happened. Quite intriguing to speculate who and how, right?"

Cynthia nodded but kept silent.

He tugged at the cuff of his threadbare jacket and continued. "I mean, there's the obvious choice of David, who was about to have his theories of human evolution vanquished by this ill-mannered American cad. There's his fossil exposures, his airstrip, his plane, all the ingredients . . . furthermore, with Shafer out of the way, David could go on fossil-hunting, shifting over somewhat to Shafer's version of human evolution, to be sure, since that's the way the evidence points. David now is the only researcher with field materials of a relevant age to pursue this line of research, so he comes out ahead with Bob gone. However, it looks as if he's got an iron-clad alibi for the night Bob disappeared."

Jones ran his hand over his head again and stared off into space. "Then there's Anthea, who'd actually threatened his life. Ruthless old woman, too! While I wouldn't put it past her, I'm not sure she's physically capable of hauling him over the Ruba and getting him stuck into a cairn. Still, she's got money, and a little goes a long way out there."

Cynthia shuddered. *Bob Shafer on his knees, pleading with Anthea Pierce not to shoot him!* "I've decided to have another drink, after all!" she said, smiling weakly at Jones.

As he signaled to the patrolling waiter, Jones took up his recital. "Now then, there's your own illustrious professor, who was in Wangara and who, from all the gossip, has as much motive as anyone to want to kill Shafer. I mean, what a way to treat a lady!"

As Cynthia opened her mouth to protest, he held up his hand and pressed on. "However, I think several factors count against her in this case. First, she doesn't fly a plane and would have to have had an accomplice who did—at least if the theory that someone got Bob out there before the end of the congress is true. So let's shelve her until we exhaust our list of other suspects."

He took another sip of beer and gazed out into space. "Anyway, I tend to believe what she told me last year when I teased her about doing Bob in—of course that was before we knew it was really an established fact! I mean, I may exceed the bounds of propriety sometimes, but really! Now, where was I? Oh, yes! Melanie told me that it wouldn't be worth the trouble. Damn fastidious woman, that, self-contained. Probably wouldn't risk the fuss. Plus, she'd be less likely to have got hold of a gun in this country than most of our other suspects."

Cynthia looked up to see their waiter arriving with her fresh beer and asked, "But isn't it illegal for citizens to own firearms here?"

"Well, technically, yes, and one can't go about brandishing guns the way you Americans do. But if you wind up shooting a thief with one in your own home, the police simply provide you with a postdated registration form. And, like just about everything else out here, they're available for a price. Firearms, not the police, but now that one comes to think about it . . . Ahem! In any case, I'd rule out Melanie Baine."

Jones waved off her attempt to pay for her beer and continued. "Then there's that bloody fool van de Hoven. It's simply not possible that he pulled off anything like this, he was on the museum tour, at the Belgian Embassy dinner, or in bed, by his wife's testimony, during the span in question."

"That leaves," he said, glancing around to check the other tables and leaning significantly toward her over his drink, "your hosts."

Cynthia stared at him, speechless, but Jones, in the grip of his narrative, pressed on. "Well, don't look so surprised, my dear. I'm sure you've wondered what went on between T. Junior and Shafer to instigate a transfer to your university right on the heels of a major find?

"Old Michel told me last summer he was sure something *had* gone on over in Barbore. Said the boy wasn't himself the last few days. I tell you, I wouldn't put it past Bob to have fiddled the boy out of the discovery! I think he put one over on the Belgians. Why not the boy?"

She sat silent, unable even to nod.

Jones glanced around again. "And even if the boy himself wasn't keen on revenge, the old man . . . well, that's another story. All the means in the republic at his disposal, quite easy to nip someone off

the street, arrange a quiet demise, transport away from the scene . . .
only a question of motive."

Cynthia continued to stare at him, chilled to the core in the warm
afternoon sun. *It couldn't be . . . but the disappearances! What if
they're in this together, and the fight at home was all a smoke
screen? What if Balebe's in this?*

Jones leaned toward her, concern on his face. "Oh, I say, did I say
something wrong? Bugger all! I've really put my foot in it, haven't
I? I'm so sorry, it *was* rather callous of me to go over all this with
you, in view of all you've been through, and your acquaintance
with all these people—ah, there's Balebe now!"

He leaned even closer. "Look, I should tell you that I really don't
think the boy had anything to do with it, so don't take what I said
too seriously."

They both rose as Balebe reached their table. He smiled at her,
and she tried to smile back but felt she was failing miserably.

"Thanks for the note on your door, Colin!" he said, smiling. He
turned to Cynthia. "I must say that he spared you an ordeal. That
reporter was an unremitting nuisance! Even David nearly lost his
patience at one point, with all the insinuations. But we managed to
get the man out of there, at long last. Ready for a major meat feast?"

She nodded. *I can't get out of this, can I? Oh, I just want to be
alone, to sort this out a little!*

Thanking Jones for the drinks, she let Balebe lead her out of the
bar, her mind reeling with the strengthened possibility that this
sweet friend beside her was a killer. Or his father. More likely, the
father.

Wangara, 1987: Evidence

Balebe listened to the rain pounding on the museum roof three
floors above him and cursed under his breath. He'd just finished
reading another postcard from Cynthia, and he felt the familiar
wave of frustration and powerlessness sweep over him. *Why do I*

always feel so damned inept and hopeless after reading her letters? Why? He looked down at the fossils lying on the pale green foam rubber, at his calipers and laptop computer, at that card, signed with that familiar flaring hand.

Damn! I was such an utter fool not to have asked her to stay! But she was so distant those last two days, pulling away. And there's something noncommittal about these letters too, full of details about the department but nothing of her.

He turned on his stool and stared unseeing toward the vault, its door ajar so that he could remove more hominid fossils—those from Ruba, casts of the Lake Turkana materials. *She must suspect that I had something to do with Bob's death. Damn! Something happened after we got back here to Wangara, if I only knew what. Is it something she learned about my father . . .* "Damn!" He realized he'd spoken aloud and glanced self-consciously toward the outer office where Margaret, the hominid curator, sat. She seemed to be glancing away as he looked in her direction.

Embarrassed, he turned and picked up the calipers again. *Better get back to it, man, or you'll be here until Easter rather than Christmas.* The rain outside increased in intensity, roaring against the roof and grounds outside the thick walls of the museum wing that housed the hominid remains.

As he measured the deep brown fragment of bone, he was able to lose himself in his concentration on the form, the correct placement of the calipers. He entered measurements next to the tibia's catalogue number in the computer database and picked up another of the Ruba finds, this one collected by Anthea's field crew on the other side of the river. He took up the first specimen again and held the two together in the little pool of light from his high-intensity lamp. *A lot like each other . . . don't need the measurements to see that. Very much alike, for individuals separated by at least a hundred thousand years . . . perhaps some of Bob's ideas about the stability of the adaptation are correct.* He cradled the two Ruba specimens in his right hand and lifted the cast of the little tibia from the Usno Formation, turning and comparing all three for a few rapt moments.

Through the sound of the rain, he heard hurrying footsteps. Before he could set all three bones back down on the foam rubber sheet in front of him, Colin Jones burst into the anteroom with a muttered "Jambo, Margaret," as he rushed past into Balebe's work space. He was struggling to control his breath, and Balebe was surprised by an urgency in the man he'd never seen before.

Glancing over his shoulder toward Margaret, Jones leaned toward Balebe and spoke in an undertone. "We've had an unexpected discovery down in archaeology, and I'd like you to see this before I call the Big Bwana in." Balebe opened his mouth to speak, but Jones cut in. "Now, Thanatu!"

Balebe nodded and rose to follow Jones, who was already in the doorway. He nodded to Margaret as he left. "I'll be back in a little while. Could you leave them out, please? Thanks." He hurried down the covered walkway out of the new museum building and dashed the few steps across to the shelter of the old wing now occupied by Nane and his crew and Jones and his reference collections. Jones was almost running, and Balebe tried to keep up without himself breaking into a jog.

Jones turned into his lab, where they immediately confronted a young woman perched on Colin's favorite stool and wringing her hands in clear dismay. *Ah, Mireille Delcourt, the student from Bordeaux—what possibly could have happened?* She looked up at Balebe and nodded, then burst into tears.

Jones danced around her, patting her shoulder and stammering, "Now, now, uh, *laisse-t-il,* uh, *il n'importe pas,* oh damn, Thanatu, speak to her—you know French!" He fished awkwardly in his trouser pocket and withdrew a crumpled linen handkerchief, which he proffered to the young woman, who was struggling to regain her composure.

She wiped her eyes and blew her nose, took a deep breath, and said, "No, no, please, I am able to speak English. I am sorry to cry, but this is a big shock to me." She let out a shaky sigh and swallowed. "Dr. Jones, he stopped me from touching it because he thinks there is some criminal *rapport . . .*" She looked at Balebe and

Jones and gestured helplessly. "I do not expect to find such a thing in the stone tools."

Balebe turned to Jones. "What is this about? What did she find, Colin?" Jones's mouth tightened. "Follow me," he said, and walked back through the doorway into the main collections area. He strode down the main aisle until he reached the rack labeled "Ruba: East, West." Turning down it he gestured at a heavy wooden tray still half drawn from its shelf. "There, see for yourself, Thanatu."

Balebe moved forward and peered into the tray. There, among about a dozen pieces of flaked lava and quartzite, lay a revolver. He stared at it, unable for a moment to form a clear thought, then his mind raced. *Is this the pistol that killed Shafer? Why here? What's this about?*

He turned back to Jones and was struck by the look on his face. *Why, you're genuinely angry—and you're sizing me up as a suspect, aren't you?* "Nasty piece of work, eh, Thanatu? It's a .32 calibre, and I'll lay odds that it's the one that killed Shafer. Seems as if someone wanted this to be found, sooner or later. Of course, only a few of us knew Mademoiselle Delcourt was coming this fall to work on the Ruba lithics. David did, and you."

Balebe reacted angrily. "Now see here, Colin, if you're trying to say I had something to do with this—"

"Now, *you* see here, Thanatu!" Jones responded, heatedly. "I want to know what bastard put this gun in my lab, and why! It's a perfect frame-up, you know, pointing at me, who's the only person who ever comes in here!"

"Except Anthea, Colin," Balebe said, trying to calm the archaeologist. "Look, it won't do either of us any good to fly off the handle like this. It's not even clear that this *is* the gun that killed Bob. We have to get a grip on ourselves and proceed methodically. First, we've got to keep Mireille from phoning someone and letting the cat out of the bag . . ."

Colin rolled his eyes. "Oh crikey, yes! I suppose we had all better see David. Damn! This is the first time I wish I'd let them install a phone down here!"

"Never mind," Balebe said, "you just stay with Mireille, since you know her better, and I'll go directly over to David's office. It's better to let him know face to face."

Twenty minutes later, Balebe watched in admiration as Pierce spoke attentively to the young Frenchwoman, whose agitation calmed considerably as he explained what he was about to do. *If I live to be a hundred, I'll never have his resourcefulness,* Balebe thought. *Here he is, having just five minutes ago seen the probable murder weapon turn up in his own museum, acting as if calling in the CID was the most natural thing in the world . . .*

Pierce glanced at his watch and turned to Jones. "Look, I'd rather not have the whole staff see the police troop in here, so I'd like to wait until the end of the day to have them come over. Why don't you and Miss Delcourt go over to the New Hibiscus and have some tea, or something, and then come back just after closing time—it's only an hour away. Thanatu and I shall ring the AG and work out a quiet visit after hours—we needn't have the entire tourist community and three hundred schoolchildren spreading this all over town." Colin nodded and rose, offered the young Frenchwoman his umbrella, and left the lab with her.

Pierce turned to Balebe, his face for the first time revealing his own emotions. "Christ! Sometimes I swear that man Shafer is haunting me—and someone still living is clearly out to ruin me and this museum! How the hell am I supposed to tell members of Parliament that a murderer could just walk in and drop a pistol in the archaeology collections? The minister of interior is going to be livid—we may lose his support, God knows, I may be fired. This is absolutely the worst time for a power transition here! The ministry still isn't totally committed to support us. God! What a bloody awful mess!"

He turned and paced back toward the collections, then whirled. "Look here, Thanatu, you must tell me—what went on with you and Shafer in Barbore? It's all tied up with this, somehow, and now that the fate of the museum's hanging in the balance, you owe me the truth."

Balebe sank down onto Colin's stool, his heart racing. *He suspects me, too! I have to tell him the truth now, though God knows, it will only make me look more the culprit. But is all this show David's way of covering his own guilt and getting me to take the fall for him? Is he so afraid that I'll take his position that he'd do this to me? I don't know. I DON'T KNOW!*

He looked up and met Pierce's intent, dark gaze, noting the lines of worry around his mouth and eyes. *Can I trust him? Can I trust anyone?* He took a deep breath. "David, I don't know whether I can trust you with that information. How do I know that you won't use it against me?"

"For Christ's sake, Thanatu! Don't you see? Someone is playing us against each other! It's not just you and me and our jobs here— it's the whole damn museum I've struggled so hard to build. This is the only research institution of its kind north of South Africa, and it's still so vulnerable. You know as well as I that there are al-together too many members of Parliament who'd just love to see me, the white Asalian they don't trust, go down, and who'd gladly sacrifice everything—the facilities, the collections, the staff—to see it happen." Pierce half-turned away and for an instant looked close to tears, then he set his chin and turned back to face Balebe. His brown eyes looked levelly at him.

"Look, Balebe, we've known each other over ten years now, and I truly don't suspect you of killing Pierce. But I can't for the life of me work out who did, and now, it's absolutely essential that we do. We've got to start by trusting each other enough to work out how to deal with the CID." He sighed and looked away. "I need to know, to tell you the truth, because I've suspected that your father might have . . ."

Balebe cut in. "I've never told my father what happened in Bar-bore. And no one else knows enough of the story for Ezekiel to have squeezed it out of them . . . but you know, sometimes I've suspected him, too." He stared at David and made a decision. "Okay, David, what the hell, here's the truth, God help us both if you use this against me. I didn't kill Shafer because of it."

After Balebe finished recounting the events in Barbore and his subsequent confrontation with Shafer in Wangara, Pierce fished in his tweed coat pocket for his pipe, found it absent. He snorted and eyed Balebe with an ironical expression.

"Yes, that was Shafer, incredibly quick on his feet and unscrupulous to the core. I must say, Thanatu, that you might have used your head more wisely at the outset and thus avoided getting tangled up in *this* affair so badly. But I understand the pressures you were under—and I do believe you that you didn't shoot Shafer, though God knows, I'd have been sorely tempted, were I in your place."

He cocked an eyebrow at Balebe. "Now, you positively didn't give your father any indication of this?"

Balebe shook his head. "I told my mother I'd had some trouble with Shafer, but nothing specific, and I know she kept it to herself. She always does."

Pierce looked at the young man impassively for a moment, then nodded. "Right, Thanatu, now, let's go call your Honorable Dad." He rose and swept the room with his eyes, shook his head, and stepped out into the thin late-afternoon rain.

San Felipe, 1987: The Call

The fossil monkey skulls on the table in front of her seemed to stare back, grinning. *Now, try again, Cavallo, let's have a little more enthusiasm for these splendid early Pliocene cercopithecids who gave their lives for science . . . and whom Dr. Melanie brought all the way back from Zaire at the taxpayers' expense.*

She checked the connection of the cord that ran from the electronic calipers to the digitizer, feeding data into Melanie's computer. Picking up the calipers, she began to measure the cranium. A minute later, she set down the instrument with a muttered "Shit!" and stared out the window at the snowcapped Santa Elena peaks. Two stories below her on the grounds outside the anthropology lab, tamarisk trees tossed wildly as the afternoon wind stripped off their dead foliage. The ventilators whirred relentlessly, yet the air in the lab was dead.

She dropped the calipers to the desk, rocking the bones on their foam rubber beds, rose, and walked over to the window looking west toward the Rio Salido. "This is hopeless," she said aloud, to no one in particular. She turned and stared at the bones for a moment, then turned back to look out the window. *No, let's face it, what's different is this distance between him and me. I miss him so much, and I dread his coming back. His letters have been so formal, not a word of the investigation.*

Her thoughts went back to their drive home from the dinner with David Pierce at the Meateater. They each had avoided speaking with the other for most of the way. Cynthia had been so wrapped up in a fog of fear and disorientation. Dinner had been a blur for her. She tried to keep a jovial conversation going with Juma, Andrew, and the others, to avoid interacting with Balebe. He'd sensed her distance and had put on his formal British manner. *So like Ezekiel in these moods—oh, damn them! How can I care so much and suspect them so much!* she'd thought, huddled inside her dress jacket.

As they'd begun climbing up Mbagama Valley Road, he'd cleared his throat and said, "After we got rid of the man from *Newsday* today, David and I talked things over a bit. He asked me to stay on for a few months, to describe the season's fossils, to be a second author with Elias on the hominid—to oversee the production, he's not going to be on as author at all! I'm a bit overwhelmed, but if David truly wants us black Africans to take the front seat, I can't very well say no—so I won't be coming back to San Felipe with you this fall."

Something inside her had frozen then. *Is David paying him off, for something to do with Shafer's death? Maybe they're all three in it together—Christ, I'm becoming a raving paranoid! But who can I believe, they could just about sew up the whole thing, David and Ezekiel . . .*

She'd managed a quiet, "I see," and they'd driven up to the gate in silence. As they waited for the askaris to come open it, Balebe turned in his seat and blurted, "Cyn, I'm sorry, this must take precedence right now. I'll miss you."

She nodded, looking down at her hands, feeling something she'd never fully acknowledged was slipping away. *God, why am I so— it's not just Shafer—I do want to be with him, I realize that now, and it's too late. Will I ever be able not to suspect him?*

Now, four months later, she was no more resolved in her feelings. The letters had been full of news of his family—except Ezekiel—of Elias, Andrew, Maleti, the fossils—but not of David, nor of the investigation into Shafer's death. He had only laconically reported what she'd already heard: the attorney general of the Republic of Asalia had rejected the operation of overseas investigative agencies on Asalian soil, although he welcomed any information that Interpol or the FBI might be willing to provide regarding foreign nationals and the case.

For the thousandth time since August, the first glimpse of Shafer's skull filled her mind. She pressed her forehead against the window, trying to blot it out. Tears welled up in her eyes as she stared sightlessly toward the river. *I'm so alone, this is all too hard. I can't go on like this. Maybe I should see the campus shrink.* She heard a door open down the hall and the distinctive swift tap of Melanie's fashionable flats coming down the hall.

The door to the lab burst open, and Melanie leaned in. "Phone, Cavallo, it's Balebe, from Wangara. Hurry it up."

Cynthia surreptitiously wiped her eyes and hurried after Melanie back to her office.

Melanie held the door open for her. "Go on in. I'm going over to the Union for a cup of coffee—want one?"

Cynthia nodded and rushed over to the phone on Melanie's preternaturally neat desk. "Balebe?"

A barely perceptible lag preceded his reply. *Is it the satellite transmission, or is it hard for him to talk to me?* "Hullo, Cyn, sorry to give you a turn by calling like this, but something's happened I thought you ought to know."

"What?" she asked. "Are you okay?"

His response to her first question intercepted her second, through the delayed transmission. "It's Colin, he's been detained by the CID in connection with Shafer's death."

"*Colin?* That's absurd! What can he have to do with it? What the hell is going on?"

"It's rather a mess, Cyn. Just listen for a moment, and I'll try and explain it. Remember the graduate student from France who Colin told us was coming out to study the Ruba artifacts? No? Well, anyway, she got here in late November and started going through the old collections in the back of Anthea's lab, the ones where only Colin ever goes. The second week, she pulled out a drawer labeled "Miscellaneous Tools" and found a .32 caliber revolver lying there among the lithics."

"You're kidding!" Cynthia interjected.

"No, and let me be on with this, before my father decides we've made a large enough contribution to Asalian Telecommunications for one evening."

Cynthia nodded, then realized the absurdity of her gesture.

"To make a long story short," he said, "it's turned out to be the gun that killed Shafer—you'll probably hear all this on the wire services soon, but there are some twists you should know."

"Such as?" she said.

"Such as, oddly enough, there were fingerprints on the pistol, and they weren't Colin's—nor David's, nor mine, nor my father's, in case you're interested—in fact, the CID can't make out whose they are and are currently asking Interpol to check their files. But you know how long that could take, especially since most of our European colleagues are not likely to ever have had prints made, and since the CID can't yet make a strong case for hauling anyone in to be fingerprinted."

Unexpectedly, he laughed. "You'll be relieved to know as well that Anthea's in the clear—I'll leave it to you to imagine what having her in for fingerprinting was like. Poor old Malongo is said to have aged ten years in the process!"

"But what's happening? Are there any suspects?" Cynthia interjected.

"This is where it gets troublesome, Cyn. Colin's in the clear as far as prints on the murder weapon go, but he's being strangely obstinate about discussing his views with the police. 'I didn't use the

gun, and you've no right to question me further,' is all he'll say."
Balebe sighed audibly. "But the police do have a right to detain
anyone whom they believe is a material witness or whom they
suspect is withholding evidence, so they've had Colin in the slam-
mer for four days now, despite David's and Anthea's best efforts to
get him out."

"And your father, what's he been doing in all this?" Cynthia
asked.

"Well, he certainly doesn't believe Colin's the murderer, but you
must understand that he has to uphold Asalian law by supporting
the CID's right to detain him. It would be a breach of his official
responsibilities not to do so. We none of us can figure what Colin's
up to," Balebe said, sounding exasperated, "other than that he's
trying to protect someone, but the damn fool's being unbearably
stiff-necked with all of us. I went to see him today, and he actually
had the nerve to parrot back to me the same line he's been using
with the police, plus saying that he had, quote, 'Complete confidence that the workings of the Asalian judicial system would result
in his release,' end quote! I could have struck him!"

"Is he okay? I mean are they . . ." Cynthia began, realizing in mid-
sentence that she might be slurring Ezekiel.

"Yes, Colin's being handled strictly within the confines of the
law, Cyn," Balebe replied. "My father's keeping a close eye on it,
and Malongo's not known to use excessive force in his interrogations—unlike some others," he added.

"BT, who's he protecting?"

Balebe sighed again. "Cyn, I don't know, and I wish I did, since
the whole thing is just mushrooming out of proportion. I shouldn't
have to tell you that party with the hand on the gun needn't be the
only one involved, and it's wearing all our nerves to a frazzle."

She felt a chill. *So you're still not in the clear, not with the police,
nor with me . . .* She drew herself together. "Is there anything I can
do, we can do? I mean, can pressure be brought to bear for Colin's
release?"

There was a short lag, then his voice came again. "It is the right of
any person to address correspondence to the attorney general of the

republic, expressing concern over any matter. I would say that an expression of concern about the detention of a prominent archaeologist would lend weight to voices already being raised in this country," he replied in formal tones.

He added with a wry chuckle, "The British high commissioner is already exerting his persuasions, despite Colin's totally disrespectful attitude to him, too!"

Cynthia picked up a pencil from the desk. "What's the address we can write? I think we can get a good showing through Melanie's connections."

"It's Office of the Attorney General, P.O. Box 76248, Wangara."

The silence while Cynthia noted the address on a pad of paper on Melanie's desk lengthened awkwardly. She finally broke it. "Well, I'd better let you hang up, this is costing a lot of diyanis."

He laughed. "Yes, the Guvnor's going to have a fit when he gets this bill. But in fact, he agreed with Mum that I should ring you up to let you know what's been happening. They've thoughtfully vacated the study for me and are probably trying to hear what I'm saying through the sitting room wall!"

She laughed, despite her mixed emotions. "How's the work been going?"

"Oh, quite well, actually," he said. "Elias is a master of comparative analysis. He's seen relationships between our skeleton and other materials I wouldn't have in a year's study. Maybe museum administration is what I'm cut out for! And you?"

"Okay, it's been a little slow . . . I've missed you, BT."

"And I, you, Miz Cavallo," he said, with a note of tenderness in his voice. There was a pause, then he said, a shade awkwardly, "Look, is Melanie still there? I need to talk with her about my return. The fact is that I actually am not permitted to leave the country until the investigation's wound up—yes, I'm also being scrutinized. I need to talk with her about the Ruba materials she wanted to me to carry out to her."

Cynthia glanced at the door and saw a shadow through the frosted glass window. "Hold on—I think she's just outside. Say hello to everyone for me—bye!" She put the phone down and strode to the door. Melanie stood outside, blond coif mussed by the wind, balancing a cardboard tray with a paper coffee cup and doughnuts in one hand while drinking from another cup.

"Balebe wants to speak with you, too!" Cynthia told her.

Melanie handed the tray to Cynthia and strode to the phone. She waved Cynthia out of her office. As the office door closed, Cynthia glanced at her watch. "Six or seven minutes! It seemed much longer," she muttered. She leaned against the wall for a moment, staring across the hall at Melanie's poster for the Third Paleoanthropological Congress that covered the door to the computer room. *That's when all this started . . . well, at least that's when the Shafer story turned fatal. Who the hell can Colin be protecting?*

Melanie yanked her door open and looked out. "Come on back in Cavallo, before your coffee freezes." She walked back and dropped into her desk chair, gesturing toward an old overstuffed chair wedged between the window and a bookcase behind the desk. "Have a seat, Cavallo. Yes, in the Comfy Chair—and don't look so surprised! I know what you guys call it, *and* all the stories about whom I will and won't allow to park their butts in it! Now, have a doughnut and tell me everything Balebe said he'd told you."

Cynthia glanced around the room from the unexpected vantage point of Melanie's own reading chair. Although her main desk was, as usual, neat, the side tables and bookcases overflowed with stacks of photocopied articles, letters, and books. *How the hell did Melanie learn about the Python's "Comfy Chair" routine? Weller probably told her to get into her good graces.* She brought herself back to the moment and took her coffee and doughnut.

"Well," she began, "it's about Colin and some new developments in the Shafer case." Melanie took a sip of her coffee and picked up a doughnut, nodding for her to go on. Ten minutes later, after intense cross-examination from Melanie, Cynthia licked the last of the doughnut's sugar from her fingers and sighed. "So that's about it."

Melanie sighed and muttered, "Jesus," then reached into her drawer and got out a battered pack of cigarettes.

"You don't smoke, not even under stress, right? I haven't for years, but I still keep a pack of cigs handy in case I have a Big

Freakout. This sounds like one. Crack the window, Cavallo. This really takes the cake. Colin! I'm sure he didn't do it, but he's clearly got an idea who did."

She rummaged again in her drawer for matches and lit up, grimacing at the first drag. "Looks like I'd better go on down to University Police and get them to send a copy of my prints to Asalia," she said, smiling slightly. "I might as well join the ranks of The Vindicated." She leaned forward and flicked her cigarette ash out the window, leaving her hand hanging on the edge of the windowsill. She glanced sideways at Cynthia. "Ever think I did it, Cavallo?"

Cynthia swallowed and said, "Uh, no, not really. You might have had reason to, but it just didn't seem your style." She was immediately seized by embarrassment. "I mean, you didn't seem the kind of person to—"

Melanie leaned back in her swivel chair and laughed at Cynthia's discomfort. "You're right that I didn't kill him, *and* that it wouldn't be my style! There was a time I might have—no, to be perfectly frank, I was far too crushed back then to even consider revenge." She wheeled her chair around and stared away into space for a moment, then swiveled back to face Cynthia, shaking her head to clear a wisp of hair from her face.

"As long as we're having this cozy little session, let's get it all out into the open. What's been eating you since you got back, Ms. Cavallo? It wasn't just having found the body, right?" She took another drag on the cigarette.

"No, that was pretty awful, but I didn't really know him—" She stopped short, realizing she was discussing the corpse of the man who'd been Melanie's lover.

"Don't worry," Melanie said, after the silence lengthened, "I came to terms with just about everything to do with Bob a long time ago. It's what's up with you that I'm concerned about." She took another drag on her cigarette. "You've been worrying that Balebe had something to do with Shafer's death, right?"

Cynthia let out a laugh that sounded too much like a sob to her own ears. "Is it that obvious? It's like, we got to be pretty close in the field this summer—not lovers, but he wants to have a 'serious relationship,' to marry, I don't know." She stopped, acutely embarrassed to be discussing her personal life with Melanie, who'd never shown the slightest inclination to be on confiding terms with any of her graduate students. She glanced at Melanie, surprised to find an unaccustomed expression on the older woman's face.

She took a breath and went on. "I was up in the air enough about all that, and then it became clear that he, or his father, or both of them, were likely suspects in killing Shafer." She sighed. "I've just been miserable. My intuition tells me he's got nothing to do with it, but his father—I've wanted to believe he's not involved either, but he's so powerful, there are all these rumors about his having people disappeared, and even now, so what if his fingerprints aren't on the murder weapon?" She hunched forward in the chair and sighed.

Melanie nodded. "I've heard the rumors. So you've been wondering if the object of your affections is a murdering swine, and if he isn't, if his father is, right?" She looked at Cynthia over the rim of her cup as she took another sip of coffee.

Cynthia nodded. "And then, when David Pierce asked Balebe to stay on this fall, I began wondering if all three of them were in collusion—am I certifiably paranoid yet?"

Melanie laughed bitterly. "Cavallo, if being involved in both paleoanthropology and the East African political scene doesn't make you paranoid, then you really *are* a loony!" She dropped her cigarette butt into the dregs of her coffee and tossed the cup gently into the wastebasket. "To tell you the truth, I've had some pretty seedy suspicions myself." She turned again to stare across the room for a long moment.

Turning back, she leveled her gaze at Cynthia. "Look, I'm going to tell you a couple of things that, if they ever get any further than you, I'll drop you from my research team like a hot rock. This stuff has got to be in confidence, right?"

Cynthia nodded.

Melanie made a move to take out another cigarette, then forestalled the motion. "When Balebe came here, you can bet I wondered what the hell had happened between him and Bob. I mean,

Bob wasn't in the habit of dropping me telexes from exotic spots, asking me to take a Fulbright scholar off his hands." She smiled wryly. "The fact that this came almost precisely at the moment that Bob announced the Barbore find was pretty fishy. I made some discreet inquiries with Michel—Laporteau—who'd been in the field with Bob and Balebe, and what he said only added to my gut feeling that something bad had happened between the two of them over the find."

She toyed with the cigarette pack. "Then, when Bob turned up missing in BT's home country, well—it seemed totally out of character for Balebe, but his father's another story, as you said."

Cynthia drained the last of her cold coffee and tossed the cup into the trash. "Colin seems to be protecting someone else. Do you have any suspicions who?"

Melanie was silent for a long time, tapping her cigarette pack against the desktop. "Yeah, I have," she said. "But they're too unfounded—it's too much of a long shot. Let's let time and the Asalian CID work it out, Cavallo."

She paused for a moment, then went on. "Now, about this 'serious relationship.' It's not my habit to pry into the private lives of my grad students, Cavallo, but it's been driving me crazy to see you moping around like this. You're easily the best student I've ever trained, and definitely have a great future in front of you. There are so few women in the field who can stand up to the relentless male pressure and competition, and I know you can." She paused, ran a hand over her eyes in an uncharacteristic gesture, and sighed.

Cynthia remained silent, uncomfortable with the unexpected intimacy of this conversation.

Melanie gazed across the room at a travel poster of Zaire. "It may be that I'm identifying too much, or projecting, whatever the psychologists say. But you've got to handle the matter of this relationship before it eats you up. I'm not in a great position to give advice about involvement with professional colleagues, but I do know that you need to stop sitting on the fence—either go for it with BT and work out how you'd be a paleoanthropologist in Asalia, or tell him no way and both of you go back to being the best of friends."

She stopped for a moment, withdrawn in a somber reflection. Then she actually gave herself a small shake and leveled her gaze again at Cynthia with a little smile. "Cavallo I *order* you to handle this matter as soon as possible. I can't afford to have *two* of you mooning around my lab, eating up my NSF grant and producing nothing!"

Cynthia smiled back. "Yes, ma'am, first thing, handle relationship, and not on company time. Anything else?"

"Yes, I have a surprise for you. You get to do all this kiss and make up sooner than you think. I've got to get those Ruba monkeys measured before the deadline for the Zaire monograph, and now that the police won't let Balebe carry them over here, I'm between a rock and a hard place. David was willing to get me the export permit for the loan of the specimens, but now he refuses to let a courier service bring them out. Says the ministry won't let anyone but authorized persons hand-carry museum specimens. So, *you* are going to spend Christmas vacation in Wangara, collecting the data!"

Cynthia sat in shocked silence, then shook her head. "But where will you get the plane fare? I mean, won't this put a big hole in your research grant?"

"Yes, dammit, but I can't complete the analysis of the Biki fossils without the Ruba data!" Melanie threw the cigarette pack into her desk drawer and slammed it shut. "I've got a January deadline breathing down my neck, and only this month to play catch-up with all the other people who've been working on other parts of the monograph for a year. I simply can't complete analysis of the postcranial material without the Ruba cercopithecid data for comparison!"

Her face shifted into a crooked smile, and she glanced at Cynthia again. "Besides, I managed to save a little money on the airfares last field season by using my frequent flier mileage, so you're in luck, Cavallo! I'd go myself, except I'm already locked into the primatology conference in Osaka. How soon can you leave?"

Cynthia swallowed, her mind reeling, and scanned the East African Wildlife Society calendar hanging next to Melanie's desk. "Um, I'll need to complete my independent study with Don Smith, but it's just an annotated bibliography, and I'm pretty well up. I can probably finish it up in a week, if I pour it on. Then there's our tutorial . . ."

Melanie waved her hand. "Consider it done, consider it done! No, to keep the dean happy, how soon can you turn in the survey and data analysis of the Miocene stuff? Next week, too? Great! You can catch up on your sleep on the plane. Plan on turning in the Pliocene monkey stuff when you get back from Asalia—and I'll want you back before spring semester starts, so don't plan any long safaris, okay?"

She pushed herself back in her seat and fixed Cynthia with a sharp stare. "Now, go send out for a pizza. I need to get this manuscript for *Science* done and out by tomorrow morning. That means I need those statistics on the femora by five at the latest. Go in there and get them done. We've lost enough damned time with all this detective novel crap already. I swear, sometimes I think Bob's still out there, hassling me from beyond the grave."

Cynthia rose from the chair. "Will do—do you also want me to run some comparisons with the published stuff on the Omo monkeys? The oldest ones are almost the same age as the Biki material."

Melanie looked up from the mirror in which she was repairing her hairdo. "Hmmm, good idea, Cavallo. Your brain may be getting back into gear! That'd probably make this paper too long for *Science's* report format, but get right on it anyway. Maybe we can do something together for *AJPA* after you come back. It wouldn't hurt to get your name out on another publication. Now get out of here, and let me get back to my writing!"

Cynthia stepped into the corridor and took a deep, shaky breath as the door swung shut behind her. Asalia again! Am I glad or afraid? Both, I guess. It seems more dangerous than ever. Is the killer still there, trying to cover his tracks? Her tracks? She walked down toward the lab, fishing in her pocket for the keys. Who's Colin's protecting? And who's Melanie not mentioning?

Wangara, 1987: Motive

The rain poured down in torrents as they rushed to the Citroen under Balebe's huge umbrella. At six in the morning, the halogen lamps still lit the misty air at Pankolo Airport.

"God, why did I wear these nice shoes? I should have worn hip waders!" Cynthia exclaimed, laughing, as they tossed her bag into the trunk.

"Yes, but think of coming through immigration wearing hip waders and your fetching travel outfit!" Balebe replied, holding the umbrella over her as she got into the car.

Cynthia had a moment to sit alone in the car as Balebe walked around to the driver's side. The rain pelting on the roof had a calming effect on her. The struggle of getting through the crowd and across the tarmac in the rain had masked her own breathlessness and pounding heart, which had not let up since the plane landed and had only worsened once she'd actually seen Balebe.

Balebe swung into the seat and tossed the umbrella into the back. "How was the flight? No, I've already asked you that, haven't I? Am I nervous? Hardly!" He grinned at her and stretched his arm over the back of her seat. "A rather unexpected pleasure, Ms. Cavallo! Welcome back to Asalia, home of ancient hominids and unsolved murder cases!" His eyes belied the lightness of his tone.

She smiled back and laid a hand on his arm. "Thanks, BT, I can't say whether I'm more glad, terrified, or nervous, right now, to tell you the truth."

He nodded. "That just about sums up my emotions as well. Look, the Djibouti Cafe's open this early, what say we go get some of their Somali tea and *maandazis*. Then we can have a decent talk in something other than a fogging-up vehicle in a torrential downpour!"

A half hour later they were sipping ginger-flavored milky *chai* and nibbling the sugary deep-fried squares of dough for which the little cafe was famous in Wangara. An assortment of early morning tourists and long-distance truck drivers were nursing their tea and *maandazis* at other tables, but the place was still half-empty. Balebe had chosen a corner table well away from the other customers. There was an awkward silence after they'd carried their food from the counter and seated themselves.

"So, what else is going on with the Shafer case?" she asked.

Balebe sighed and rubbed a hand over his hair. "Well, they've had so few leads, apart from the murder weapon and the mystery prints, with no one volunteering information, least of all that damned Colin, who's now been through deportation proceedings! I wonder how he'll fancy December in London—I doubt he's spent more than a fortnight in Britain since he graduated from Cambridge!"

He looked out through the Djibouti's foggy windows for a moment, then at her again. "Since they do know Bob was shot at the site, they've been scrutinizing the records at Matope Airport, and all the flight logs, for the planes that flew out to supply the conference and to pick up people and gear afterwards, to see if anyone could have managed to fly into West Ruba on the sly. Malongo and the others on the case can't imagine any other means for Bob getting out there, alive, that fits the time frame. With the rains coming so soon after the conference, they've got a pretty good sense of the interval in which he was shot."

Cynthia looked at him expectantly, and after a moment's pause, he continued. "So far, my father says they've pretty much drawn a blank. Last week he confided that they're following up on two flights that have slightly longer than absolutely necessary turn-around times. But 'the matter is complicated by the international aspect,'" he said, mimicking his father's tones. "He's also concerned that the case is tying up his best investigative team, and there's considerable pressure from higher up to get on with the so-called 'sedition cases' against Asalian dissidents. It's only a matter of time until the press of other work draws Malongo's team off."

"At which point, the Shafer case effectively goes into the deep freeze," Cynthia said.

He nodded and continued in a lower tone. "I couldn't write any of this to you in a letter, because I'm not at all sure that my mail isn't being read—it happens, you know, and there are plenty of people

who'd love to compromise my father by alleging his son was revealing state secrets to foreigners, or some such nonsense."

She shook her head and matched his lowered tones. "What's all
this about rejecting the help of foreign investigators? It looks bad
from the outside."

"I know," he said, "but you have to understand that there are
matters of national sovereignty at issue here. Although the Office of
the President is pressuring my father to solve the case, because it's
a grave embarrassment to the republic, they insist that he do nothing to indicate our dependency on more developed countries. The
effects of the colonial period linger on, Cyn, you should know
that."

She nodded, silently.

He sighed and tapped his fingertips on the tabletop. "Look, it's
time I told you the whole story of Shafer and me in the field in
Barbore. I've already explained it all to David. You've probably
heard so many rumors that the truth will seem a little bland, but
here goes."

After he'd finished his narration, she asked, "Where are the negatives now? They could be very damaging to you."

He smiled. "You may not believe this, but once I'd got to San
Felipe, I burned them. In the bathroom at Mrs. Simms's boarding
house. Flushed the ashes down the loo. Don't look at me that way—
they'd served their purpose in getting me away from Bob, and I'd
no interest in proving that I was the real discoverer of the fossils.
I'm not *that* kind of paleoanthropologist. So long as Bob thought I
had them, I figured he'd mind his p's and q's. I knew he'd never in a
million years consider that I might destroy them!"

She laughed out loud. "BT, I can't figure if you're the most honest, foolish, or cunning person I've ever met!"

He smiled back, a little grimly. "Maybe all three together, Cyn. I
can see how you could think the worst, even without knowing all
the fine details. And I don't blame you. I can only say that as of
now, I do believe my father, both that he had nothing to do himself
with Bob's death and that they're doing the best they can on the
case." His face tightened. "But I swear to you, if I ever find out that

218

he did have a hand in Shafer's death, I'll leave Asalia and never come back, and I'll tell the world why!" He rapped his fist on the table so hard that their tea splashed on the table.

She leaned over and touched his trembling arm. "Oh, I've been so sad and angry these last months. I *have* suspected you, and your father, and it's just been awful. I believe you, I want to. I've realized that I'm more attached to you than I thought, and I'm scared. I don't know what to think about your father, either."

"He's a hard man, Cynthia, as you saw, I suppose. But I just don't think that he has it in him to have Bob killed for a rather petty and personal reason, by his lights. I mean, even if the rumors about his role in the disappearances is true, he's the sort of man who'd only turn to such methods for national ends, not this. But dammit, I can't be sure, and I don't know that I ever shall!" He drew away from her, rigid with emotion.

She got out a tissue from her purse and began to mop up the spilled tea, her mind racing. She suddenly stopped wiping and exclaimed, "You know, BT, I think we and the police have been going at this all wrong! We've been looking at all the people with a motive to kill Shafer." Now she rapped her knuckles on the table. "Maybe we should look for someone without a motive."

Balebe looked at her, puzzled. "What do you mean? Doesn't anyone who'd commit a murder have a motive?"

She shook her head. "Yes, but maybe not an obvious one. Look, you and I and the CID and God knows how many other amateurs have been doing the classic thing, right? Going over all those people with the motive, means, and opportunity to kill Bob. And we've fixed on the people with grudges against him."

She laughed. "God knows, there are enough of them! The problem is, all those people with motives have pretty good alibis, or lacked the means to kill him, or to get him out to West Ruba. Except for your dad, and if he'd not got word of your real problems with Shafer, he's out of the picture, too."

She gestured with her cup. "So, what if there's someone who had the means and the opportunity, but not the obvious motive? That's the only option left."

Balebe nodded. "I get your point. We need to make a second list: there's Colin, Juma, I discount any of the rest of the fossil team. But Colin was here in Wangara with an alibi—at least if the Victoria's night manager can be believed—and anyway he doesn't fly. Juma was at his farm, which is too far away to get from and to quickly enough, and he doesn't fly either. That leaves . . ." Balebe looked up at Cynthia, a wide-eyed stare on his face.

"Michel." They both spoke together.

"But why?" he asked. "Whatever could he have gained from shooting Bob and dumping him out there in Ruba? Bob had never done anything to him, that I know of, anyway."

Cynthia wagged her finger warningly. "Yeah, but remember, we're looking for an unclear or hidden motive here."

"It's just too weird, Cyn. Yes, he flies, and I suppose he could have readily got hold of a .32 in one of those shady nightclubs he likes to patronize, but really, why on earth would he do it? Remember, I've been in the field with him, and he's completely imperturbable—detached, more like it. And he's the guy everybody likes."

Cynthia nodded. "Yes, I know he's a great guy, if a little heavily into his sensual pleasures, but who else had the means and the opportunity?"

Balebe shifted in his seat and mumbled, "My father, for one— Cyn, I just can't keep from coming back to him . . ."

"Well, let go of that for a minute, BT and think if there's anything to indicate some motive on Michel's part."

He shook his head, pondering for a few moments. "Nothing, unless . . ."

"Yes, what?" she asked, leaning forward.

"The notebooks, Cyn, remember? The stuff about Anthea and Juma, and the page ripped out. What if that ties in somehow? God! I've still got those notebooks! Michel went back to Brussels before I could swap with him again. They're in my trunk at the museum!"

"Let's go get them—it's not much, but it's some new angle on the case. Malongo and company don't know anything about this, do they?"

Balebe shook his head. "To tell you the truth, I'm not so eager to let them know either. What if we're wrong? This is the flimsiest of stories we're making up right now, without anything substantial. What if we drag him into it without reason, with him so ill?"

"I know, BT, but let's ransack those notebooks for anything like a motive! We've only got a few more days before they kick Colin out of the country forever!"

Escape

"Oh no!" Balebe exclaimed as they drew into the museum parking lot. "What now?" Five dark blue police cars were drawn up around the entrance to the office building. Armed policemen were circling around the main building and heading for the labs behind them. As they drove up, Inspector Malongo emerged from the office building with a very agitated David Pierce. Malongo got into his chauffeured Volvo and roared out of the parking lot, gravel flying.

Pierce spotted their car, strode over and leaned on Balebe's side of the car, oblivious to the drizzle on his back. "That tears it!" he nearly shouted. "That damned fool Jones escaped from police custody as they were transporting him to the British High Commission for final processing! The police are currently ransacking the museum, looking for him. His car's been impounded, so he can't use that, but God knows what he'll do now. He knows this city like the back of his hand, and if he gets out of Wangara, it may be weeks till we find him!" Pierce slapped his hands against the roof of the Citroen in a hopeless gesture. "And to top it off, the police are now treating him as a suspected felon!" His voice broke and he turned away.

"Oh my God," Balebe muttered softly. In response to Cynthia's questioning gaze, he explained grimly. "Asalian police are free to shoot suspected felons on sight, no questions asked."

Cynthia felt numb. "But why? Don't they know he isn't guilty? And why is he doing this? Could he really be the murderer?"

Pierce turned back, shaking his head. "I'm virtually certain he's

221

not the murderer, but I haven't a clue why he's gone and done this—unless being held in detention all this time has driven him around the bend. Malongo doesn't really seem to think he's the culprit either—but he's furious at Colin for escaping, and he refuses to rescind the felon declaration."

Cynthia turned to Balebe. "Can't you get your father to do something?"

He shook his head hopelessly. "I seriously doubt it. It's really beyond his control now. As I told you before, he's walking a tightrope with this case, and he can't interfere with due process too much." He slammed his hand against the steering wheel. "Bloody damn fool! What did he have to gain by running off like this?"

"Perhaps he's playing for time," Pierce said quietly. "Or perhaps the prospect of leaving his homeland made him more desperate than we'd bargained he'd be. I only wish I could figure out where he'd head for."

Balebe stared through the windshield for a moment, then said, "I think I might know, David, at least I've a hunch. You know, Colin used to talk a lot about his boyhood up in Nyandidu. Running with the Wachacha boys in the forest, exploring all the way up to the caves on Mount Tidinga."

Pierce straightened up and glanced around for a moment, then bent down to the car window again. "Yes, he knows that area extremely well—and he's an expert tracker and hunter. If he made it up there, he could easily keep out of the way of the police for weeks, living off the land."

Balebe reached out and placed his hand on Pierce's arm. "David, let me go after him up there! I think I know where he'll fetch up, and if I could get to him and persuade him to turn himself in quietly, perhaps we can get this mess to turn out okay after all."

Pierce heaved a sigh and wiped the moisture from his face. "It's worth a try. This is a tragedy in the making. Look, in this rain, you'll need a four-wheel-drive vehicle. Take my Land Cruiser—it'll get you up the side of Tidinga. The museum driver can lift me home and around town until you get back." He reached into his pocket for his car keys, but Balebe forestalled him.

"David, I don't think you should get involved here, at least not to the extent of loaning me your car. We're moving perilously close to aiding and abetting a criminal, and the museum is already too much at risk right now. I can get a short-wheel-base Land Rover from my parents' neighbors."

Pierce cocked an eyebrow at Balebe and after a moment nodded. "I hate to say it, but you're right. And you must be very careful up there—God knows, I don't want to lose the investment we've made in your education!" Leaning further into the car window, he made eye contact with Cynthia. "Welcome back to Asalia, Miss Cavallo. I'm afraid you've come at a very bad time for us. But I shall be happy to get you started on the Ruba cercopithecids as soon as you wish."

Cynthia nodded acknowledgment but said, "I think I should go with Balebe. In this weather, it's best to take two people. He could get stuck along the way."

"Absolutely not!" Pierce cut in. "It's bad enough we're withholding information from the police, but getting a foreign national involved—that's beyond what I'll permit!"

Balebe abruptly started the car. "She's right, David. I could use a companion on this trip, and Colin knows her." Above Pierce's objections, he threw the car into reverse and began backing away. "Don't worry, David, we'll be all right! You really should get in out of this rain!" he shouted. They reversed out of the parking lot, leaving an infuriated Pierce standing in the drizzle.

Cynthia sat in silence, shocked at Balebe's treatment of Pierce. He gave her a quizzical glance. "What's he going to do, go to the police?"

Despite herself, she burst out laughing. "Oh you're bad, just bad!" He joined in her laughter for a moment, then became serious. "Look, it's now quarter to nine, and by the time we get home, both my parents should be gone—my father was going to drop my mum at Saint Crispin's this morning. That should give us a little leeway to dump your stuff and get out of the house. I'll tell Kaniugi and Mariamu I'm taking you to see the flamingos at Lusugi Island. We can swing by the MacPhersons' on the way home and ask the missus for the loan of their old Rover. I've borrowed it before for short trips—it just sits there when they're not off on safari." He glanced at her again and said, "Say, are you okay? I just remembered you've been traveling over a day now. You don't have to go along, you know."

Cynthia shook her head. "No, I want to go. This is such a mess. I'd go crazy if I had to stay here and worry about both you and Colin." She sat back, her mind reeling. *How dangerous is this? What if the police figure this out too? We could get shot out there!* She watched the verdant lawns of the suburbs flash by her window.

Balebe broke the silence. "We may not find him, you know. I'm only going on a hunch. He spoke so much about a certain cave on the upper slopes of Tidinga, the good water, the abundant game. Even without a gun he can get enough to eat, setting traps and using sling stones."

"Can we get up there in this rain?" she asked, watching pedestrians with umbrellas negotiate huge puddles on the unpaved margins of the road.

"Good question." He shifted down as they began to climb up Mbagama Valley toward home. He turned into the second driveway at the top of the hill and pulled up in front of a large stuccoed house. Two enormous Irish wolfhounds ambled around the end of the building, wagging their tails in a desultory way. "Wait here," Balebe said, getting out of the car and calling to the dogs, who came over to be patted. Balebe rapped on the front door with an elaborate brass knocker and was soon admitted.

Cynthia sank back in the seat with her eyes closed. *This is too much. First I find Shafer, now the police want to shoot Colin, and I'm going to rescue him. I've been on airplanes for almost twenty-four hours, and I haven't even figured out whether I trust Balebe a hundred percent . . . this is just too much.* She felt tears begin to prickle under her closed eyelids and fought to keep them at bay.

A snort next to her ear shocked her back to reality. The huge, wet nose of one of the wolfhounds was pressed against the car window. Under hairy brows, soft brown eyes were regarding her in a friendly gaze. Face to face with the huge dog, Cynthia just had to laugh. She rolled the window down, only to be nuzzled by the dog.

"Okay, okay, I want to be friends, too!" she said, scratching behind the dog's ears. "God, you're big!" The window was totally obscured as the second wolfhound pushed his head inside. She laughed, tousling their wet fur.

The dogs drew away at the sound of the front door closing. Balebe walked to the car and leaned in. "Do you think you can drive the Citroen the rest of the way home? It's only a few hundred meters. I'll lead you in the Land Rover."

Half an hour later, Cynthia smoothed and folded her rain poncho and stuffed it behind the seat of the Land Rover. Balebe hustled out the back patio door, carrying a large plastic sack and glancing furtively over his shoulder. As he wedged the sack into the small space behind his seat, he muttered, "I hope to God Mariamu won't notice my extra plundering of the kitchen pantry for a while—want a banana? They won't keep! Here, take these chocolate bars and stick them in your jacket, okay?"

He hurriedly started the Land Rover, whipped it in a tight circle, and drove toward the gate, waving to the askari who emerged from his hut into the continuing drizzle. Once clear of the gate, he breathed a sigh of relief. "I told Kaniugi we were off until tonight sometime, but if they see the amount of food I've nipped, they may get suspicious." He reached across and pulled a road map from the dash. "Here, have a look at where we're headed. I'm picking up the L4 road down the other side of the ridge, then heading northeast. The base of Tidinga's about a three-hour drive. After that, we take the Rumuginga Road—that little blue squiggle. That'll put us halfway round the southern side of the mountain. From the town of Tidinga Tuu on, it's unpaved road up the mountain."

She shivered in her jacket as they bucked down the ridge road. "How far is the cave, by your reckoning?"

He shook his head. "Well, I've only been up there in dry weather, and that was an hour's drive to the trailhead, then another hour on foot. In this weather, God only knows."

She laughed. "I sure hope we're not on a wild goose chase, BT!

We're gonna be two very unhappy campers if Colin's made a break for some other part of the country."

"I know," he replied, grimness replacing his smile. "But I think it's all the more likely that he'd try for Tidinga, given the weather. He knows the police will probably be reluctant to hike into the forest in this kind of rain."

"And we're not?" she rejoined. "Hey, how dangerous is it up there?"

"Well, there's still plenty of game on the mountain. Elephants can be a problem, but the buffalo are probably the worst." He lapsed into silence.

"So, how do we cope with them?" she asked, glancing sideways at him.

"Um, by being very careful." He reached over as she snorted cynically and tapped her arm gently. "Look, I suggest that instead of worrying about imaginary buffalo, you get some sleep these three hours. You'll need to be rested for the climb up to the cave."

"Yeah, and if I'm asleep, I won't have to watch your compatriots' driving!" She wrapped herself in the sleeping bag they'd smuggled out of Balebe's room, wedged her backpack against the window as a pillow, and settled herself into the corner of her seat. After a moment, she opened her eyes and stared at Balebe's profile. "BT, what'll happen when your father finds out about this? I mean, we are close to aiding and abetting, aren't we?"

His mouth tightened and he kept his eyes on the road. "I don't know, Cyn, and frankly, I've decided not to let myself be bothered about it. If we can keep Colin from getting himself killed, that's the most important thing. And the worst that can happen to you is probably persona non grata status and deportation."

"Oh great! Just the ticket for success in my career! And what about you? Ten years of hard labor and twenty strokes with the cane?"

He glanced at her with a mix of amusement and irritation on his face. "More like two years and ten strokes. And do go to sleep now—you're putting me off my driving!"

You're not kidding, are you? Oh, Cavallo, what have you got yourself into? Please, just no more dead bodies, especially not Colin. She wriggled into a more comfortable position and closed her eyes.

Tidinga

"Wake up, Cyn!" Balebe's voice broke through into her sleep. For a moment she was totally disoriented. Then their place and purpose brought her into complete wakefulness. They were winding up a narrow tarmac road toward a row of one-story buildings, their varied colors and galvanized metal roofs shrouded in the rain. The drizzle had turned into a full downpour that nearly overwhelmed the windshield wipers. She glanced at her watch. *Two-thirty. We've made pretty good time, but we've still got further to go. God, are we going to walk up after sundown?*

Balebe steered the Rover around major potholes in the main street. "Welcome to Tidinga Tuu. I've decided to top up the petrol here, and to get some tea for the thermos. Stay in the vehicle—and keep the hood of your anorak up, okay? We should keep a low profile here. Let me do the talking. I don't stand out quite so much as you do. "

A miserable-looking station attendant emerged with an umbrella from his shelter to pump gas. As Balebe paid him, he added a thirty-diyani note and handed out their thermos. "Please, man, help us with some *chai* from that *duka* over there, and keep the change. We'll meet you over there." The young man nodded with a smile and jogged toward the tea shop.

As they pulled up outside the shop, Cynthia watched the rain pouring off the tin roof and shook her head. "How the heck do you think Colin got up here, with no car and half of Asalia looking for him?"

Balebe wiped the fog from his window. "This isn't as godforsaken a place as it looks right now, Cyn. The Tidinga Safari Club's only ten kilometers down this road, with daily shuttle service from

Wangara, and the country buses come through here several times a day. Plus, you've forgotten the *matatu* guys. If Colin had a little money on him, which apparently he did, since he wasn't being treated as a criminal when they took him to the High Commission, he could readily get someone to take him up here—no questions asked and in a big hurry. Ah, here's our tea!" He accepted the thermos from the young station attendant with thanks and bade him good-bye.

Pulling the Rover out onto the main street, he smiled at her. "Better drink most of that tea now, we'll be off the tarmac in another few minutes, and I'll bet we'd be getting most of it on our outsides rather than our insides from then on!"

An hour later, Balebe gingerly braked the Rover to a halt on the slick red road. Both heaved a sigh of relief.

Cynthia looked through the mud-splattered windscreen at the road ahead. "How much further, BT? I can take over for a while. Don't give me that look—I've driven on icy roads back home in Kansas since I was sixteen, and this mud is nearly exactly like it. Piece of cake!"

He looked at her ruefully and managed a smile. "I didn't know it was going to be this hard, Cyn. I swear, coming down that last hill sideways, even though we're in four wheel drive, was as much as I want to handle today."

She smiled back. "Yeah, with a cliff on one side and tropical timber on the other, a thrill a minute! Look, let me drive for a while. I've never been wider awake! Seriously, I'm pretty sure I can manage this stuff."

He nodded. "Okay, I am getting pretty tired. We've only about five kilometers to go, although that may take us some time. Can we manage to swap sides without getting out into this mud?"

As they clambered past one another in the cab, their bodies touched. Cynthia caught her breath as she felt his warmth, and as they settled in their seats, his hand came to rest on her arm.

"Oh Cyn, I've missed you so!" he began.

She reached to embrace him awkwardly over the gearbox for a moment. She murmured, "I've missed you, too, BT." Pulling away, she took hold of the steering wheel. "I think we'd better keep our minds on finding Colin right now, yes?"

He nodded, withdrawing his hand from her back. "Right, do you remember how to handle a right-hand-drive car?"

"No problem—at least there's no other traffic!" She started the engine and began to creep forward on the slick road.

After several minutes' driving, she felt more confidence in handling the Rover and glanced over at Balebe. He was deep in thought, a concerned look on his face. She looked back at the road and asked, "Worried about Colin?"

"Actually, I was thinking about us."

"Uh-oh!" she rejoined.

Balebe sighed. "Cynthia, I've some things I need to say to you, so bear with me—I fear I'm about to deliver myself of one of my semi-annual personal monologues."

"Okay, BT, fire away," she said feeling much less casual than she sounded.

"I have been going utterly mad having this distance between us. And I don't mean the miles," he quickly added. "I know you've been keeping me at arm's length. Which I don't blame you for, under the circumstances, but now that I'm nearly clear of all this, well. Cyn, you've been my best friend, and I fear that I'm still devoted to the idea that we could be more than that. And I've no idea how in hell we can ever work out a life together, even in the best of times."

She felt the old confusion well up inside her, loving yet fearing the commitment in his words. "Oh, Balebe, I wish I had a clear answer for you." She felt the car begin to skid and steered into the direction of the slide. As it regained purchase on the slippery surface, she felt the silence lengthen awkwardly. "I'm kind of at a loss for words right now, and I need to keep my mind on this damn road!"

"Sorry, didn't mean to distract you." He reached out and wiped fog from the windshield.

"It's okay, BT, I know we should talk—just not now!"

After another half hour of difficult driving, Balebe gestured ahead. "The trailhead's just around the bend."

They reached the end of the road and turned off the engine. Balebe unfolded a topographic map of Mount Tidinga. "Here's where we are right now, and here's the cave I think Colin may head for. It's about five kilometers more." He checked his watch. "Four-forty. If we really move, we can get there well before the light fails."

The roof resonated with pouring rain as they parceled out their food supplies into their backpacks. Balebe stuffed the sleeping bag into its sack and tied it to his pack. "Okay, that looks like it! Ready for a little rain?" He grinned.

Cynthia struggled to get her poncho over her back pack. "Boy, Thanatu, if this turns out to be a wild goose chase, *your* goose is cooked!"

He climbed out and stood in the downpour. "Come on out, the water's fine!" He laughed. Cynthia jammed her hat on top of her poncho hood and clambered out.

Water ran in streams down the steep trail, and they tried to stay on the grassy verge of the narrow pathway. Nonetheless, their boots collected the heavy mud, weighing them down.

As they stopped to kick it off, Cynthia panted. "How high are we, anyway?"

"About twenty-five hundred meters—over seven thousand feet." Balebe shook his leg to kick off more mud. "We'll be going up close to nine thousand by the time we reach the cave."

"Oh great, sleep deprivation, jet lag, and hypoxia—a winning combination!" She knocked one boot against the other.

"You forgot near-drowning!" He chuckled and glanced up at the sky. "Though it does seem to be dying down a bit."

"Yeah. Let's make tracks before the downpour resumes, okay?"

The rain continued to slacken, and soon only a thin, cloudlike mist touched their faces as they walked along. Cynthia thought she saw a trace of blue sky once, through the clouds shifting above the narrow gap in the forest vegetation. They'd walked for the better part of an hour, making reasonable time. Then, as they rounded a curve in the road, Balebe said softly, "Stop! Don't move!"

Craning her neck to see around his poncho, Cynthia saw at least eight buffalo standing on the trail only fifteen feet ahead of them. The lead animal, an incredibly large and ugly male with scabby knees and heavy, flaking horns, peered at them shortsightedly, nose raised, testing the air. Lowering his head, he took a plodding step toward them, then let out a huge, wheezing breath. The rest of the herd jostled behind him to peer over his back, rolling their eyes and snorting.

"I think they're confused by our funny shapes with these ponchos," Balebe muttered. "I'm going to give them a shout in hopes they'll take off. But if they charge, try to get into the woods and up a tree. You just stay silent, in case they turn out not to like shouting people in rain ponchos."

Cynthia tried to imagine running swiftly in her pack, poncho, and muddy boots and gave up.

"Ho! Get away!" Balebe shouted, waving his arms. The lead buffalo backed up a pace and bumped into the animal behind him. The herd seemed to waver for an eternity between flight and charging forward at them. Suddenly, they pricked up their ears and scented the air frantically. A high-pitched whine grew into the heavier roar of an engine, with the whopping sound of rotors.

Before either Cynthia or Balebe could move, a small helicopter flashed over the trail, spooking the buffalo, who crashed off into the forest.

"Police! Damn! Get off the trail!" Balebe plunged toward the trees on the side opposite that taken by the buffalo, and Cynthia slid after him. They heard the helicopter banking and coming back for another pass. Balebe pulled Cynthia into a crouch under a heavy shrub. The copter hovered above the trail for a moment, quartered the forest for another, then headed up the trail.

Balebe tried to still his shaking hand and cursed. "Damn it to hell! They must have seen our Land Rover. I had no idea they'd be out here this soon. I wonder if someone tipped them off?"

"How do you know it's the police?" she asked.

"They're the only ones in the country with that model copter. My father's used one on a couple of occasions—landed on the back lawn at the house. If they're using them in this kind of weather, they're serious about finding Colin."

"Do you think they saw us?" she asked, checking her canteen.

He shook his head. "I can't be certain, but I think they might not be sure what they saw. They only had a second, and these camouflage ponchos may have looked like buffalo from above, but then again . . ." He wiped the moisture from his face. "Look, we need to get up there, if only to make sure they don't shoot him in cold blood! I think it's only another kilometer or so to the cave. Let's get back on the edge of the trail and push as hard as we can."

Twenty minutes later Cynthia was panting heavily, laboring along with a stitch in her side. Balebe's breath came in audible rasps ahead of her, and he was nearly staggering.

"Hey, BT, let's take a break! Over there, under that tree."

She smiled at him as they leaned against the massive trunk of the tree, catching their breath. "I've plumb run out of the adrenaline boost that encounter with the buffalo gave me!"

He nodded, panting. "Me, too, but not far now. We've really got to try and get to the cave before that copter comes back."

Pressing on, Cynthia glanced at her watch. "Six-ten! No wonder the light seemed to be failing! It'll be dark in less than an hour!"

"Yes, I know," he gasped. "On the bright side, I don't think they'll fly the helicopters after dark. And we're just about there, Cyn. See that clearing ahead through the trees? It's where the falls and the cave are."

Five minutes later they stood panting at the edge of the small clearing. Cynthia struggled to get her breath and rubbed her aching side. "God, this is a beautiful place!"

Balebe nodded. "My Wachacha ancestors believed the fairy people lived here." He pointed to their left. "Look, see that cliff face with the vines on it? The cave's about halfway up, to the right of that waterfall! You know, I think I smell smoke. Do you?"

She nodded. "Yes, I caught a whiff, too. You think he's here, then?"

He grunted assent. "I think we should announce ourselves straightaway. If Colin's there, he may be in quite a state after the pass the copter made. If he knows who we are, he'll be a lot easier to talk to—I hope!"

"Then let's get these ponchos off, so he can see us better and not mistake us for police!" She began wriggling out of her rain gear. As she did, the high-pitched whine of the helicopter pierced the air.

"Oh bloody, bloody hell!" Balebe exclaimed. "Let's run for it! We've got to reach him." He dropped his poncho and pack on the ground and sprinted off across the clearing, shouting, "Colin! Colin! It's Balebe and Cynthia! We're here to help!"

Cynthia's breath tore at her lungs as she ran toward the cliff face. Balebe, better adjusted to higher altitude, increased his lead over her. *We aren't moving fast enough!* she thought, while the whine of the helicopter grew to a crescendo behind them. As they got to the base of the cliff, it roared over them, banking abruptly to avoid the precipice.

Balebe was already clambering up the hillside. "Up here, there's a little path to the falls, we can get to the cave from there. Quickly!" They could hear the copter turning and coming back toward them. As they reached the waterfall, the copter dove along the face of the cliff and hovered only twenty feet away. Cynthia stared for a moment into the wide eyes of a policeman holding a rifle, then clambered after Balebe, who ducked behind the hissing veil of waterfall and was inching along a slippery ledge toward the other side.

The water fell on her back. *Icy cold! Oh, my heart is going to burst! Will they shoot us?* Balebe was already out the other side, shouting something blotted out by the slapping of the falling water and the demonic roar of the helicopter. She heard another voice as well, shouting against Balebe's. *Colin! He's here!* Her foot slipped, and she fell to one knee.

As she rose, a shot rang out. Then another. "No!" she screamed and threw herself past the wall of water. Ahead, Balebe staggered to his feet, his chest covered in blood, waving his arms. "No!" she screamed again. The helicopter was settling in the little meadow below, and as her eyes raced back to Balebe, she noticed a crumpled body just down slope from where he stood, caught on a little rock outcrop. Blood gleamed on Colin's head.

She raced toward Balebe, arms outstretched, only to see him shake his head, screaming, "Get down! Get down! They've shot him! I've got to get to him before they finish it!" He threw himself over the edge of the path and slid down to Jones's inert body. Tearing his shirt off, he began wrapping it around the man's head, meanwhile covering the body with his own.

Cynthia whirled around to face the metallic pounding of cleats on the ledge behind the waterfall. The first of the policemen was beginning to emerge through the veil of water. She turned back to Balebe and shouted, "Give me your identity card! Quick!"

He looked up at her, puzzled, then reached in his hip pocket and tossed her his wallet. She caught it clumsily, then opened it to the card and began walking back along the ledge. "Don't shoot! This is the son of Attorney General Thanatu! Put your guns down! Look! Here's his identity card, see? It's Ezekiel Thanatu's son! Don't shoot! We're friends of the police! Jones was surrendering!"

The first of the policemen continued walking toward her, his rifle leveled at her chest. Their eyes locked as he came closer and closer. It was the same man she'd seen from in the helicopter. They were now only a few feet apart. Cynthia smelled cordite. *This is the gun that shot them! Oh God, we're dead!* The man's mahogany face was impassive, his dark eyes fixed on hers. The end of his rifle barrel was now only three feet from her. She held her ground and struggled to breathe evenly. "Look, see, Balebe Thanatu—the attorney general's son. Don't shoot! We are *not* resisting arrest."

She glanced over the man's shoulder to the policeman behind him, an older man in an officer's cap, training a revolver on her. "Please, take this, check our identities. And get help for them, please!

"*Acha tu,*" said the older policeman to the one in front. "*Nipa cheti chako!*" he barked at her. "Give me that card! But don't make tricks, or we shoot!"

As Cynthia leaned forward and handed the wallet gingerly to the man with the rifle, the barrel grazed her breast. She shuddered and stepped back, watching him pass it back to the officer. Before he started to read, he barked an order to the rifleman, who pushed past

234

Cynthia and trained his gun on Balebe. The policeman behind the officer moved forward and aimed his rifle at her. Cynthia started to shake uncontrollably. *Oh, God, please. Don't let them shoot us!*

The officer brushed by her and commanded in Swahili for Balebe to rise and face him. He scrutinized the identity card and the young man for what seemed an eternity. Balebe stood silently, his bare chest heaving.

Glancing at Balebe, Cynthia started. *He's not bleeding! Where did all that blood on his shirt come from? Colin?*

Finally the officer nodded. "*Basi.* Arms at rest, men." He turned to Cynthia, his face still grave. "And who might you be? Tourist? Asalian citizen? ID, please!"

Cynthia drew a shaky breath. "I'm a foreign guest of the Thanatus. American. Working at the national museum." She gestured weakly across the clearing. "I'm afraid my passport's in my pack over there."

He nodded curtly. "You will show me when we get down." Glancing past her to the third policeman, he said, "*Piga radio* call HQ . . ."

Cynthia broke in, "We know Inspector Malongo! Please tell him we're here—he'll vouch for us!"

The officer looked at her with some irritation, then at Balebe, who nodded silently, and then called his man to guard them while he made the radio call himself, to handle this increasingly tangled affair.

As the officer turned to go, Balebe said, "Look, we need to get this man medical attention, and quickly! He has a head wound. Please get him out of here!"

"You leave the arrangements to me!" the officer said sharply. "I am in charge here, not you!" He ordered his other man forward to guard them, and he made his way back down toward the helicopter.

Cynthia felt hopelessness swamp her relief. *They won't get him to a hospital! He'll die, and they'll pin Shafer's murder on him, and we'll never know who really did it.* She sat down abruptly on the ledge and put her face in her hands. She glanced over at Balebe, who was gazing at her with concern. She called, "I'm okay!" He nodded and crouched down over Jones again.

She sat, chin on hands, on the damp ledge, watching the rotor turn lazily on the dragonfly-like helicopter in the clearing. The light was fading quickly in the now partly-clear sky. A profusion of bird song filled the air, mingling with the muffled crackling of the radio. She heard the policeman on the ledge near her shuffle his feet but decided not to look at him. Finally the officer emerged from the copter and made his way back up the cliff, a blanket over his arm.

Shaking the water from his blue hat, he approached Cynthia and Balebe. "Okay, we are going out before it is too dark to fly. We have orders to carry this man Jones to hospital. You," he pointed to Cynthia, "will come with us. You, Thanatu, will go back in your Land Rover, with these two guards. You will come straightaway to Central Police Headquarters in Wangara, no matter when you arrive, to make a statement. Inspector Malongo and your father," he said, emphasizing the last word, "will be there to meet you." He gestured toward Jones's inert body. "Now, we need to get his man down. We will pick up a medic at the air force base the other side of the mountain, then proceed to Wangara. He is not supposed to die before giving us a full report."

Balebe glanced up at Cynthia, a ghost of a smile on his face. She nodded and smiled back. As they struggled down the path, Balebe supporting Jones's head and one policeman holding his legs, Cynthia fell in behind Balebe. The unconscious man's face was waxy white below its makeshift bandage. "Do you think he'll make it?" she asked.

"I don't know. I think it's only a scalp wound, but there was so much blood! I know I saw bone. It didn't do him any good lying there for the better part of an hour in the chill, either," Balebe muttered softly. "If they get him into Wangara General, he's got a good chance."

At the copter, the police officer, who explained that his name was Lieutenant Odaka, expertly bandaged Jones's head and had him placed in Balebe's sleeping bag. He then set the still-unconscious man into the narrow space behind the copter's seats and gestured for Cynthia to climb in beside the pilot. He turned to Balebe and the two policemen as he climbed into the copter himself. "Better start walking. You have a long way to go. Buy these men some dinner in Tidinga Tuu, then come posthaste to Wangara. You have some explanations to make."

Balebe stood back and grinned ruefully at Cynthia through the copter's bubble as the pilot revved the engine. The grass around the three standing men flattened as the rotors whirled faster. The copter rose, tilted forward, and swept into the twilight sky. Cynthia watched the figures on the ground dwindle. Then the clearing disappeared in a mass of dark green forest. Cynthia glanced back at Jones, whose face distorted in a grimace for a moment, then went slack.

Rounding the side of the mountain, they flew through a cloud into the last bright rays of sun. The twin peaks of Tidinga, rocky and snow-covered, glinted pink and gold, cold, remote, and pristine. "Our traditions say this is the house of Ngai, of God," said Lieutenant Odaka, gesturing at the mountain. "Few people ever see it as you are now seeing it."

Cynthia nodded silently. *So beautiful, so cold. Oh, Colin, who have you been protecting?*

Wangara

Cynthia yawned mightily and shifted in her creaking straight-backed chair, listening to the bird song outside the ward's window. *Whatever else its medical merits, Wangara General certainly doesn't go in for coddling their visitors. Just as well, I'd probably fall completely asleep again if I had a comfortable chair . . . Comfy Chair, God, I wonder if Melanie has seen this yet?* She glanced down at the copy of the *Standard* she'd bought an hour before from a street hawker near the hospital, with its headline, "Archaeologist Death Suspect Shot in Tidinga Raid." *They never get the difference between archaeologists and physical anthropologists right.* She stifled another yawn and peered down the hall to the uniformed policeman sitting outside Jones's room.

It had been after nine the night before when the helicopter set down on a floodlit pad behind the dark bulk of Wangara General Hospital. Lieutenant Odaka had bustled her out of the copter to clear the way for the waiting emergency team. She'd stood at the edge of the floodlights as Colin had been lifted down, still connected to the IV drip the air force medic had put him on at their refueling stop at the air base, then rushed into the building on a gurney. As the doors closed behind the medical team, Inspector Malongo had stepped from the shadows to confer with Lieutenant Odaka and the air force medic for a moment on the tarmac.

Then, as the two younger men shook hands with him and climbed back into the copter, Malongo turned to her, raising his voice to be heard above the helicopter engine. "Well, Miss Cavallo, we meet again, once more under unusual circumstances."

She nodded, her hands still jammed into her jacket.

Malongo gestured toward the door. "Let us go inside now. It will be some time while the doctors assess Dr. Jones's condition, and I can take your statement as we wait." Cynthia had nodded mutely again and preceded the inspector through the door.

After she'd finished her narration, Malongo said, "So, you never actually entered the cave?"

"No, the shooting started just as Balebe got to the mouth of it." She shuddered as the sound of the two rifle shots rang in her memory.

"Ah, yes, a most unfortunate occurrence, and very distressing for you," Malongo said, appearing slightly uncomfortable. "We try to avoid such incidents, but Dr. Jones appears to have brought it on himself by his erratic behavior." He shifted his bulk in the chair. "We will take full depositions from young Mr. Thanatu, as well as from each member of the police team, to see if any irregularities took place." He glanced at his watch. "I will wait here until the doctors have something to tell us. The Land Rover with Mr. Thanatu and his, er, escorts, shouldn't be reaching Wangara until around midnight. May I lift you somewhere, after we've heard from the doctor?"

Cynthia considered her options. "I suppose I should get some sleep, but I'd like to wait for Balebe. Could you ask him to pick me up here, once he's done with making his statement, unless he'll have to, uh, stay with . . ."

Malongo waved a large hand and his faced creased into a smile. "Not to worry, Miss Cavallo, we do not plan to press criminal charges against him—or you!" He gave her a sardonic look. "It is true that you both withheld information from the police, but we understand that your goal was to encourage Jones to give himself up, rather than to abet his escape. So we are inclined to view this escapade benevolently—unless evidence to the contrary comes to light."

Cynthia opened her mouth to reply but stopped as a tall black woman in a white coat approached them. Malongo rose to shake hands with her. "Dr. Mbira, allow me to present Miss Cynthia Cavallo. She is a friend of Dr. Jones and was at the scene when he was apprehended. Miss Cavallo, this is Dr. Mbira, head of neuro-surgery."

The woman nodded, taking Cynthia's hand in a firm handshake, then opened the stainless-steel-covered clipboard she carried in her left hand. "I think we are going to be lucky here, Inspector. Dr. Jones has a hairline fracture of the right parietal bone of the cranium and a small haematoma beneath, caused by the bullet's impact as it glanced off his head. Moreover, he had lost quite a lot of blood from the scalp wound. However, we have dealt with these problems and stabilized him." She snapped the clipboard shut. "I see no reason why he cannot make a full recovery, with no impairment to his faculties."

Cynthia sank back down in her chair, heaving a sigh of relief. The woman looked down at her and favored her with a brief but brilliant smile. "I trust this is reassuring news, is it not? But we must be very careful with him the next twenty-four hours. He is very weak, and with head wounds, one can never know for sure until the patient begins to show clear signs of recovery."

Malongo broke in, "Has he regained consciousness?"

Dr. Mbira gave Malongo a slightly mischievous glance and hugged her clipboard. "Ah, now, Inspector, you are too eager! He has not, and we shall ring you when he is in sufficient condition to be interviewed. For the time being, you must leave him with us. We are putting him up in Matthews Ward. You may post a guard, if you wish, but make sure he is someone who understands hospital protocol!" Nodding to them both, she turned and disappeared behind the surgery doors.

Malongo chuckled and shook his head. "That woman is always putting me in my place when I have business with her! 'Hospital protocol,' indeed! Pardon me, now, I must go tell my sergeant to come in and stand guard. He knows the proper etiquette."

Cynthia nodded and settled back down in her chair. She picked up her backpack and placed it on her lap. Hugging it to her chest, she slumped back, eyes closed.

She started at the touch of a hand on her arm. Balebe was now sitting in Malongo's chair, his face haggard and stubbly but smiling. "Hullo, there! It's two in the morning, and I think we'd better get home."

She wiped her eyes and stretched. "God! I've been sitting here asleep for five hours!"

He laughed softly. "Yes, the matron at the desk said they'd just let you be, since you were clearly exhausted." He reached over to take her pack. "You'll be relieved to know that my father and I have already completed the reentry formalities from our Big Adventure, and if we sneak in now, we'll be able to avoid a grilling from both Kaniugi and the kids!"

She rolled her eyes and moaned, "Oh, good, I couldn't handle that right now."

As they walked out into the cool night air, Balebe said, "I've got some other news that isn't so good, Cyn. The journalists have got hold of the whole thing—the gun in the collections, everything— and it will be out on all the wires in the morning."

"Oh boy, wait until Melanie hears about this—she'll kill us!"

Balebe hunched his shoulders against the wind. "Well, Cyn, on the brighter side, it might do some good. Maybe we'll get the real killer flushed out, somehow."

"Do you think Colin will tell us something now?" she asked as she climbed into the Rover.

Balebe shook his head as he opened the door on the driver's side. "God only knows. Hopefully, that head wound will have knocked some sense into him."

The next morning, Cynthia and Balebe waited in the hospital for Jones to regain consciousness. They had agreed over a hurried cup of tea at the house that museum work was out of the question today. A nurse emerged from Jones's room and hurried down to the senior matron's station, only a few feet from where Cynthia sat. Glancing briefly at Cynthia, the young woman entered the head nurse's cubbyhole-like office. The two women emerged after a few moments and returned to Jones's room, arousing the police guard's curiosity but saying nothing to him as they entered.

She heard footsteps on the stairs, which turned out to be Balebe, balancing two steaming mugs. He smiled at her and shook his head. "If you knew what I went through to get these cups out of the cafeteria! Say, what's up? Is Colin awake?"

"I don't know, the nurse just fetched the matron, and they both went back to the room. They didn't seem to want to say anything to the guard."

"Hmm, scoot over a little on that chair, okay?" Balebe gestured with his cup. "We can share what little sitting room they provide here."

The matron emerged from Jones's room and spoke briefly to the guard. She walked down the hall toward them, her ring of keys tinkling rhythmically with each step. When she reached the door to her office, she glanced at them impassively for a moment, taking in their shared seat with an almost imperceptible twitch of her mouth. She said, "Your friend is close to fully regaining consciousness. I shall ring through to the CID. But you will have to wait until after the police are finished with their enquiries." With a rustling of her stiff white skirt, she was gone.

"Great!" muttered Balebe. "The first faces he sees when he opens his eyes will be the cops! Well, the stupid sod deserves it, I guess! What he's put us through!"

"And himself, BT, and himself," Cynthia rejoined, sipping her coffee.

The matron emerged from her office and came directly over to them. "Chief Inspector Malongo wishes you to come to headquarters at once. He says to tell you that there is something you will want to hear."

They stood up so fast that their chair canted over and nearly hit the floor. Cynthia grabbed it with her free hand, spilling some coffee on her jeans. "Damn! Uh, sorry!"

Balebe interposed. "She means to say, thank you very much, sister. We'll be back later!"

Rushing down the steps to the ground floor, Cynthia spoke over her shoulder. "What do you think has happened?"

"I've no idea, but it sounds like the break we've been waiting for. Maybe there's been an arrest! Oh, damn!" he exclaimed, stopping short in the corridor. "Speaking of arrests, I've got to get these mugs back to the cafeteria, or the cashier will put out a dragnet for us!"

"Hurry, BT! I think this is it!" Cynthia said. But he was already gone.

The End of the Game

"Damn and blast this town!" Balebe exclaimed as a battered Toyota pickup swerved around them into the parking space they'd spotted. "Nobody's done any traffic planning since the Brits left, and the number of cars on the road have increased a thousand percent—we'll never get a parking place this time of day!"

They'd been circling the city block with the central police headquarters in it for nearly fifteen minutes, fruitlessly seeking a place to park the MacPhersons' Land Rover. Both were becoming increasingly jittery as the time lengthened.

Cynthia pointed across from them. "Look! That man over there's getting keys out of his pocket! We could—whoa!" she cried, gripping the dash as Balebe made a fast U-turn in the middle of the broad avenue and headed for the business-suited African man now getting into his Peugeot.

Balebe flashed her a reckless grin. "Asalian driving at its best, my dear! I wasn't about to go down to that roundabout and make a more legal turn—not after what we've seen this morning!"

"Well, you could've at least told me to hold on," she smiled back, glancing around for traffic control officers. "Hanging a U-y a half block from central police headquarters sounds like a sure recipe for disaster."

"Not to worry, *they* do it all the time! Now, have you got some change for this meter? It just might be functional, you know."

As they walked up the stairs of the headquarters building, Balebe muttered, "Get your passport out, we'll need to identify ourselves straightaway." A guard headed them off as they made for the entrance, interposing himself between them and the doorway. After a quick exchange in Swahili, Balebe gestured for Cynthia to follow him to the registration desk.

The uniformed woman behind the high counter took their papers and scrutinized their faces impassively, then checked a note on government letterhead lying next to her pens. She initialed two yellow chits and handed these, plus the note, to Balebe. "You will go directly to the chief inspector's office, twelfth floor. Hurry, you are behind time!"

As they passed through a checkpoint where their chits and letter were rechecked and mounted the stairs to the elevators, Balebe muttered, "From the look of it, we'd get there faster if we took the stairs." A mass of people, depressed-looking Africans in threadbare city clothes with a few disoriented-looking white tourists, stood around the doors to three elevators. One had an "Out of Order" sign on it. As the doors of another opened, the people surged forward to pack themselves into the space, leaving four times that many standing outside its sliding doors.

Cynthia glanced at the stairs and sighed. "Looks another day of interval training for the sea-level-adapted, yes?"

Reaching the twelfth floor, they stopped to catch their breath before going over to a window in the wooden wall barricading the stairwell from the rest of the floor. Balebe leaned in and showed their chits and letter to the policewoman sitting at the window, while two armed policemen leaned over her shoulder and inspected them with professional curiosity.

"Identity papers!" the woman demanded.

"We've already shown them!" Balebe protested.

"For entry to the twelfth floor, you show them again!" the woman declared, with an arrogant stare at Cynthia.

Cynthia fished her passport out of her bag.

"All right. Give in your bag now," the woman said to Cynthia.

The policeman on the left opened it and sorted through its contents as the other man looked on. Balebe shifted from foot to foot impatiently. The policeman closed the bag. "*Sawa,* okay," he said.

"You may enter," the woman said, maintaining her cold formality. "The chief inspector's office is just there, at the end of the corridor."

Balebe and Cynthia went through the door opened by the policeman, only to be halted again. "Body check," declared the second policeman, beginning to frisk Balebe. Another policewoman emerged from a side room at a word from the woman at the desk. "Lift you arms, please," she said dispassionately to Cynthia, and ran a metal detector, then her hands, over Cynthia's body, her eyes never meeting Cynthia's, her face remote.

As she submitted to the body search, Cynthia heard the woman at the window demand of someone in Swahili, "What do you want?" Her tone was rude. Cynthia could not catch the murmured reply, which was met by, "He is away. You just go sit over there, and I will call you."

Small consolation to know she's as nasty to her own countrymen as she was to me . . . just like Guatemala.

Released from their inspection, they walked down the hall. Balebe glanced at Cynthia. "Holding up okay?" he asked quietly.

"Yeah, I've seen as bad in Latin America."

He shook his head. "I'd like to apologize on behalf of my country-

men—Christ! There's David!" They hurried down the hall to a polished wooden door that Pierce was holding ajar, beckoning them
inside.

"There you two are! I was beginning to think you'd gone off on
another escapade!" His dark eyes flashed in irritation. As they
stepped into Malongo's anteroom, the receptionist looked up and
nodded, intent on a conversation into her telephone headset.

Balebe opened his mouth to protest Pierce's tone but stopped as
his father stepped out from an inner chamber. Father and son eyed
each other tensely for a moment. Then Ezekiel's eyes moved to
Cynthia, and his grim expression softened slightly. "Well, Miss
Cavallo, you and my son appear to be fated to have an 'interesting'
life. We'll chat about the CID viewpoint on your excursion to
Tidinga later. Meantime, come into the chief inspector's office.
We've decided you two may as well be here, since you seem to have
become so entangled in this case. The call's just coming through."

They entered and approached Malongo's large mahogany desk.
The chief inspector and two officers were fussing with a tape cassette hookup to his speaker telephone. Malongo gave them both a
brief glance, then nodded into his phone receiver, pressed a button,
and replaced the receiver. As static came through the amplifier,
Pierce murmured to Cynthia and Balebe, "He sent me a telex a few
hours ago, saying he was going to ring through with a statement . . ."

As Cynthia and Balebe both began to form the word "who" on
their lips, an accented voice came over the speaker. " 'Allo, is this
the chief inspector of the CID?"

"Michel!" Balebe whispered. Cynthia nodded, then shook her
head sadly.

"Yes, this is Chief Inspector Malongo. As well, I have here Attorney General Thanatu, his son, whom you know, Dr. Pierce, and
Miss Cynthia Cavallo, the American student you met last summer."

A weak chuckle came over the line, followed by coughing, then a
brief silence. Finally he spoke. "*Ah, nous sommes donc en fa-
mille—très bien!* Yes, I am Michel Laporteau. For security, I have
asked a member of the Interpol, a Monsieur Bouvier, to attend to
my conversation."

245

There was a pause. Malongo leaned forward and folded his hands. "Very good, I am also assisted by two of my staff. You should know this conversation is being tape-recorded."

"*Bien,* precisely as I wished."

"Now, Dr. Laporteau, you telexed to Dr. Pierce that you wished to make a statement regarding the death of Dr. Robert Shafer."

They waited tensely through the satellite transmission lag.

"Yes, I wish to make a statement. I had hoped to end this all more cleanly, with something written, avoiding this disturbance." He began to cough again.

Another French-accented voice broke in. "This is Inspector Bouvier of Interpol. I must inform you that Dr. Laporteau is very weak, and that we are speaking from his hospital room under the supervision of his medical staff. Please try to be brief and to the point. Ah, *oui,* here he is again."

"Yes, let me commence now, Inspector." He laughed softly. "As much as I have hated those hypocritical crows, the curse of a Catholic boyhood lingers. So, now that I am composing my atheist soul, perhaps confession will help me. It will certainly keep poor Colin, the chivalrous fool, from being charged with Shafer's murder!" He began to cough, then resumed. "I beg that you forgive if I am a little vague, I am now given drugs to control the pain, and sometimes I become dispersed."

Cynthia caught Malongo's eye for a moment and looked away.

Laporteau cleared this throat. "So, yes, Inspector. I killed Bob Shafer."

Pierce and Ezekiel muttered under their breath, and Malongo hastened to ask, "Will you tell me when and how you did so, Dr. Laporteau?" They waited again for a reply.

"Well, it was really quite simple. I had one last flight to Anthea's camp, the afternoon of the first day of the congress. I was to carry food and other supplies to the East Ruba airstrip, where a few of Anthea's men were waiting to meet me with a Rover for the supplies. It was easy to have Bob hide in the back of the plane while we unloaded the cargo hold."

"But," Ezekiel began, to be cut off by a curt gesture from Malongo, who said, "Yes, go on."

"We arranged that he would come out with me to Matope Airport," Michel said, "and that he would quickly get into the back of the airplane. You know how disorderly is the small plane area there, with people circulating constantly. It was easily accomplished."

Laporteau paused. The listeners could hear murmuring, then Laporteau's voice again. "Bob simply hid in the plane while I dropped the supplies with Anthea's crew. That was a tense interval, but I was able to pretend a great hurry and stand in the doorway of the plane, passing out the supplies and supervising. No one saw Bob." Laporteau chuckled. "Do you know, I had such a sense of aliveness during these proceedings. At that point in my life, such feelings conveyed a profound pleasure." He lapsed into silence.

Malongo clasped his hands more tightly and leaned over to speak into the telephone. "Could you please tell us about the actual, er, act, as well as how you got the body to West Ruba?"

"Yes, of course, the criminal details. Well, I took off, heading the plane for Wangara, and then turned back toward West Ruba once out of sight of Anthea's camp. There was a vehicle left waiting at the West Ruba airstrip, to be used in the excursion. It served to carry us to the Memlolo. It was there, near the cairns, that I shot him."

Ezekiel broke in, leaning over the telephone. "But how did you induce him to accompany you? And what was your motive?"

"One thing at a time!" Malongo whispered urgently to his superior.

Again Laporteau chuckled. "Yes, how did I induce Bob to accompany me? I think David and Balebe will laugh when I tell you. On the morning of the opening day of the congress, I confided in him that I, too, had developed sentiments against David Pierce, because of some incidents in the field season in Ruba, and that I wanted to revenge myself. I told him that in the course of my surveying, I myself had found a hominid fossil, which I would take him to see that afternoon, so that he could "discover" it during the tour I was going to lead through the area on the field excursion."

247

He paused. "I proposed that not only would he again be famous for making a new find, but he would be demonstrating his superiority right in David Pierce's own territory. He could not resist."

Balebe and David stared at each other a moment. An ironic smile formed on David's face, and he shook his head. Malongo spoke again. "I hope you are not becoming too fatigued, but could you please give us the details, Dr. Laporteau?"

"Yes, well, the details. They are a bit sordid, *n'est-ce pas?* But I understand your professional concerns . . . *Bien,* after landing at West Ruba, we went quickly down to the Memlolo, to the place where the cairns stand. I led him up near the cairns and pointed at a place on the ground, near a lava cobble. This was actually the hardest part, since I wanted to place him near to the cairns, to save myself time, and yet it was not such a logical place for a fossil to be found as one of the gullies. But Bob was not in the least suspicious, and he went down eagerly to inspect the place I had indicated."

There was a pause, then a sigh. "It was simple to draw the pistol out and to be ready when he looked up with his question. His last expression was disbelief. *Incroyable,* unbelievable, that his old friend Michel Laporteau was about to shoot him. The last person in the world with a motivation."

In the pause that followed, only vague electronic sounds came over the loudspeaker. Then Malongo cleared his throat and said, "Please go on. How did you, er, proceed after . . ."

"You are very insistent on the details, eh, Inspector? Well, it is your business, I know. After I shot him, I cut the clothes from his body with my little Swiss knife—a tedious affair—and dragged him over to one of the cairns. It took longer than I anticipated to cover him with stones, and I had to hurry, to make the return to Wangara before nightfall. I suppose I should have looked more closely at the stones, and put more on, from what I read in *Newsday.* And I did not notice the matter of the teeth. This young *américaine* of Melanie's was very observant!" He broke off coughing.

Cynthia found Malongo's eyes on her, glanced away, and met Ezekiel's gaze. She looked down.

Malongo pressed forward toward the phone again. "And the clothes?"

"I disposed of the clothes by wrapping them around a stone and then dropping them in the Ruba as I flew over. A gesture learned from the mystery novels, yes."

Laporteau sighed. "The pistol—alas, I thought I was being so clever about the pistol. You see, I wanted it somewhere accessible, but also somewhere where it would not be found until after my death. Then the letter my advocate was instructed to send to you would reach you, revealing the location of the pistol in the old Ruba locality's "Miscellaneous Tools" drawer."

He cleared his throat, muttering, "*Merde,*" softly. "Colin and I had often joked that no one would ever go to look at those materials again. I had no idea of this Mademoiselle Delcourt's project, and of the trouble I would bring on my friend Colin. I deeply regret that he has had to suffer from the discovery of the weapon before my death. And now, I am afraid I have put his life in grave danger." His voice broke and he fell silent.

They waited a long minute. Then Laporteau resumed. "Colin, he knows absolutely nothing of all this, but I believe that he suspects that I am involved. To vindicate him, and to clear my personal honor, I am instructing the Interpol go to my safe box in the Banque du Bourg de Bruxelles—my advocate has the entry card. There you will find a set of my own fingerprints I have made myself, to check against those I left on the pistol."

Malongo glanced up at Ezekiel, who nodded. "Yes, please have Inspector Bouvier do so at his earliest convenience." He seemed to be groping for words for a moment, then went on. "Now, Dr. Laporteau, we really must ask about the, er, motivation for your act. Did something happen between you and Dr. Shafer?"

The transmission lag seemed to drag on forever. Then Laporteau laughed sardonically. "Yes, why did I, of all people, wish to take Bob Shafer's life? This is the part hardest to comprehend, I am sure. And it is the most difficult to explain. Sometimes I myself cannot believe that I took such a step." He took a wavering breath and cleared his throat. "Forgive me, I am unaccustomed to speak of the personal. Here is the story."

He paused again for a moment. "Last summer, as I mapped the West Ruba exposures for David, I already knew about my condition. The doctors could not inform me of the precise course of the disease, but they gave me no more than two years to live."

Balebe and Cynthia exchanged glances, and Pierce sighed quietly as they waited for Laporteau to continue.

"I had a lot of time to think, as I did my surveying," he said, at long last. "I made a review of my life, as one is supposed to, and I found it to have been usually interesting, often pleasurable, and occasionally truly intriguing. As with a new locality, or a very resistant lover. I had known moments of joy in my flying, and the various pleasures of physical love."

It seemed to Cynthia that everyone in Malongo's office was trying hard not to meet anyone else's eyes. Malongo squirmed in his chair and cleared his throat, eyes on the telephone.

Laporteau continued. "However, from the new perspective of the condemned, I found something lacking. I, who had so carefully avoided the dreariness of bourgeois ties, of the church, procreation, the dreadful family Sundays, suddenly wanted to have my life count for something. I felt that it would be unbearable to depart without making a significant gesture. How ironic life turns out to be."

Cynthia raised her eyes and looked out Malongo's window toward the clouds building up over Wangara's green hills, sensing what would come next.

"But what to do?" Laporteau said. "I could not imagine myself in an orphanage, emulating the Mother Teresa. My own illness disgusts me far too much for me to tolerate anyone else's. As I explored the exposures, I searched for a means by which my life and death could have an effect." He sighed. "At the same time, my own detachment was crumbling, victim of unaccustomed emotions of sympathy, of loyalty, *merde alors.* I found myself viewing that formidable old woman, Anthea, with pity. I don't need to explain the circumstances, but it was clear that she was suffering deeply because of Shafer's actions."

Balebe and Cynthia glanced at each other. *The notebooks.*

Pierce rose, walked over to a chair near the window and sat, burying his chin in his hand, struggling with emotion.

Laporteau continued, sighing. "And Juma, for whom I had the utmost respect, was suddenly smaller, a bit insecure, worried about the future for David, and for him and his men, if Bob carried his assault on David's credibility to the maximum. I saw his manhood diminished, and I was preoccupied."

Laporteau paused a long time, and Malongo began to speak just as the Belgian continued. "I was sure as well that Shafer made some dirty deal with the young Thanatu. Perhaps you know more than I do about that affair."

Ezekiel and Malongo both fixed Balebe with intent stares, and the young man nodded, swallowing hard and averting his eyes.

"So, at any rate," Laporteau said in a stronger voice, a hint of defiance in his tone, "it occurred to me that by removing Shafer, I was doing many persons a great favor. I saw no reason for him to continue to make mischief for so many people, in his ambitiousness. There was also my friend Melanie, who still suffers . . ."

Cynthia looked over at Balebe again, and he shook his head.

Laporteau again spoke. "So, I determined to kill him, before he engaged in another set of humiliations. The rest was, as I have said, surprisingly simple. To obtain a pistol in Wangara was not even very expensive. To pick a place for the execution, and for his burial, also came readily, given my knowledge of the area."

He laughed softly. "I must say, nonetheless, that a few times it was touch-and-go, as you say in English. Personally, I found the process of seducing him into coming with me as immediate and exciting as any other seduction I have ever attempted. The lack of a predictable outcome, the risk, they gave me a great sense of aliveness." He paused a moment. "You must think me very callous. Perhaps I am."

They could hear the smile in his weak voice. "Even now, I still feel no regret for the act. In the end, I judged that Bob made more trouble for others than he contributed to the field. Without a doubt, the fossils he discovered will be described by others. And others will fill his place, I hope with more kindness in their ambitions. I don't know. Perhaps this is a futile hope. I have never understood the ego-involvement of their genre."

He laughed softly, then coughed. "Balebe's father has already attempted to question me through Interpol about that flight, but I put everyone off by pretending to be a bit closer to death than I really was. Now, with my friend Colin in such danger because of my actions, I decided I must present a full confession. I hope this is sufficient."

Low murmuring came over the line, and indefinite rustles and thumps. Then Bouvier was back on the line. "That must be enough for now. He is completely exhausted. I will make the appropriate inquiries of the advocate and telephone to you again later in the day."

"Hmm, yes," said Malongo, stretching back in his chair. "Thank you, Inspector. In case you wish to fax us evidence, let me give you our number."

As he did so, Cynthia glanced around at the others in the room. The police assistants were still intent on the call. Pierce sat sunk in his own thoughts, his hand obscuring his eyes and mouth. Ezekiel walked to the window overlooking Wangara's streets, hands clasped behind his back. Balebe stood with his hands in his pockets, chewing on his lower lip.

They were all startled to hear Laporteau's voice again. "I want to ask a favor of Miss Cavallo, please."

Shocked beyond any clear thought, Cynthia came forward to the telephone. "Yes, I'm right here."

"When you see Melanie again, please tell her that I always understood that she did not answer my letter, and that I send her my affection."

In the silence that followed, Cynthia felt both pity and confusion well up inside her. "Yes, certainly, I'll do that."

"Thank you. Now, I am finished, and I will say good-bye. Good-bye, Balebe, *bonne chance!*" The line clicked off and static filled the air.

252

Reflections

Balebe shook his head as they headed down the stairs from the twelfth floor. "I feel as if I'm in a dream. But you heard the same things I heard, right?"

"Yeah, I'm having a hard time believing it's happening, too." She brushed the hair back from her face and moved out of the way of a uniformed messenger toiling up the stairs.

He glanced at his watch, then spoke over his shoulder to her. "The Neville's bar is just opening up. Let's get something to drink there."

"Amen! Let's!"

Twenty minutes later, at a table in the darkened bar, Balebe raised his gin and tonic slightly off the table, then shook his head. "No, dammit, there's nothing to toast to here. I mean I'm relieved as hell to have this suspicion lifted from me, from my father, and David, but . . ."

She nodded. "I know what you mean. With Michel dying, it's not like we have much to celebrate."

"But if he weren't dying, it would be even more of a disaster," he said, taking a sip of his drink.

"Yeah, but if he weren't dying, well . . ." she broke off.

"Bob wouldn't be dead, right?" he asked.

She nodded, then shook her head. "BT, I just don't know what to think. How to judge."

He waved his hand, then laid it over hers. "Maybe we shouldn't try sitting in judgment, Cyn, not on this one."

His hand, as always, felt warm on hers. She looked up and met his eyes, then managed a smile. "Well, at least Colin's going to be all right."

"Hmm, yes, great news, that. Good of Dr. Mbira to call us." He glanced at his watch. "Afternoon visiting hours begin at two. We can get some lunch and then go on out, if you like."

She nodded. "And I guess I'd better get on with what I was sent here to do—we've lost two days of my fourteen, with all this."

"Not to worry, David's given me permission to get into the collections on the weekends, and I'm sure he'll extend it to you. So we can work straight through till you leave!"

She grinned. "Oh great! When my friends ask about my travels in Asalia, I'll tell them about the inside of the primate fossil room! So much for wildlife and scenery!"

"Ah, but you forget the up-close-and-personal encounter with African buffalo on Mount Tidinga, arranged by your own special safari guide!'

She laughed out loud and squeezed his hand. "Oh, yeah! To say nothing of the thrills and chills of impromptu mountaineering!" As their laughter died, she recalled him standing on the ledge, his chest covered in blood.

"Oh, BT, when I came out of the waterfall, I thought you'd been shot!"

He glanced at her, then looked away. "Yes, I must have looked a sight, with Colin's blood all over me. To tell you the truth, I didn't know whether I'd been hit or not, for a moment. I was trying to hustle him down the path when he was shot. We were so physically entangled that I felt the impact myself and was knocked down."

They sat together silently for a long interval. Then he cleared his throat. "Is this a good time to have the rest of that conversation we began on the muddy road?"

"I guess so." Her voice was soft.

He removed his hand and straightened in his seat, then laughed and said jokingly, "Madam is entitled to madam's lack of enthusiasm, I suppose."

She tried a weak joke in return. "As long as I ain't memsahib, Thanatu. That I can't abide!"

He looked across the table, serious again. "That's a real problem for you, isn't it? Well, frankly, Cyn, I can't abide it either. But things are changing here. Maybe in another ten years, there'll be no more memsahibs. But God knows what will be in its place. After the example of Ethiopia, I'm not sure that I'm wild about 'comrade.'"

She nodded. "Well, there's always the Tanzanian example, 'brother' and 'sister,'" she said, taking a sip of her drink.

"Yes, but let's not emulate their economic disasters!" he snorted, rattling the ice. He sighed and began to draw patterns in the condensation on the side of his glass. "It's a dicey one, Cynthia. Sometimes I'm full of hope for Asalia, when I see all the guys like Andrew and Elias coming on, and the others I knew while at university, in agronomy, engineering, biology, progressive guys, who want to serve the people and not just get rich."

She nodded, and he went on.

"Even some women are making it into the professions now, and they're super. Strong, determined, and organized! Like my grandmother and aunts, only living in the modern world, too. I'd always thought I'd hitch up with one of them, once I'd got my degree." He glanced at her briefly and sighed. "Other days I can't imagine we'll get through another decade without a violent revolution in which anyone who benefited from the present state of affairs gets thrown out or just put up against a wall. Look at Uganda."

She nodded again, recalling the army roadblock they'd passed through on the way back from Ruba, the hostile, arrogant sergeant who bullied them all, his nervous teenage soldiers.

He straightened up in his seat. "Yet this is my home, and I'm coming back here after my dissertation's done. I've got to try to be part of the solution to the country's problems, not another piece of the problem. Sometimes I think my father's right—I should have gone into something more 'applied,' but this is what chose me . . ."

The silence at the end of his words lengthened, and she glanced up at him. His eyes were on her face, and he smiled, a little sadly. "I know I'd be asking a tremendous amount of you, over and above the personal commitment, to join me here. Asalia is a gamble, and we are all staking our futures in the game. Being born here is one thing, choosing to become part of it is something else . . ." He sighed. "Moreover, I know you'd have to give up a lot. You'll probably have your pick of jobs in the States, once you've got your degree."

She began to protest, but he shook his head. "No, don't make modest noises, I've read your work. Melanie's right to encourage you to publish that theoretical paper you wrote last spring in *Journal of Human Evolution*. You'll be ahead of her, Johnson, or Shapiro in a few years, I'm sure of it. Melanie knows it, and she's big-hearted enough to be involving you in the very richest part of her Zaire project. They'll be beating down your door with job offers, just wait and see."

"Yeah, let's," she said. "I'm somewhat less impressed with my abilities than you are."

He reached out his hand and touched hers for a moment, then removed it. "I think you know that it wouldn't be the same in Asalia. Oh, you'd probably be given a little office at the museum, and free rein to work with some of the collections. But the best materials, the paid positions, and the pitiful amount of research funds the government can dole out would be going to the black Africans, not to some expat wife. Even were you to renounce your US citizenship, I doubt the situation would change."

He smiled sardonically. "I'm painting a pretty grim picture for a suitor, aren't I? There'd be consolations, I suppose—the proximity of the fossil localities, people who love you—you've made a great hit with the family, you know, including the Nyau contingent. But it wouldn't be the fast track, the money you need to do decent research projects, the National Academy of Science at forty-five, and all that . . . And you've never told me what your family would think of your bringing home a black husband, either."

He folded his arms and sank back in his seat. "But I needed to let you know that the invitation stands."

She blinked and sighed. "BT, I love you as much as I love anyone, outside of my family—and, incidentally, they would probably be concerned about an interracial marriage—you know what it's like in the States—but the Cavallos are *not* racists, and anyone I wanted to—oh, I don't know! You really are dear to me. And I care for your family, too, even Ezekiel—he's got a crazy sense of humor under all that stiff-upper-lip stuff."

She shifted in her seat. "It's just that I have worked so hard to get where I am, and I can't just walk away from it. I'm the first person in my family to go to college. They're so proud of me." She was silent for a moment, groping for words. "It's been a struggle—nothing like your dad's, but you know some of it. Sam McIntyre wasn't the first sexual harassment I've had to deal with, and I'm so tired of struggling along on almost no money. It's hard to think of letting go of the goals I've been sacrificing for. Asalia is a wonderful, fascinating, heartbreaking place, and I am still sorting out its effects on me. I'll never be the same—and that would stand even without this whole Shafer thing."

She looked at him, shook her head, and looked away. "It's just that I can't give myself over to a lifetime here, to leaving what I've managed to get to in my life—not now, at least. I don't know what else to say."

She felt his eyes on her for a long moment. Finally she looked up at him, near tears. His face softened and he touched her hand again. "Do I take it from the 'not now' that the subject is not completely closed, however?"

She nodded. "You take it right. I'm not saying 'never.' I'm just not saying yes, now."

He laughed. "Ah, the *mañana* attitude! Well, then, friends for now, eh?"

"Yes, friends!" she smiled. "Look, that was my stomach rumbling—can we get some lunch here?"

He nodded. "Yes, ma'am! Then we'll go see Colin."

Driving home from the hospital in silence later that afternoon, Cynthia suddenly laughed out loud. "I don't know who's going to suffer most out there, Colin or the nurses!"

"Yes, he's still weak, but he's already putting up a fight!" Balebe shook his head and shifted down as they started up the hill toward home. "I'm glad we've engineered it for him to call Michel tomorrow morning, though."

"It was really nice of you to think of it, BT. I think it'll be good for both of them."

He nodded. "Speaking of phone calls, should we ring through to Melanie?"

"Yeah, it's probably best that she get as much of the story from us as possible." She glanced at her watch. "She should be in the office by now. I wonder what the business about the letter is?"

"Maybe we'll find out, Cyn," he said, turning into the driveway. "Or maybe not. You know Melanie."

She laughed. "Yeah, at least we can tell her that her two star students won't be cooling their heels in some picturesque outpost of the Asalian penal system, either! Big of Malongo not to press charges!"

Balebe murmured as they got out of the car. "I wouldn't speak too much about that around here, Cyn. I think the only thing that got us off with our wrists slapped is everyone's desire to avoid any more adverse publicity. Let's go on and try putting the call through to her. We can use the lines in the sitting room and study and speak to her at the same time."

Melanie answered on the second ring. After a couple of quick questions about the newspaper stories, she listened to their recitation of the day's events with minimal comments. As Balebe finished his description of Laporteau's disposal of the corpse and the gun, Melanie murmured, "Jesus. I was right."

"So he's the one you suspected?" Cynthia asked.

"Yeah, it's hard to pin down exactly why, but when Colin started acting so strange, I began wondering about Michel. He's really near death now, isn't he?" She fell silent after they assented.

Cynthia felt a flutter of nervousness. "Melanie, at the end of the phone call, Michel asked me to tell you something."

Balebe broke in, "I can hang up now, if you wish."

Melanie laughed shortly. "Why bother, Thanatu, you were in the room when he told her, right?" She went on in a softer, more serious voice. "No, go ahead, stay on the line. What was it, Cynthia?"

"Uh, Michel said to tell you that he understood about your not answering his letter. He sends you his affection." She swallowed hard and fell silent.

The line filled with electronic bubbling and static for a long moment. Finally Melanie broke the silence. "Graceful to the end." Her voice choked off, and when she continued, they had to strain to hear her. "Well, to satisfy your curiosity, the letter Michel wrote to me was after Bob had dumped me, and I'd been thrown out of Barbore. The word about me and Bob was out all over the gossip network, and some people were willing to believe the spy story, too."

She fell silent again, then continued. "I was back here in San Felipe, wondering if I'd make it through the tenure review and the scandal, drinking too much and generally in a downward spiral. Jerks like Sam McIntyre were having a field day, making cute remarks about my love life. I could barely force myself to go into the departmental office to get my mail, much less contemplate ever attending a professional meeting again in my life."

Cynthia stared out the sitting room window at the trees outlined in black against the deepest purple evening sky. *I can't even imagine how she made it through all that . . .*

Melanie spoke again, softly. "Out of the blue, Michel wrote me. He offered me a civil marriage and a home in Brussels. We'd spent months together in the field, but aside from a casual pass at me the first season, he'd just been a good friend and colleague. I was so stunned, it was so out of character. The guy wasn't the marrying type, to say the least."

Another pause, then her voice came over the line more strongly. "His letter was the kick in the pants I needed to pull myself together and get on with my work and my life. I never replied to him, and he never brought it up again. He's that kind of person."

Cynthia could hear Balebe sigh softly on the other extension. She stared out through the window, barely able to discern the feathery black-on-purple skyline in the darkness. A breeze seemed to be stirring the trees.

Melanie's voice came over the line again. "I'm going out for a walk down by the river now. You guys get the right measurements, okay?"

The line went dead. Night had descended on Wangara, and raising her gaze again to the window, Cynthia was confronted by her own reflection.